MAKING MUSIC WITH SAMPLES

Tips, Techniques & 600+ Ready-to-Use Samples

Daniel Duffell

Making Music With Samples

by Daniel Duffell

A BACKBEAT BOOK
First edition 2005
Published by Backbeat Books
600 Harrison Street,
San Francisco, CA94107, US
www.backbeatbooks.com

An imprint of The Music Player Network United
Entertainment Media Inc.

Published for Backbeat Books by Outline Press Ltd,
Unit 2a Union Court, 20-22 Union Road, London, SW4 6JP, England.
www.backbeatuk.com

ISBN 0-87930-839-7

Art Director: Nigel Osborne
Editor: Paul Quinn
Design: Paul Cooper Design

Origination and Print by Colorprint (Hong Kong)

04 05 06 07   5 4 3 2 1

Contents

Introduction

If the electric guitar was the revolutionary musical instrument of the 1950s and 1960s, then by the end of the 20th century the same claim could justifiably be made for the digital sampler. Sampling is also *the* production technique that has influenced the evolution of popular music more than any other in the last 20 years.

OK, so sweeping statements like these are usually spurious at best – but this time, they happen to be true. So what is sampling, and why is it so important...?

A sampler is like a sonic digital camera – point it at a sound, hit a button and the sampler will play back what is hopefully an exact replica of the sound you just fed in. There's an awful lot you can do to your sonic snapshot from that point on, as we'll see in the course of this book, but that's the starting point for the whole affair.

Its most obvious uses emerged in the dance music field of the 1990s, but sampling is by no means restricted to any one genre of popular music. In fact, nowadays you'd be hard pushed to find many recordings that *don't* employ some sampling technology. That snappy acoustic guitar part in the latest singalong pop hit, or the luscious string pad on that romantic ballad, or the wheezy organ riff that warms up a funky new dancefloor tune – there's a pretty good chance those are all samples.

The parts themselves might have been performed by 'real' musicians, maybe even recorded specifically for the track in question… but then those performances will have been cut up into chunks (samples), edited and rearranged using a sampler and/or sequencer. Or the whole part might have been selected from a sample CD – like the one attached to this book (CD2); or else lifted, in the now time-honoured but controversial fashion, from an existing composition, recorded years, perhaps decades earlier, and now recrafted into an entirely new piece of music.

Some die-hard traditionalists call this approach to music-making lazy, or even shameless plagiarism. Some maintain it's downright immoral – whether or not a royalty is paid to the original artist and record company, which increasingly it tends to be. But sampling is a fact of modern musical life, and an undeniably creative one when used well. As sampling proponents will point out in their defence (not that many feel defensive), music-makers have always borrowed from what's gone before – sampling technology just allows this to be done more easily, more accurately, and sometimes even more inventively. (See the History section in Chapter 8 for more on the precedents of today's sampling culture and technology.)

It's the ultimate in democratic, DIY music-making: you no longer even need to know how to play the minimalist three chords beloved of iconoclastic punk rock acts – you can sample someone else playing those three chords, if you feel the need. Or, with the addition of a sequencer, you can build a complex piece of music from scratch, note by note, instrument by instrument. Of course it helps if you can tell which end of a keyboard is which, not to mention being blessed with a good sense of rhythm, so you know whether or not your creation possesses those two magical elements that machines simply can't create by themselves: groove and musicality.

Sampling is no longer simply a matter of ripping off a James Brown drum track – that's way too obvious now. Many sample users spend weeks trawling through record stores seeking out obscure and often (to put it kindly) less-than-classic records, which nonetheless might contain a few seconds of musical sparkle that could inspire a fresh composition – like prospectors searching for a tiny golden nugget amid the riverbed mud. At its best, and most innovative, sampling can provide such a lost gem with the platform and presentation it has always deserved, but perhaps never had.

In the process you might be giving a long-forgotten vintage track or artist a new lease of life – dusted down, dressed up in a smart new arrangement, introduced to a new group of admirers – and at the same time encouraging another generation to seek out older musical forms and recordings. And if you play by the rules, you may even be generating a new source of cash for a veteran musician or songwriter (check out the section on Copyright in Chapter 8 for more on the legal ins-and-outs of sampling).

The unprecedented power that the personal computer can offer music-makers nowadays promises yet more radical and sophisticated developments to come.

This book

The core of *Making Music With Samples* concerns creating your own innovative, exciting and very personal sound palette using a sampler. Ideally you'd want to read the book from cover to cover, but because reading about music is clearly not as much fun as *making* music, and as everyone has their own preferences, and a different level of understanding and competence, you're obviously going to be drawn to some sections before others.

If you feel you know all about the basics of music, sound frequency, and the theories behind sampling, you can probably skip Chapter 1. And if you're not so interested in an equipment rundown (if you already have the sampler you want, for instance), and just wish to jump straight into working with samples, you could go directly to Chapter 3. Having said that, it's just possible the sections you miss out might contain things you don't even know you need to know... yet. And don't, whatever you do, skip Chapter 8 – it might be an eye-opener.

What this book *isn't* really about is offering you advice on which specific sampler to buy. For the most part it presumes you already have a sampler of some sort and are looking for a bit of help getting your system to do what you want it to do, and sound how you want it to. As a happy by-product, if you *are* looking to buy your first sampler, or to upgrade from a basic system, there's a lot of helpful stuff in here to guide you to the type of system that might best suit your needs.

Making Music With Samples is not intended to replace your product manuals either, but rather to complement them. Equipment manuals have generally improved over the years, and most of the professional systems mentioned in this book are blessed with excellent instruction books. Manuals will tell you which buttons to click or push on your particular system – each brand and model will have its own idiosyncrasies. Even more importantly, a manual will tell you about the little shortcuts and extra facilities of your gear which, because of the universal nature of this book, simply can't always be covered here. It's a lamentable fact that most enquiries received by equipment helplines are from people whose problems could have been avoided with a quick look through the product manual. So go on, read it...

And happy sampling.

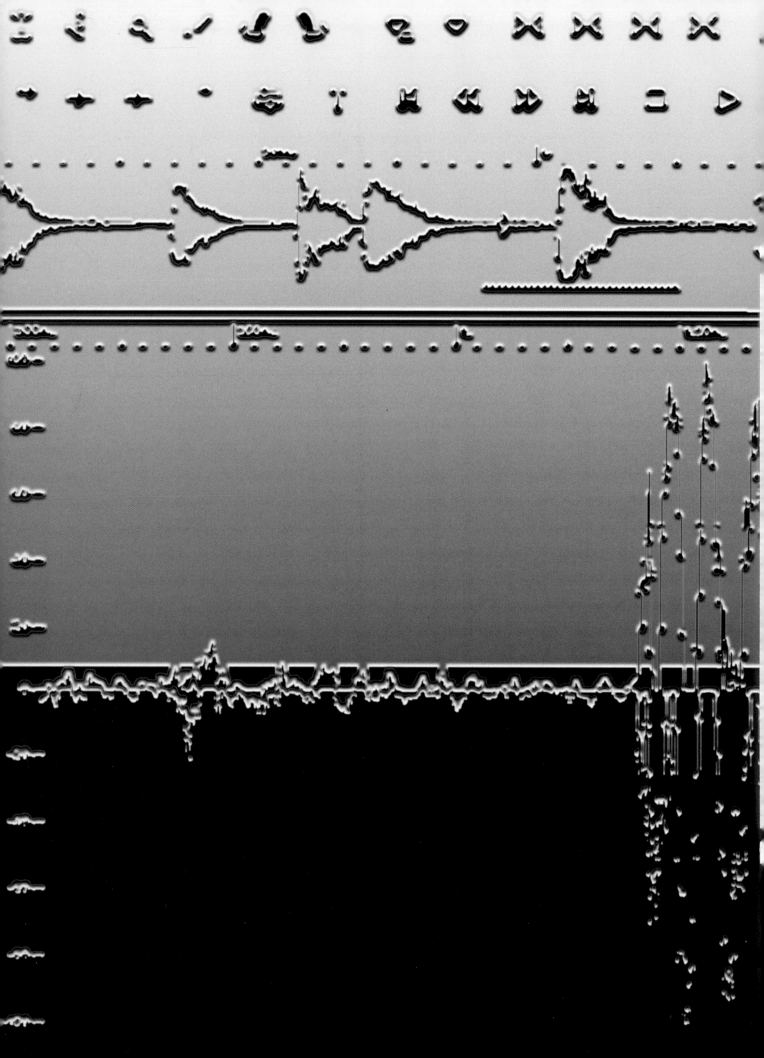

CHAPTER 1

sampling
basics

As Julie Andrews put it in *The Sound Of Music*, "Let's start at the very..."

No, wait, on second thoughts maybe it's best not to use that quote without getting permission. Don't want to infringe anyone's copyright, do we?. Let's just say, if you're unsure of the fundamentals of musical structure, or what it is a sampler does, from a technical standpoint, this is where you should begin.

This short chapter includes:

● A very quick run-through of musical building blocks like bars, rhythm, pitch, and frequency.

● How samplers do what they do: analog-to-digital conversion, binary numbering, bit-rates, sampling resolution etc.

The learning curve

Using any kind of music-making equipment – whether it's a guitar, keyboard, drum kit, saxophone or whatever – involves a certain degree of learning and honing of skills. Using a sampler is no different in this respect. It takes time to master.

And of course music itself can be complex and contradictory. For some people the reality of making music turns out to involve far too much actual hard work in proportion to how satisfying it is, and quite frankly they waste a lot of time and money finding this out. For that reason it's a very good idea to start with one simple piece of music-making technology, and learn it thoroughly. When you've used it for a while and know it well enough to realise it might be starting to hold back your creative process, you are probably ready to go out and either add to it or replace it.

Sampling is a great place to start the whole process because it's the most versatile tool in the sound-makers toolbox. The choice of either hardware or software sampler is something we'll look at in detail later, and depends on a few personal factors – such as your preferred working methods, and whether or not you want to play live gigs.

There are dozens of different music tools out there that offer sampling facilities. Most of them combine the ability to sample sounds with a number of other facilities… some of which you will want or need, and others you may not. They're presented in very different formats, and offer different levels of complexity – again it depends what you want. And the only way to be sure what it is you want, is to start creating something, anything, and see if you like the result.

If you're a DJ, or a music-maker wanting to create dance-based tunes, a great place to begin is with one of the crop of simple, inexpensive hardware samplers (see Chapter 2). It will give you a good understanding of basic sampling operations, and how easily a piece of music can be sliced into convenient, re-usable chunks.

If you've worked as a DJ, you'll know it's about putting together and blending several pieces of pre-recorded music. Messing about with game-style loop-based music software is similarly about re-constructing a load of building blocks made from pre-recorded material. Taking the next step, the great leap forward to creating your own original music, requires learning about what those building blocks are made of. Once you know that, you need to know how to make new ones. It's about learning how to create or where to find the right sounds to use, learning how to sculpt individual sounds, and then about how to make a loose collection of noises gel together to form coherent music.

In other words, making music with samplers is just like making any other kind of music – once you know your way around the instruments, the rest is all about inspiration and practice.

Building blocks of music

If you have spent any time learning to play a musical instrument, or created your own successful DJ set, you will already know a fair bit about music, perhaps without realising it.

You'll have a pretty solid understanding of tempo and how different styles of music and different rhythms tend to be fundamentally linked to how fast the music is. You should know about crucial stuff like phrasing, and that music tends to be made up of beats and bars – sets of

---

A WORD ABOUT WORDS

The trouble with words and names is that, in order for them to work, we all have to agree on them. If I say 'banana,' you know I mean a piece of fruit rather than a cow, or a jumbo jet, or anything else. Unfortunately, when it comes to standardisation, sampler manufacturers seem to have given up after the word MIDI...

I've tried to stick with the more popularly recognised terminology. For instance, throughout the book I've used the term 'sampler instrument' to mean a collection of samples responding to a single MIDI channel. The majority of manufacturers do call it an instrument, although Akai and Steinberg and a few others call the same thing a 'program'. You'll see terminology/jargon boxes, like this one, explaining any phrase where the meaning may not be clear.

four bars, or eight bars, or 16, 32 etc. You'll at least be aware of the existence of musical key – though in fact many great pop music producers don't learn the intricacies of musical theory until well into their careers. But from very early on they know if you try to mix some notes or tunes together they complement each other musically and sound wonderful… while others clash horribly. You don't need to know the theory to know whether it works. Most importantly, you'll know how the music you love makes you feel, and that can drive you on to learn more.

Thinking about music in this way involves more than simply enjoying it as a consumer. When we listen to music purely for pleasure, we might notice blatant errors and know when we don't like something, but we don't go searching for little faults or inconsistencies in the detail of the performance, or the way all the instruments sit together in the mix. We don't consider how it was done, and whether we could master the techniques ourselves. But that's the way you have to start listening to music now – and it's a change for the better, opening up a whole new world.

Instruments, pitch and volume

Beyond tempo, rhythm and musical key, we have to consider the role of different instruments, the role of sound frequency (or pitch), and the role of relative volume levels. All notes produced by all instruments within a piece of music have two roles to play: they help define rhythm and musical pitch.

Drums and percussion instruments illustrate this perfectly. We know that a kick drum (or bass drum) on a drum kit is a strong rhythmic instrument – its primary purpose is to beat out the rhythm. Similarly a snare drum is a strong rhythmic force, but is higher pitched. A hi-hat, the pedal-operated pair of cymbals used for ticking out a rhythm, is much higher pitched still. We generally say that the kick drum is a bass instrument, the hi-hat is a treble instrument, and the snare is a 'mid' instrument, because it sits in the middle.

A conga drum, or a bongo, or a tom tom, and many other drums, produce frequencies that sit between the bass tones of the kick drum and the mid tones of the snare. In fact, because there are so many instruments producing noises that sit in this middle ground, we tend to carve up the mid area into two further frequency zones. So the snare is usually said to be a high-mid type of instrument, and the conga would be said to be a low-mid instrument.

Once you've grasped this concept, it becomes clear that all instruments, whether acoustic or electronic, can be said to produce sounds that fit into various frequency ranges. It's fairly obvious that an acoustic piano will produce a huge range of frequencies (you can tell from all those keys and strings), but perhaps less obvious that drums also produce musical notes – though clearly in a more limited range than a piano. Drums can be tuned just like all other instruments. So a series of different drum sounds not only creates a rhythm, but also produces a melody. In fact, more or less any series of noises can be said to form a rhythm and a melody of some kind.

As you'll quickly realise when you start experimenting with EQ (which we'll come to in Chapter 6), the idea of instruments belonging to a particular frequency range is a bit of a simplification. Although most

FREQUENCY

We perceive sound as a variation in air pressure. When the air pressure alters, a membrane inside the ear is either pushed in or pulled outwards (by tiny amounts) depending on the frequency and 'amplitude', or volume, of the sound. Musical instrument sounds tend to be made up of a variation in sound pressure that's repeated many times very quickly, like ripples on water. A bass sound, for example, will consist of a regular, repeated ripple or wave that happens anywhere between 40 and 150 times per second. An average bass soundwave might cycle at around 80 times in a second. This can be expressed on paper as 80 hertz (80Hz) – named after the German physicist/inventor Heinrich Hertz who first proved the phenomenon. Hertz is a measurement of 'occurrences per second' and is therefore an expression of frequency – how many times something is repeating per second. It's used to measure soundwaves, cycles, or 'oscillations'. In the case of a high-frequency sound it might be 10kHz, which is 10,000 cycles per second. (There's more on frequency and analysis tools in Chapter 6.)

instruments produce sounds that are predominantly within a particular range, they in fact contain elements within several frequency ranges. A kick drum is mostly bass, but also has some low and high mid tones produced by the impact of the beater on the drum skin. It's a little more precise to say that we perceive the kick drum to be a bass instrument because the bass elements of the sound are far louder than the mid elements. The dominant frequency within a sound is said to be the 'fundamental' or 'first harmonic'; the next loudest element is said to be the second harmonic, and on it goes through the third and fourth harmonics, and so on. The fundamental is what gives a frequency its note name (for instance 261Hz is the fundamental frequency of the note middle C).

Which brings me neatly to the role of relative volume within music. When we perceive our kick drum as more or less a single note, this is defined by the loudest element, even though it contains two or three or ten or 20 different, subtly interacting harmonics. The same thing happens when you hear five or six instruments at the same time. All of the different sounds blend together to form a combination of notes known as a chord, or 'harmony'. It's the relative volume of each instrument that defines the tonal character of that chord. And of course some instruments, such as guitars and piano, are polyphonic, meaning they can produce more than one note at a time – essentially creating their own internal chords.

You might be wondering what all this has to do with sampling. It's simply demonstrating that music is just a collection of instruments beating out rhythms and melodies. The sampler is the only instrument ever created that can produce the sound of all the other instruments in the world. So to use a sampler successfully it helps to understand how these different sounds can be used, crafted and blended together to make a piece of music.

How a sampler works

All digital audio recorders, including samplers, record sound by slicing it up. As the sound arrives they chop off a slice, measure what's in it, and store those measurements as data, which includes details like pitch, volume etc. Then they do the same with the next slice, and so on, ending up with a string of consecutive slices. When you want to play the sound back, the same process is done in reverse – technically known as digital-to-analog, or D-A, conversion, – so the sound should come out exactly the same as it went in.

The number of slices used for A-D conversions was determined by a bloke called Harry Nyquist, who came up with the idea that if you wanted to accurately digitise a sound you'd have to slice it up at more than twice the highest frequency within the sound. Based on the theory that people can hear sounds at frequencies ranging from around 20Hz at the bass end to around 20kHz at the top, Nyquist calculated that to capture all the audible detail (all 20kHz of it) you'd need to chop each second of sound into a minimum of 40,000 slices. This is where we get the standard CD sampling frequency of 44.1kHz (the 4.1 added to give a little extra 'headroom'). Filters are then used to remove the unwanted frequencies above 20kHz.

Unfortunately it turns out that some of us can in fact hear sounds at frequencies above 20kHz, so after years of complaining by audiophiles extra slices were later ordered – hence the new professional standard of 48kHz, as used in much top-end digital audio recording gear.

DIGITAL AUDIO

The term used whenever sounds from the 'real' world are brought into the digital domain, whether via samplers or other recording means.

FILTER

If you think of the way a filter in a coffee machine works, allowing water through but not coffee solids... well, an audio filter controls the flow of sound, letting some frequencies through but stopping others.

There are those who believe we can perceive (even if we can't actually hear) frequencies still higher than this, so to be on the safe side, some professional gear opts for 96kHz, or even 192kHz. It must be said that not everybody believes there is any perceivable difference or useful benefit gained from using sampling rates above 48kHz, but others will swear the extra headroom allows for almost-subliminal extra-high harmonics to be appreciated by those with ultra-sensitive ears. The downside is that sampling at higher rates obviously creates more data, which means lots more hard disk memory space to store the results.

The bits that count

The accuracy of how we measure what's in each slice is just as important as how many slices we take. This depends on the 'resolution' of the measuring scale itself. To take an example from the outside world, if we could only measure distances in kilometres, it would be difficult to describe a very short distance. We need to increase the resolution of the measuring scale, dividing our kilometre into 1000 smaller units, metres, which could then be subdivided by 100, into centimetres, or even smaller units, millimetres. This allows for greater detail and accuracy.

In the non-digital world, our standard counting system is decimal (or 'base ten') – presumably based on the fact that we have ten fingers and toes – which means we measure things in groups of tens, hundreds, thousands etc. Computers, samplers and other digital devices use base two, or binary, which only involves the digits 0 and 1. In effect digital machines are simply responding to a series of on/off messages: 0 is off, or negative, and 1 is on, or positive. But because it means measuring in small chunks, very detailed information can be transmitted in long strings of 0s and 1s, or 'binary digits' (bits for short).

Binary is very simple, to a computer at least, but can seem confusing for an average decimal-using human. Instead of powers of ten (10, 100, 1000 etc), its measuring groups are powers of two (2, 4, 8, 16, 32, 64 etc). If this sounds baffling, don't worry, it's not vital to understand it – it's just to help explain what is meant when you see terms like 8-bit, 16-bit, 32-bit and so on. An 8-bit digital system operates in a range from 00000000 (eight zeros) to 11111111 (eight ones), which translates back into decimal numbers as 0 to 255 – in other words a total of 256 individual data options or measuring units.

An 8-bit sampler, it follows, would be able to divide each slice of a sample (and there are over 40,000 per second, remember) into 256 measuring units. This might seem like a reasonable amount on paper, but it's not really detailed enough for music reproduction. If you try converting a good-quality sample down to 8-bit, you'll instantly hear the rough edges (like looking at a low-resolution digital photo). A 16-bit system can divide each slice of the sample into 65,536 units, which is a lot more accurate and smooth. A 32-bit system can divide slices into a staggering 4,294,967,296 units – that's over four billion data options per slice.

OK, now all that number stuff is out of the way, let's look at the kind of equipment you'll need for sampling...

OVERSAMPLING

Oversampling is a process whereby samples that have been created at the standard rate of 44.1kHz – or even at 48kHz or 96kHz, for that matter – can be refined further by inserting (interpolating) tiny new slices of sound between the existing ones. In oversampling, these new slices are automatically generated by taking the information from two consecutive slices and calculating what should/would fit between them to link them up.

The idea is that, as well as a smoother, more detailed sound quality, the extra slices also provide the high-frequency filters used with more to play with, resulting in a less harsh and drastic cut-off – certainly when compared with a lot of early digital equipment, which had no oversampling. When you see a specification that reads 64x or 128x oversampling, it means the machine is interpolating 64 or 128 extra slices for every existing slice – so there are that many more slices in the finished article (eg 64 x 44.1kHz = 2,822,400 slices per second). While the results of oversampling can be very impressive, it's still not the same as sampling a sound at a higher rate to start with (96kHz, say), which would supply more authentic detail from the original audio.

BITS AND BYTES

There are eight bits (b) in a byte (B), and, for reasons best known to binary, exactly 1,024 bytes in a kilobyte (kB). A megabyte (MB) is 1,024kB – that's more or less a million bytes – and a gigabyte (GB) is 1,024MB, or roughly a billion bytes.

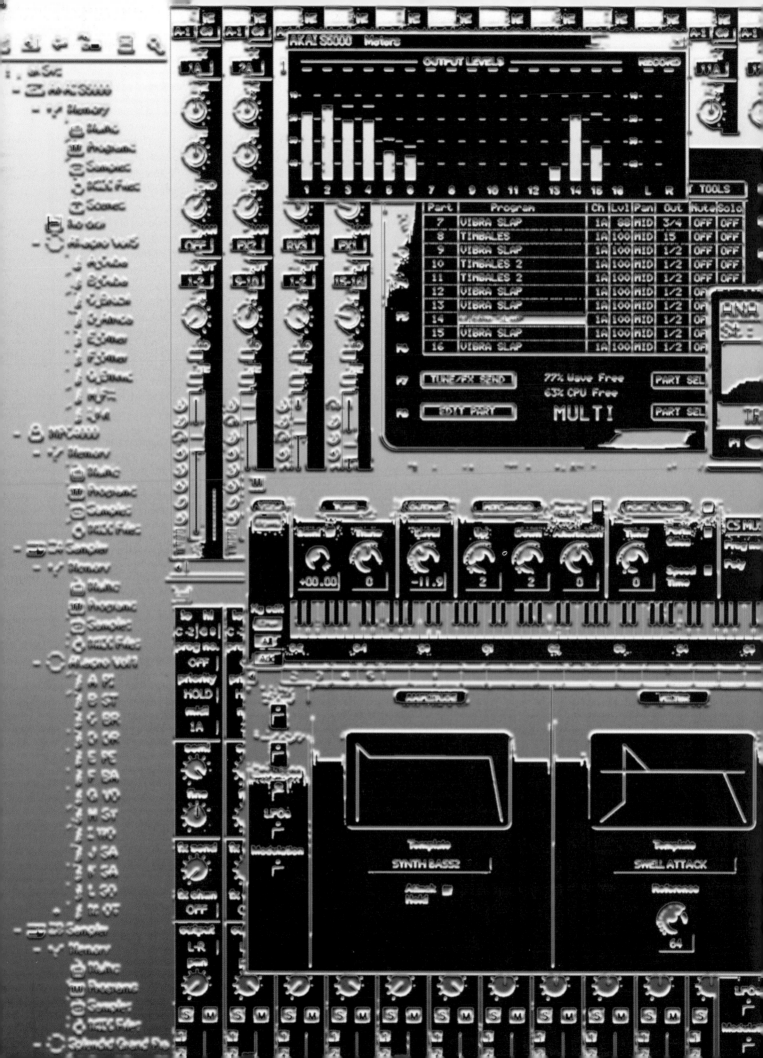

hardware
& software

If you haven't already got a sampler, or if you just want to read about some alternative options, this chapter will give you a fair idea of the general types on the market these days. The idea is not to cover every available model or brand, but simply to outline the broad types of sampling hardware and/or software you could use. For instance:

- Entry-level loop-based hardware and game-style software with sampling facilities.

- Professional hardware and software sampling options, including workstations and all-in-one integrated computer set-ups.

LITTLE LOOP-BASED HARDWARE SAMPLERS

The main purpose of basic samplers like these is to create loops. In this context loops are short sections of tracks (probably between one and four bars in length), which you believe might work being repeated. This can be particularly effective if, for instance, you loop a section of a song and mix back and forth between the looped section and the rest of the song. It's an instant remix in its purest form.

It's a little like 'back-to-back' mixing two copies of the same record to alter the order in which different sections of the track occur – only it's better. When you get bored with that you can (depending on your machine) play the loop backwards, which usually sounds pretty cool but can be tricky to mix in time. If your chosen machine has a filter or some effects, you can add these for extra colour. See the relevant sections on filters and effects in Chapter 6.

Basic samplers like this are available as either standalone machines or as 'onboard' sampling systems on DJ mixers. Each has its own merits: the onboard approach tends be cheaper, and simpler in terms of physical set-up in a 'bedroom studio' environment. A standalone unit might cost a little more, but will probably have more to offer in terms of facilities, such as basic effects, and be a little easier to integrate into a club situation. It's straightforward enough to plug a sampler into an installed mixer, but when DJs are swapping over in the course of a night, the music's not meant to stop, so there's not usually a chance to start changing mixers over between each set.

On many low-budget, so-called 'entry-level' loop samplers, the facilities for editing the start and end points of your loops can be cumbersome (even non-existent), so it's very good practice to learn to record your samples perfectly in time. You hit the record button at precisely the right moment, usually the first beat of a bar, and then hit the stop button bang in time too, usually at the end of a bar. Get this right and your loop repeats perfectly in-time without editing. Judgment of musical timing and tempo is a skill you should already have as a DJ and/or a musician.

Looping systems are also found on a lot of CD decks designed for DJ use. With many CD players there are no facilities to edit the start and end points of your loop, you simply have to hit a button at the right moments to set the correct start and end points. It's a major help if the loop facility is 'seamless', otherwise a moment of silence occurs between the end of the sample and playback starting again. Watch out for this seamless feature in the gear specification list. Non-seamless looping facilities are only any good for one-shot 'effect splashing'.

LOOP

A little word that's big in sampling mythology, and one that's been overused and abused by the media, so consequently causes some confusion. It's often misinterpreted as meaning *any* sample, but a loop is specifically a small section of sound that's repeated continuously. It plays from the start to the end and then, without a gap, plays from the start to the end and then, without a gap, plays from the start to the end… and round and round it goes forever – or till you make it stop. (There's lots more on loops in Chapters 4 and 5.)

ONE-SHOT

A sample played without immediate repetition. The sound plays from the start to the end and then stops. It can be played again at any time, but it *isn't* a loop.

EFFECT SPLASHING

One of the oldest forms of sampling is often called the effect splash… the name comes from sound effects production for film, TV and radio. It refers to the practice of using a short recording of a sound (passing train, thunderclap, bleating sheep and so on) as a background noise or sound effect. The tradition lives on in music production, where dropping in a single sound at a choice moment can create a sense of drama, fun, humour, pathos etc etc.

GAME-STYLE SOFTWARE

If you have a home computer or games console you'll no doubt already be blessed with quite a few options for testing the waters of making music with samples.

At the simplest end of the scale is a collection of game-style products, all of which retail for well under £50 ($75). These can give an extremely useful insight into the music production process in a very straightforward way. There's quite a selection available, but some of those particularly worth investigating, in no particular order of preference, are Acid Screenblast, eJay, Magix Music Maker, and FruityLoops (FL) Studio.

The way these products tend to be put together, they take a finished piece of music, separate each instrument, generate a sample of each, and then hand all the samples to you, the end user, for you to re-assemble as you wish.

Most then provide you with a standard 'block' style arrange window, which will be familiar to anyone who's used a software sequencing program. As seen in image 1, the main area of the screen is divided into a kind of grid. The screen-wide horizontal strips that are numbered down the left-hand side represent 'tracks'. The idea is that you can drag the provided samples (from an 'explorer' or folder-style browser window) out onto the screen and drop them wherever you want them. The samples are represented onscreen by the rectangular blocks. Usually each track is used to play back a single instrument, so you drag drum samples and place them on tracks you want to use for playing back drum samples, bass samples to tracks used for playing back bass samples, and so on.

Spreading out from left to right along the top of the main area is a ruler, which indicates time – appropriately called the 'timeline'. The left-hand side represents zero and the scale spreads out to the right. When you press Play, a vertical line, a time counter, moves across the screen from left to right. As it moves along, any samples you have placed on the screen will be played according to where they are on the timeline. How fast this counter moves across the screen is determined by you setting the 'tempo' of your song (we'll have more on tempo later).

In this beautifully simple manner you get to arrange your own version of the piece of music. If you try it you'll get the hang of it very quickly indeed. This system of tracks, blocks and a timeline happens to be the same format used by all of the professional audio+MIDI sequencing packages on the market today It's a perfect introduction to the first principles of sequencing, and of course manipulating samples.

It's hard to go wrong with this kind of 'painting-by-numbers' software. All of the samples you'll need are gathered together in groups that are at the same tempo, in the same musical key, and stylistically suited to each other... so it doesn't really matter what order you arrange them in, they will produce something that sounds like a reasonably coherent piece of music.

There are of course other games console products that

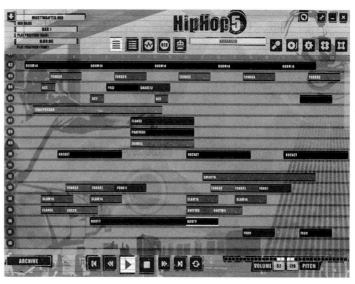

image **1**

SEQUENCERS

All music can be broken up into sequences. A sequencer is simply a hardware or software device that helps you structure a piece of music, playing a series of sounds back in a certain order and with specified timing relationships. Often it's done with the help of MIDI (Musical Instrument Digital Interface), the language that electronic instruments use to communicate with each other. With MIDI sequencing the sounds may be samples played back by a sampler, or sounds from a synthesiser, sound module, drum machine etc. But it's also possible just to control the timing and spacing of sounds manually, using an audio sequencer to rearrange blocks of sound onscreen. Many composers now tend to use a bit of both approaches to sequencing, hence the evolution of what's described in this book as audio+MIDI sequencers. (There's more about using MIDI in Chapters 3 and 7.)

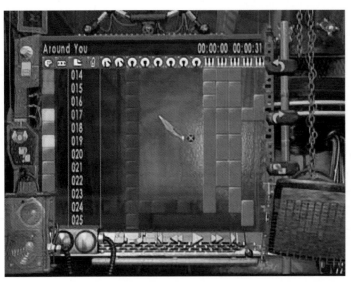

image **2**

endeavour to bring a little more traditional video game visual styling to the package – like MTV Music Gen2, seen in image 2). But they still employ the same basic underlying principles as the rest of the game-style genre, and the visual styling often doesn't make the actual music-making process any easier, or even more fun.

In terms of features, these products usually incorporate basic versions of some of the professional facilities and processes described later in this book: for instance you get to control the volume of each of the tracks; you can 'pan' any samples placed on a particular track (make them come from one speaker or the other); and there is usually a simplified set of effects that can be applied to individual tracks. There's always a basic stereo sound recording and editing window too. The really big differences between the features provided with these packages and the ones on professional systems are sound quality and depth of sophistication.

There are also some hidden hitches. The reason why these 'games' are as immediate as they are is that they remove the need for you to think about a number of first steps normally essential in music-making. By providing a jigsaw puzzle of ready-made samples that automatically fit together, they've made it possible for you to leap straight into the fun bit of arranging songs and playing with effects. But as soon as you deviate from the pre-prepared material, the whole enterprise tends to crash and burn. If you try to combine samples that have come from different songs, you very quickly realise that attempting to play two rhythmic samples together that were recorded at different tempos sounds terrible (like really bad beat-mixing). The same goes for musical key, musical style, and a fair few other factors.

There are several packages that rather cleverly get around the problem of combining samples recorded at different tempos – most notably Acid by Sonic Foundry. Provided your sample is four beats long, or you can inform Acid of the number of beats or bars within your sample (assuming it's a whole number), and you can specify the original time signature, Acid is able to automatically calculate the tempo of the source material. When you drag the sample out on to the screen, it is automatically stretched (or shrunk) to fit the tempo of your song.

Its ability to automatically alter tempo, and to a lesser extent musical pitch, has won Acid many fans, and brought the software into use within many professional studios as a tool dedicated to this job. More recently, Ableton Live may have snatched the crown here, thanks to an equally adept automatic stretching system, combined with a stack of additional live-performance-friendly features.

You can get some impressive results from entry-level audio sequencing packages, particularly if you utilise many of the reprocessing techniques explored throughout this book. In fact there are examples of hit records that have been produced with such basic products – after all, music is about your ideas and determination to make them a reality, not the technology you use. But at some point you begin to hanker after inventing your own rhythms, your own sounds, your own melodies. Which is where the learning curve steepens a little, and the rest of this book begins... The next step is to look at the more advanced sampling systems and platforms you can choose from, and explore the pros and cons of each.

PROFESSIONAL HARDWARE SAMPLERS

For around 15 years, rack-mountable hardware samplers ruled the roost – they were the only way you could get your hands on all the essential tools and techniques you'll find in this book. Now suddenly, in the past few years, software samplers have become the tool of choice in many studios, where, among other advantages, they can be easily integrated into a computer-controlled set-up.

But although new hardware models are thin on the ground, the traditional rack-mounting studio sampler is not quite dead yet. It still has a great deal in its favour, and is well worth investigating as a second-hand purchase if you're starting your first studio.

A professional studio hardware sampler is generally built into a sturdy metal box that will screw into a proper studio/live rack; on the front it has a smallish screen, a load of real buttons, usually a slider or two and a data wheel, and some have a number of multi-function knobs (more on this later). They store samples on either an internal or external hard disk, or onto a computer, so they have plenty of storage capacity. Most can be fitted with CD drives.

They play back all of their samples from a dedicated amount of RAM, so you always know how many samples they can cope with playing simultaneously. They come loaded with good quality filters, effects and all sorts of great tools for cutting up and twisting sound. Round the back they might have up to 32 high quality audio outputs for connecting to a mixer. They have their own internal power adapter, and are stable and rugged enough to survive life on tour... so if you're a live musician they will serve you brilliantly.

Hardware samplers are generally excellent value for money. They'll remain fully functional samplers for many years – unlike a computer, which is almost guaranteed to be obsolete very soon indeed. They represent a superb combination of facilities, reliability and value for money.

The predictable storage capacity of hardware samplers is also particularly well suited to the reproduction of professionally prepared multisamples of real instruments. (See Chapter 5 for more on multisamples.) Hardware samplers have always come with (often very large) libraries of traditional instrument samples on CD which can be loaded easily and fairly quickly. Many users never bother to make their own samples at all, they simply load up the factory-prepared libraries and start composing. As a result, the sampler manufacturers took to releasing machines that play back pre-prepared sound libraries but don't actually allow users to make their own samples. This brought down the cost of the machines and has proved to be a popular format... one that could well outlast the hardware sampler itself. These machines came to be known as 'sound modules' – models by E-mu, Roland, Korg and Yamaha remain popular.

But the future is not looking rosy for the trusty rack sampler. The cold hard facts are these: industry giants Yamaha have entirely ceased production of their 'A' series at the A5000; Roland no longer produce a dedicated rack-mounting studio sampler; and E-mu have ceased production of their E Series (their E6400 is shown in image 3). The other legendary name in hardware sampling, Akai, is the only company still active in this particular market – and it's with a product that's undoubtedly a hybrid between hardware and software. The whole idea of creating hybrids between computers and dedicated hardware looks like the way forward for all production systems, so we'll be exploring the concept more in a minute.

SOURCE MATERIAL

A sample in its original state – before it even becomes a sample – is called 'source material'. This helps remind us that all samples are recordings of a sound that originally came from a different source – whether you've recorded yourself playing acoustic guitar, or grabbed a drum sample from a CD – and so they will keep certain important attributes of the original sound, specifically tempo, musical key and tonal properties.

Layout of a hardware sampler

Although they're no longer in production, there are still plenty of old E-mu, Akai and Yamaha rack samplers circulating on the secondhand market.

The traditional Akai and E-mu way of doing things involves an LCD screen where literally all information is displayed. It can be helpful to visualise this screen as a little window onto a really big map... you can move the window around to look at different bits of the map but you can never see the whole picture. The map is three-dimensional, so you can move left, right, up, down, in and out. Moving the screen around the map is done via six 'cursor' buttons – usually configured in a little diamond of four arrow-shaped buttons to move left/right or up/down, plus a pair of enter and exit buttons.

image **3**

image **4**

image **5**

Editing what's on the screen at any moment is done via a set of 'soft' buttons, a numeric keypad, and a data entry wheel. The soft buttons are real hardware buttons placed immediately below the screen, whose effect depends upon what's on the screen – so they're a little bit like having a touch screen. Some models of sampler allow you to attach a computer keyboard and a mouse. The package is usually rounded off with a main output volume control, a headphone socket with level control, and an input recording level knob.

The Yamaha A series user interface (seen in image 4) is quicker to use. It provides an LCD screen accompanied by a row of soft dual-action knobs, whose effect is determined by what's on screen. These knobs have both a rotary and a push-click action, like a button. Navigating is done via a matrix, which consists of a grid with a row of buttons along the top and another column down the left side. At each intersection on the grid you find a particular editable function; so with just two button pushes – one from the top and one from the side – you can reach any parameter (a 'parameter' means any settable value controlling a process or sound). The A series also shipped with a software application called Wavesurgeon, an onscreen waveform editor and beat slicer – to use it you have to rather slowly transfer samples to the computer and back either via SCSI or MIDI (the latter is unbelievably slow at this job).

The only rackmounting hardware samplers still in production in 2004 are the Akai Z4 and Z8 (the Z8 is pictured in image 5). These retain some of the traditional control surface elements of older-style hardware samplers – such as the data wheel and soft function buttons for getting around – but also add one or two useful twists. The most obvious of these is that the Z range is popularly used as a hardware extension for the AkSys software (as discussed later in this chapter). Using AkSys is much like using a software sampler, but with the added advantages of a hardware add-on: a ready-made audio/MIDI interface with quality connections, greater stability and fixed capacity. The hardware connects to the computer via USB and the software offers more graphic control of the hardware. The samples stay on the hardware at all times.

Sampling workstations

Rack-mounted samplers have only ever been one part of the hardware story. Some people clearly prefer an all-in-one hardware solution to music composition, where you can create, play, record and edit your music all on one instrument. Products that fall into this category are called workstations.

The basic workstation formula is very simple – it's a combination of a hardware case, friendly dedicated control surface (with either keys or velocity sensitive pads for playing-in notes), a sequencer, onboard effects and a source of sounds. Some workstations provide a library of factory-prepared sounds, others provide sampling and some provide both.

Confusingly there are also a number of hardware-based digital multi-track recorders (with onboard effects etc) that are also often called 'workstations'. To avoid misunderstandings, we'll refer to these as digital audio workstations (DAWs). This format can be used in conjunction with a sampling workstation to form a very workable, fully hardware production set-up, and is a viable alternative to using a computer sequencing package.

As for sampling workstations, there are two different basic physical formats – the keyboard and the desktop style.

Keyboard workstations

The keyboard workstation grew out of the early synthesiser design ethos of providing a piano-style keyboard, a sound creation engine of some sort, and either an arpeggiator (see next page) or a basic sequencer.

The format has evolved enormously and is now very sophisticated. The keyboard is accompanied by the usual knobs, sliders and buttons for parameter control/sequencing, but there's also an extensive array of realtime control hardware like pitch/modulation wheels, MIDI controller knobs, touch pads, light beam controllers etc – all very tactile and immediate to use (there's lots more on the various controller options in Hands-On Sampling, Chapter 7).

The built-in sequencing facilities combine many different approaches to basic pattern and score sequencing. But they also offer interesting innovations in live sequencing tools, based around the notion of being able to physically 'play' entire sequences from the control surface to create new arrangements on the fly – as such they are considerably better suited to live arrangement improvisation than most computer-based sequencers (with the possible exception of the Ableton Live software sequencer).

The onboard effects are usually very high class, as are crucial elements like the audio quality of the A/D D/A conversion, and the rugged, reliable standard of audio input/output connections – we're talking about professional studio hardware here. Most importantly, the

SCSI
Small computer serial interface is a system for transferring data from one place to another within a computer system, or between a sampler and computer, for instance, using a multi-pinned D-Type connector. You can link as many devices as you like into a chain (using through connections in much the same way as MIDI), but it's vital that the last device in the chain is 'terminated' (check your manual for details). SCSI connections are gradually being replaced by USB, Firewire, and mLAN.

USB
Universal serial bus is a system that uses a specific type of cable (with square/rectangular plugs) to integrate 'peripheral' devices into a computer – for instance audio or MIDI interfaces, hardware controllers, and external data storage devices. Up to 127 devices can be connected in a series. The older USB1 has a maximum data transfer rate of 12Mbps (12 megabits per second); USB2 transfers data at up to 480Mbps.

FIREWIRE
Firewire is the more catchy name for IEEE1394 (or iLink) and was developed as a high-speed alternative to USB. Though its original data transfer rate is 400Mbps (roughly similar to USB2), it's theoretically going to be able to handle transfer rates of up to 2Gbps (two gigabits per second) in future. It can also connect devices directly to each other without the need for a computer between them.

ARPEGGIATOR

An arpeggio is where you play all of the notes in a chord individually, often in rapid succession, one after another, rather than simultaneously as in a chord.

An arpeggiator is a mechanical device that plays an arpeggio for you, automatically, based on the notes you hold down on a keyboard. The word dates from analog synthesisers in the 1970s, in the pre-MIDI and pre-sequencing era. The 'chord' you hold can be anything from a single note, which the arpeggiator simply repeats, to as many notes as the keyboard's polyphony will allow (see Chapter 4 for more on polyphony). The user can also adjust the speed to create or fit with a specific tempo.

Arpeggiators have remained reasonably popular, precisely because of the mechanistic feel they give to sequences of notes, and therefore to the music they produce. They're commonly used in the creation of techno and trance.

sampling facilities are highly sophisticated, with many innovative automated procedures. These compensate nicely for the slightly diminished visual display area of the user interface (the LCD panel).

Over recent decades, all the major keyboard/synth manufacturers have produced systems that have contributed to the evolution of the workstation. For quite a few years Korg seemed to have the edge with the Triton range, which has continued to evolve and still remains an extremely strong product. But it's now joined by the Motif range from Yamaha and the new Fantom range from Roland. The Roland Fantom can be expanded to offer 1GB of sample time – enough to undertake song-length samples that amount to multi-track recording capability.

Desktop workstations

The desktop workstation grew out of the classic sampling drum machine format. Some offer almost identical sequencing, sampling, effect facilities and so forth as keyboard workstations do, but served up in a wedge-shaped box that sits on top of a desk (or wherever else you want to place it). The top plate of the box is angled up away from the user and the controls are arranged ergonomically within a relatively small area.

Instead of providing a keyboard for playing-in rhythms and melodies, the desktop workstation retains the velocity-sensitive pads that are the hallmark of the drum machine, often arranged in a traditional rectangular format – as still employed by Akai with their MPC range. Other manufacturers arrange their pads slightly differently, often in a straight line, which is a layout that neatly suits step/pattern sequencing, and coloured black and white so they more closely represent an octave of keys on a piano keyboard. Roland have the MC-909 ('Sampling Groovebox') and four different SP models;

Yamaha have the RS7000; Akai have the MPC range (their MPC4000, as seen in image 6, has the advantage of utilising the AkSys computer-based operating software); while Korg have the likes of their Electribe SX (which includes their 'Valve Force' tube circuitry).

The appeal of the hardware workstation format lies in a simple combination: the versatility of sampling as a sound source, the tactile appeal of creating rhythms by hitting buttons and pads, and, probably most importantly, the suitability of such a compact all-round hardware solution for working live.

It's an option that's been loved and relied upon by several generations of hip-hop producers because it works particularly well if all you want to work with is drum patterns and sampled loops from records – which you can then take onto a stage to rap over.

To many people's surprise, the all-in-one hardware workstation seems to be undergoing a bit of a revival. And there are some pretty good reasons why this might

image **6**

be so. The most obvious is the resurgence of live performance, because hardware solutions like this are better suited to transportation and the stage environment. Not to mention the general stability of such systems compared to relatively unpredictable, crash-prone computer set-ups Having said this, the overall trend in music production, especially in studios, is towards having a computer at the heart of operations. Which brings us to...

USING COMPUTERS

The reason for the slow demise of the dedicated hardware rack sampler was the rise of the computer. A lot of studio hardware is simply a computer in a box – a computer that only does one job. This job could, theoretically, just as easily be done by a multi-purpose computer that's used for all other studio work too – an idea that's been attracting a lot of attention for a few years now. Obviously a very enticing and potentially cost-effective solution, it's turned out to be a bit of a false promise.

In a truly professional commercial studio – one fit to respond to the demands of different artists and projects from one day to the next – you need a lot of different things: multi-track audio recording and playback (a working minimum of 24 tracks), a mixer, compressors and other effects to balance the sound; then there's the issue of where you get your synthesiser or other instrument sounds from; then there's running a sequencer, mix automation... oh and of course sampling.

A state-of-the-art computer armed with an audio+MIDI sequencer can do all of these things. But not all at once – at least not consistently and reliably in a professional sense. Not without a bit of hardware help. It will happen, some day, but it hasn't yet.

The closest we have so far is Pro Tools, manufactured by Digidesign. The uninitiated might look at Pro Tools running and think, "There you go, one computer dong it all" – but there is a trick going on. The Pro Tools software requires that you install some additional hardware inside your computer – a PCI card, connected to an external hardware rack, which contains extra processors and extra RAM. So basically it's a piece of dedicated hardware lurking behind the scenes within a computer.

It's a very neat solution, which works very well, but it illustrates that even a state-of-the-art computer is not up to the job of powering a software-based studio unassisted. A Pro Tools HD system costs at least £4000 ($6000) – it's a superb, professional set-up, but is not as cost-effective for a beginner as buying a computer and using traditional studio hardware to lighten the load on the computer.

The Pro Tools approach is known as a DSP-based system, because it comes with its own digital signal processor, a specialist chip, on the PCI card, designed for recording and playback of music, which provides that extra hardware helping hand.

The two main software sequencing rivals to Pro Tools are Cubase, made by Steinberg, and Logic Audio, made by Emagic. Both of these are what's known as host-based applications, because they rely on the power and speed of the host computer's own central processing unit

COMPUTER ABBREVIATIONS

PCI means peripheral component interconnect; a PCI card is a printed circuit board that can be slotted into a computer to expand its capabilities – for instance a soundcard or audio card that might offer advanced music recording and playback, plus often high quality audio, digital and MIDI interface connections.

DSP stands for digital signal processing, where a specialist processor chip (often part of a PCI card) is used to translate analog signals into digital ones for more convenient manipulation and modification, easing the strain on the host computer's own central processor.

A **CPU** (central processing unit) is, strictly speaking, the term applied specifically to the single, sophisticated, often large silicon chip that is the heart, or rather brain, of a computer. Its speed determines the core speed of the computer. In practice, the term CPU is often used to refer to an entire computer hardware system in general.

RAM (random access memory) is the active memory of a computer, required to run the system software and other application programs. The more RAM your computer has, the better – especially nowadays, when just running the computer's basic operating system can be very demanding, not to mention using heavyweight music production software. The computer's RAM (measured in MB or GB), in conjunction with its CPU speed (measured in MHz), will indicate the practical power of your computer.

(CPU). There are now several significant host-based competitors to these packages, each of which can boast many happy customers – these include the increasingly popular PC-based Sonar by Cakewalk; the Mac-based Digital Performer by Mark Of The Unicorn (MOTU); Nuendo by Steinberg; and Vegas Pro by Sonic Foundry. Digidesign have also released their own host-based version of Pro Tools in the form of Pro Tools LE.

As computers improve and become even more powerful, it's quite likely that eventually host-based systems will become the industry-standard solution. This could still be some years away yet, so in the meantime a new way forward is emerging, which I'll discuss later in this chapter under 'The Third Way'.

Pro Tools, Cubase, Logic and their competitors offer hard disk audio recording, realtime effects processing, advanced mix automation and sophisticated MIDI sequencing – but unlike their hardware workstation cousins, they don't provide sampling facilities as such. Each platform does offer sampling functionality (and other add-ons such as software synthesisers and effects) via separate pieces of software known as plug-ins.

The idea is that the software sampler runs on your computer alongside the audio+MIDI sequencer, sharing the CPU and the RAM etc. MIDI from the sequencer is routed internally to the software sampler, and the sound from the software sampler is routed internally to the mixer of your audio+MIDI sequencer. The sound from the soft sampler is then dealt with and processed in exactly the same manner as sound recorded to the hard disk by the sequencer itself. It's a clever solution that works remarkably well… within the limitations of the power of a single computer.

Each sequencing package offers its own software sampler that will not work with the other platforms. Pro Tools has Soft Sample Cell (previous versions of Sample Cell needed their own PCI card with its own DSP and RAM, but Digidesign have discontinued this in favour of a host-based version). Logic works with Emagic's own EXS24 – which, from Logic 6.0 onwards, has become a standard part of Logic. Cubase uses Steinberg's own Halion.

In terms of functionality, each has its strengths, weaknesses and unique features, and is again a matter of personal preference – although you're governed to a large degree by your choice of sequencer. To some extent this buying decision has also become partly computer-platform based: since the 2003 purchase of Emagic by Apple Computer, Logic is no longer being developed for PC – from version 5.7 onwards it is Mac-only. Cubase remains cross-platform, as does Pro Tools.

Standalone software samplers

One way of increasing available computer power is to use two computers. One computer would be used mainly for hard disk audio recording and MIDI sequencing, while the other's used for sampling. If this is the way you want to go, you'll need a standalone software sampler, one that's not tied to any particular sequencing package. Such a set-up would offer all the traditional functions of a hardware sampler – particularly if you equip your computer with a professional multi-channel audio card and MIDI hardware control surface – but also much more, thanks to the added processing power of a dedicated computer. This approach effectively turns one computer into a dedicated sampler, connected and used in almost exactly the same way as a traditional hardware sampler.

This is not the only way to employ standalone soft samplers. In fact, all of the current standalone software sampler packages will run a stripped-down version of themselves within the major sequencing packages as an instrument plug-in, in much the same way as the own-brand software samplers. They do, however, require more CPU and RAM than you might hope, and consequently exacerbate any issues of lack of computer power.

There are four main products available: Kontakt by Native Instruments, Mach Five by MOTU, Gigastudio by Tascam, and Emulator X by E-mu. All three systems are very good, each with its own particular strengths and differences.

Native Instruments are accepted as a leading developer of modular software synthesisers (more about this in Chapter 6), and Kontakt benefits greatly from that fact. It has a sublime set of audio processing tools for transforming sound, and a unique tonal quality.

Gigastudio (formerly Gigasampler) came up with the idea of streaming samples from the hard disk, rather than needing to have the whole sample loaded in RAM prior to playback. The benefit is that Giga can play back longer and therefore more convincing samples of real instruments. There's an extensive library available for it, which makes best use of this feature.

Mach Five is a more recent product release and employs disk streaming or RAM-based playback, a simplified interface with strong sound-shaping tools, onboard sample editing and true cross-platform compatibility, which means it works with all major audio+MIDI sequencers and reads all known types of sample file format.

Emulator X is the most recent of the bunch, and so offers a comprehensive set of facilities to match the others, but it also uses dedicated hardware.

There are a few free software samplers available too, which perhaps don't offer quite the same degree of functionality, but will work with most of the PC-based sequencing packages.

Most notable is the DS-404, available via www.computermusic.co.uk

Layout of a computer-based sampler

What you're confronted with when you first run a software sampler largely depends on which software you use, but there are common features within all of them. The first point is that, unlike a hardware system, if you are at all computer literate you already have 50 per cent of the skills you need – you'll already know about browser windows, folders, drag & drop, and all the other things that are almost second nature to the average six-year-old nowadays.

There are really only a very small number of basic functions within a sampler. They are:

- A file system that enables you to load, save and organise your samples (more of this in Chapter 4).
- A sample and loop edit area, if it has this facility (see Chapter 4).
- A zoning and layering system to help you set up how samples respond to MIDI (more on this in Chapter 5).
- A set of filters, envelopes, LFOs or other sound-shaping tools, including onboard effects, if it has any (see Chapter 6).

The differences between one sampler and another lie in three areas: organisation, presentation, and sound. Organisation is all about how each designer/manufacturer has chosen to combine the various elements – how things are laid out onscreen and which buttons you press or knobs you turn to make stuff happen. Presentation is essentially about the way the controls actually look and is therefore partly cosmetic, although it does to some extent relate to the organisational factor.

The sound of each system is different because of the underlying coding of the software. No

image **7**

two computer coders do things exactly the same way, so no two pieces of software (or hardware) sound the same. The simplest way of explaining the different approaches to interfaces is to use pictures – screengrabs taken while using various software sampling systems. So here are a few to have a look at...

Steinberg Halion 2

Image 7 shows the main screen in Halion – the 'macro view'. Halion keeps the keyboard visible in each view for easy auditioning of samples, checking MIDI activity LEDS, accessing program and channel selection buttons and file load/save buttons. The filter, amplifier, envelope and tune controls are all here too. The buttons below the keyboard swap the screen over to other views, showing things like Key/Zone View and Env/Filter View, and Mod/Tune View (these various functions will be explained in the coming chapters). The Env/Filter View is seen in image 8, showing the controls for the filter and amplifier envelopes; the tracker ball and list to the right are for quick file selection.

image **8**

Emagic EXS24 MKII

The EXS24, originally launched for the Emagic Logic sequencing package, manages to cram quite a lot of stuff into a single main page (as seen in image 9 on the left) – partly because it's a mono-timbral device, so it only has to deal with one keyboard zone of samples. The raised area is the filter, which has complex velocity sensitivity and tuning controls to either side of it. Running along the middle is the modulation matrix. At the bottom are controls for three LFOs and two envelopes. There are separate pages for key/velocity zoning and preferences.

image **9**

MOTU Mach Five

MOTU take a more-or-less single-view approach (as in image 10, right), even though Mach 5 is a multi-timbral sampler.

Running down the left side are instrument loading and mixer sections. The bottom half of the middle section is devoted to the filter, three envelopes, velocity controls and an Aux Send system for effects. The top half of the middle section shows two edit windows, one for key/zone setting and the other for actual sample editing and loop editing. Both these two windows can be expanded to fill the whole display area. Down the right edge are various tuning controls and the four-part effects sections.

E-mu Emulator X

Emulator X from E-mu is a massive undertaking. It's a multi-timbral sampler with a truly huge array of functions and features, so it would have been impossible for E-mu to stick to a single-window interface. It offers an overall main page with many of the controls for the type of tools you might wish to tweak in realtime, laid out in a graphic style. From the main page you are taken off to separate edit windows for importing/recording/organising samples, editing individual samples, organising multi-timbral collections, or more detailed editing of individual sampler instruments. (Emulator X not pictured here.)

image **10**

Akai AkSys

Akai AkSys (see image 11, right) is a software/hardware hybrid, as mentioned in the hardware sampler section a few pages back. The software aspect of the system takes what is primarily a single-window approach, with a graphic interface resembling a studio mixing console, accompanied by a set of controls representing tools for sound shaping and synthesis. A number of smaller windows can then be opened to access smaller 'floating' windows for layering/zoning, filters/envelopes, effects, and individual sample editing.

image **11**

NI Kontakt

Kontakt takes a split-screen approach. Always visible down the left half of the screen is a large explorer-style file-browsing window where you locate samples you want to use. Down the right side is a graphic representation of a studio 'rack' system. When you load a sample it's placed into an instrument (seen at the top of the rack in image 12). Buttons expand the instrument by opening up additional slots in the rack for layering/zoning, filters and effects. It's a neat system that lets you open all of the different editable functions of a single sampler instrument in one vertically scrollable window. The set-up is good for detailed editing of every aspect of an individual instrument, though not quite so good for realtime tweaking of sound-shaping tools for all instruments at once.

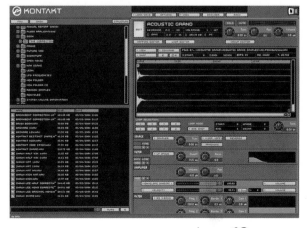

image **12**

image **13**

NI Intakt

Intakt is a dedicated looping and slicing machine, so all of its functions are laid out in a single window, as seen in image 13. The browser down the left makes locating samples quick, and all sample editing, filter and effects controls are easily accessible.

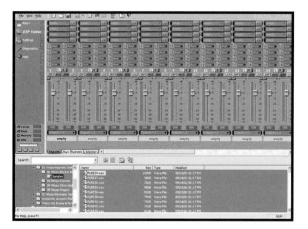

image **14**

Tascam Gigastudio

Gigastudio – which Tascam claims is "the world's most powerful sampler" – uses an interesting approach, as seen in image 14. A series of buttons in the pane down the left of the screen switch the rest of the screen over to different aspects of the system. There are two main windows, one for loading samples and setting their relative volumes and another for applying filters and effects etc.

THE THIRD WAY – MIXING HARD & SOFTWARE

The DSP-based system solution is growing in popularity as an answer to the lack-of-computer-power issue. The Pro Tools hardware is dedicated to Pro Tools software, so that's no good if you want to use an alternative sequencer – it will allow other products to play back audio through its audio outputs, it just won't lend them its DSP and RAM.

But there are several other DSP-based solutions. Powercore by TC Electronic, for instance, employs a PCI-card full of DSP to run the TC range of effect plug-ins. Plug-ins can consume an awful lot of system resource, so having effects taken care of lightens the load on your computer considerably (for either Mac or PC). Powercore does not have any audio outputs so it's not a soundcard, and won't function independently of a computer – it's purely there to provide additional system resources for its plug-ins.

The flagship of the TC computer-based range (they make traditional studio hardware effect processors too) is the recent Powercore Firewire, which offers even more DSP power and connects to the host computer via Firewire (though it's not an mLAN-enabled device as yet). The Powercore Firewire system has been 'open source' for some time now – meaning other manufacturers can create software that uses its power – and although it will still not share its power with your audio+MIDI sequencer/DAW or VST plug-in effects, an increasing range of high-quality plug-in effects and instruments is now available for it.

Related to Powercore in some ways is the emergence of the Yamaha 01x. This is an interesting hybrid that's one of the first products to employ mLAN. It's essentially a fully independent 26-channel digital mixing desk with motorised faders, onboard dynamics processing and high-quality effects. It operates as a standalone hardware product but also connects to your computer via Firewire and functions as an audio and a MIDI interface and as a fully-fledged MIDI hardware control surface (see Chapter 7). Because all your audio is passing through the 01x on its way to and from your computer, the effects and compression etc are available for processing sounds within your sequencer, and so lighten the load on host system resources. The onboard dynamics, effects and all hardware mixer controls come with software control surfaces that load into your audio+MIDI sequencer as though they are VST plug-ins – so you can edit onscreen with the mouse even though the effects are actually being generated within the hardware.

Working with the 01x is interesting because it's possible to use the hardware to perform most of the mixing functions of your sequencer entirely from the control surface. This makes you feel like all the power of the sequencer is actually within the hardware. It feels like using an old-style hardware system when you are in fact using a computer – it provides excellent tactile control combined with enormous power . But it also feels like you can control your hardware from the computer when you want to… so it amounts to the best of both the hard and soft worlds, which is surely a sign of things to come.

The 01x is also significant because in order to run the dynamics and effects, and to operate as a standalone unit without being connected to a computer at all, it's armed with DSP and RAM. It seems very likely that it won't be long before *all* the software running on your

mLAN

The 'music local area network' concept, originally developed by Yamaha, uses the Firewire cable system to create a network out of all of the hardware in your studio, transmitting both audio and MIDI information down the same cable. You take a cable from one piece of equipment to another, then another, in the same way as a through connection for MIDI or SCSI. Items can be in any order, and there can be as many as you like in the chain. This single chain of cables has the carrying capacity (or bandwidth) to carry all audio and MIDI information throughout the entire system – up to 100 channels of pristine digital audio or hundreds of cables' worth of MIDI. mLAN will drastically reduce the quantity and hassle of cabling in most studios. It's not cheap, and at the moment it's rare in samplers – though there are mLAN interface boxes available for some units.

VST

This stands for 'virtual studio technology', a term originally associated with software developers Steinberg and their application Cubase VST. This wasn't the first software package to emulate an audio recording and mixing environment – complete with mixing consoles, effects processors etc – but Steinberg cleverly licensed the drivers for their system to other software developers, quite a few of whom have created software effects 'plug-ins' to integrate with VST, making VST a de facto standard. Even Emagic have made Logic compatible with VST plug-ins.
Pro Tools and Cakewalk do not support VST technology, but you can use so-called 'wrappers' – these effectively disguise plug-ins of one format so they can be used within the 'wrong' host application.
VSTi means 'virtual studio technology instrument'. A few years after Steinberg unveiled VST, computers had increased in power sufficiently to make it possible to create and run actual software instruments, like samplers and synthesisers, rather than just effects and mixing tools. The term VSTi was coined simply to make a distinction between software instruments and software effects.

computer will be able to access and use those additional resources. This seems particularly likely with the recent announcement of a strategic development partnership between Yamaha and Steinberg, aimed specifically at developing the future of mLAN and the 01x.

In 2004, E-mu somewhat unexpectedly rose from the ashes of its demise as a hardware sampler manufacturer with the release of Emulator X. After a considerable absence, E-mu have produced a software sampler that looks to be a very strong future contender, because it features all of the patented filter technology, effects and various other sonic things that made E-mu hardware samplers so popular. Interestingly, E-mu have still kept faith with the hardware option to some extent, as the Emulator X is dependant on a PCI card with proprietary DSP onboard (which is used for effects) – this makes the Emulator X a cross between a standalone software sampler and a hardware-dependant DSP-based system like Powercore or 01x. Emulator X is the only software sampler with built-in audio recording and editing facilities – including audio in/out on the PCI card.

The release of the Emulator X presents a strong challenge not only to the new school of standalone software samplers but also to the Akai Z series of rack samplers. Akai have been treading the fine line between hard and software for a while now with this rather neat solution to the DSP vs host-based issue. The Z is a hardware rack sampler, with all the benefits of predictability and stability that brings, but as we've seen it comes bundled with AkSys software to control the sampler entirely from a computer (with the hardware connected via USB and the samples remaining in the hardware at all times, much like 01x). With the dedicated front panel hardware controls and the software editing facilities, the Z series is incredibly user-friendly, quick and versatile.

It's important to grasp the subtle difference between these two approaches: the Emulator X is very much based within your computer, so it can run as a VST instrument within your audio+MIDI sequencer. The Akai way is still married to the analog world, because its audio outputs are on the back of the actual hardware rack unit. Each approach has its advantages – the Akai is possibly better suited to the live musician and the E-mu perhaps best for those seeking a fully integrated computer studio solution.

SOFT DRUM SAMPLERS & SOUND MODULES

The drum machine hasn't been left out of the software revolution. Hardware drum machines may offer a set of (usually 16) dedicated pads on which you tap out beats, each pads playing back an individual sample of a drum sound, and you can usually switch between 'banks' of drum sounds, making 128 or 256 individual samples available. Their main strength is simplicity and speed of use. There's something very musically conducive about just reaching over and hitting a pad and knowing a familiar drum sound will appear – especially if it's a sound you like.

The format has been reborn in a series of plug-in instruments that offer you the same approach on screen – except of course you don't get the joy of tactile pad-tapping. But they do respond to MIDI, so you can tap out your beats from a keyboard instead (which, truth be told, is not as nice, but it'll do). As usual with software reincarnations you get a lot more besides: primarily hundreds if not thousands of drum sounds, so you always know where you can quickly and easily access the sounds you need. Many also offer filters, envelopes and effects on each individual sample too… and of course the ability to import home-made or sourced samples to create new banks of sounds. Good examples of this are the LinPlug RMIV, FXpansion DR008, and Battery by Native Instruments.

The one and only BFD...

There is one sample-based software instrument that stands out from the crowd when it comes to acoustic drum sounds. BFD by FXpansion is an incredible illustration of what can be achieved through a combination of a good drummer, a selection of vintage drum kits, a good studio full of the best microphones, a sampler and some exceptional skill. It's another simple idea that has been executed beautifully, using techniques similar to those described in the 'Out In The Real World' section in Chapter 3.

The team who made the BFD hit upon the bright idea that it might be great if you recorded a selection of different drum kits using the same set of microphones in the same positions within the same live recording room, and then put the results back together so the user can exchange individual instruments within the kit, in the knowledge that they'll still fit together tonally and acoustically.

The mike set-up for the recording was quite complex, and worth looking at briefly here to demonstrate just how much work is involved in obtaining high-quality samples of acoustic instruments like drums. They used thorough close-miking, including front and back mikes on the kick drums, top and bottom mikes on the snares, and individual mikes on each drum and cymbal. They also placed an overhead pair of condenser mikes reasonably close to the kit, another pair some four metres or so away, and then a pair of PZMs (pressure zone microphones) at the boundaries of the recording space. Using these three pairs of room mikes captures the natural reverb of the recording room at three different reverb times (see Chapter 6 for more about reverb). Each drum or cymbal was sampled individually, and up to 12 times each, struck in different ways every time. The mass of 24-bit 48KHz samples (an astoundingly huge 9GB in total for seven drum kits) is then built into a very subtle and sophisticated velocity-layered MIDI-responsive software drum machine... When you read the section on building velocity-layered instruments in Chapter 5 you'll appreciate what a labour of love this must have been.

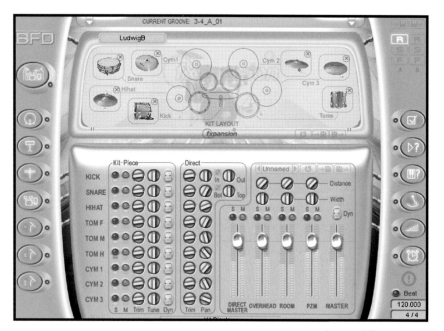

image **15**

Image 15 shows the BFD user interface. It has a few unique features: each individual kit element has its own level and pan controls, but there are also three more faders that control the level of the three sets of room mikes. These can help adjust the amount and blend of natural reverb on the kit. The really clever bit is that, because every drum was recorded with the mikes in the same places, you can swap, mix and match different individual drums between kits and they seamlessly fit together... right down to the natural reverb.

Sonically, the results are amazingly rich and utterly convincing. This is partly down to the sensitive way in which each drum or cymbal responds to different MIDI note velocities, and the presence of a clever global dynamics control that offsets all incoming note velocities. So you can get a sequenced MIDI drumbeat up-and-running, turn the global dynamics up or down, and it's like the drummer is hitting the whole kit harder or softer. It really does sound like a very skilled drummer in action.

The package is finished off with an extensive collection of MIDI files containing un-quantised recordings of an outstanding drummer playing a Roland V-Drum MIDI drum kit. In my opinion, BFD is by far the most convincing and downright gorgeous sample-based drum instrument ever made.

Software sound modules

The sound module has also been reborn in software form. Several packages have emerged – like Hypersonic by Steinberg and Sampletank by IK Multimedia – offering hundreds of ready-made instrument multisamples. This format has now become known as the ROMpler, because they are essentially samplers that don't sample (ie they use read-only memory, or ROM).

To be honest, they're not too popular with some critics, who feel that software samplers like Kontakt and Gigastudio offer better quality factory-prepared instruments, with plenty of other features thrown in. It could also be strongly argued that hardware products from E-mu, Roland and Yamaha still offer better quality sounds, and more of them, and hardware control surfaces to boot. And it's surely only a matter of time before somebody (probably E-mu, Roland or Yamaha) actually releases a really good software ROMpler.

SOFTWARE SAMPLE EDITORS

Referring to all software-based sampling systems as samplers is a little misleading. Only one of them actually records audio (E-mu's Emulator X), the rest are better described as dedicated sample *players*. But using EXS24, Halion and Sample Cell, which all operate exclusively within host sequencers (Logic, Cubase and Pro Tools), sample recording and basic editing duties can be carried out within the host software.

If, on the other hand, you are using Kontakt or Gigastudio on a computer dedicated to sampling, or you are using a hardware sampler and wish to transfer your samples to your computer for editing, you need a dedicated piece of sample editing software.

There are five main packages in common use: Sound Forge by Sony, Wavelab by Steinberg, and Cool Edit by Syntrillium (all PC-only); Spark by TC Electronics, and Peak by Bias (both of which are Mac-only). There are loads more available too, and many of them are free, but the ones listed are professional standard and very well specified.

All the packages offer very similar basic features. These sample editors are your toolbox when it comes to recording and editing the actual content of your samples. They're used for literally hundreds of editing tasks, which will be covered as and when appropriate as the book progresses.

Basic operation of a software sample editor

Regardless of whether you're using one of the five main professional software sample editing packages or one of the stack of very low-cost or free versions, the basic layout is almost always the same. Have a look at the example in image 16 on the next page.

This screengrab comes from Wavelab. The main area of the screen is occupied by a large two-part graphic display of your recorded sample. The vertical axis of the waveform display shows the volume level of events within your sample (not the frequency). The horizontal axis

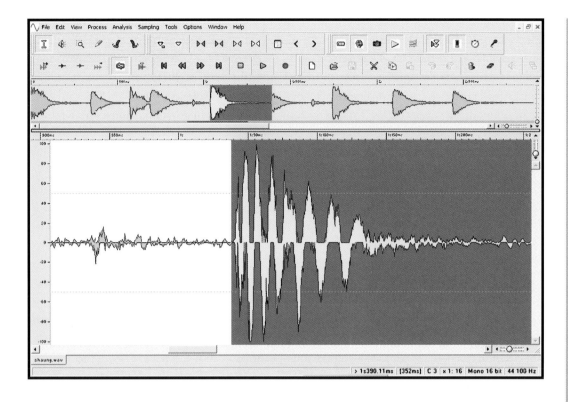

image **16**

shows time. Between them you can get a quick and highly effective picture of where all the different events in your sample are in relation to each other. Although it doesn't show frequency (which would obviously aid identifying different instruments), you will very quickly become adept at 'reading' a display because things like kick drums are always physically louder than things like hi-hats, and different types of sound have different 'shapes'.

The larger waveform display is where you do all your detailed editing etc. The smaller one above it is for navigation – it shows an overview of your sample. This can be really useful when you're working on longer samples and want to be able to keep an eye on which particular part of the overall sample you're currently editing (otherwise, when you have the main waveform zoomed in, it can be easy to get lost). For image 16 I've zoomed in on an individual kick drum within a drum beat. This means you can see the kick in great detail, but we can also look at the overview and be confident which kick drum within the sample you're currently zoomed in on.

There are several ways to zoom the display. You either grab and drag one of the little handles (in the bottom right corner of the displays), or use the little arrows on either side of the handles, or hit the magnifying glass zoom tool button and then click on the display. When you try it, it will all soon become obvious.

You should find that you can change the actual calibration of the two axes (shown to the side or above the main waveform display). There's often a range of options available, but the most important is the ability to change the horizontal axis from showing time in mins/secs/ms to bars/beats/ticks. In some circumstances (particularly when trying to cut 'sound for picture', as in video/film soundtrack editing, or in other non-musical sound design tasks) what you really want to know is the amount of time that's elapsed from the start of the sample. At other times (when working with rhythmic material in a music production environment) it's more beneficial to have an indication of where you are in terms of bars or beats.

In most applications, right mouse-button clicking (Mac = control-click) will call up a drop-down menu of options. When working with tempo-based material in this way it's essential to ensure that the overall project tempo is set correctly for the specific sample. In Wavelab, global tempo setting is done in the Preferences window, other applications have an onscreen tempo display where you can numerically alter the project tempo.

Running in a strip along the very top you can see a standard set of pull-down menu labels. As with most computer software, these menus contain everything you need to set up and use every aspect of the software – much of which is duplicated within the 'button' system (also accessible via right mouse-click menus or keyboard commands). The numerous buttons can be seen immediately below the menu tags. These are either 'one-touch' shortcuts for various operations, or they open up other more specialised editing windows and menus.

In this example, running logically from left-to-right, starting in the top left corner we have: cursor selection tools, which determine whether the cursor acts as a selection tool or an audio scrub tool that starts playback from cursor position; magnifying glass display zoom tool; pencil for drawing waveforms or editing data; and kickers that jump playback position from one marker to the next. Then there's a set of marker tools for dropping and jumping between markers, and a set of window tools that open up ancillary edit windows.

On the next line down there's a collection of transport buttons to control playback, and a standard set of loading/saving/cutting/copying/trashing tools. Running in a little strip along the very bottom of the screen, below the displays, you can see a collection of information regarding the currently loaded and selected sample: in this instance the length of sample, root note (if the sample has such embedded sampler zone information (see 'keyboard mapping' in Chapter 5), and the sample recording properties – mono/16-bit/44.1kHz.

The contents, layout, colour scheme etc of the entire set-up can be re-configured and customised to suit your own working methods or visual tastes. The way in which the various tools and so on are displayed will vary between the five main commercial sample editors, but they all offer more or less the same functionality, at least on paper – their actual sound/performance is inevitably variable.

KEYBOARD COMMANDS

Something that can come as a bit of a shock for beginners when they first see a seasoned pro using a computer set-up is that there's far more use of the computer keyboard than the mouse. This is because almost every operation in a good-quality piece of music software sampler can be executed with a keyboard command – pressing one or more keys to carry out an operation, instead of clicking on drop-down menus etc. The most obvious and useful example is that the 'space bar' is generally used to start and stop playback. In fact, by combined use of the ctrl, alt, shift, alphanumeric keys, function keys, directional arrows, enter and delete etc, you can use many soft samplers without ever touching the mouse. It can take a bit of practice to learn all the key commands for your system, but it can effectively halve the time it takes to get things done. You should find a list of the keyboard command set for your software in the Preferences; sometimes you can actually customise them to suit your own needs, or create your own from scratch.

OTHER SOFTWARE SAMPLING OPTIONS

There are a number of software products that defy easy categorisation. These take several different approaches and have their own unique features that make them noteworthy, but they have several things in common.

The most obvious similarity is their typically reasonable price. They are all, in effect, systems suited to genuinely creative music production, offering a fairly comprehensive set of sequencing and sampling facilities, plus effects, at an affordable one-stop price. They've proved easy enough to get to grips with, offering immediate gratification to first-time users, yet are extensive enough to provide long-term creative potential. They're possibly not quite as comprehensive or well-endowed as the market-leading audio+MIDI sequencers, but they give them a run for their money in other ways.

These products include Reason, Ableton Live, and Making Waves.

Reason

Reason, by Propellerhead Software from Sweden, is an immensely popular package that sits firmly between the game-style approach and more comprehensive and professional systems. Reason is similar to a workstation in concept in that it offers a complete music production environment.

Onscreen (as you'll see in image 17) it takes the form of a vertically stacked studio-style rack… and yep, it's almost certainly one of the coolest looking bits of kit on the block. Reason gives you a collection of devices you can load into the rack, including: a standard block-style sequencer; an analog-style pattern sequencer; two synthesisers; a drum machine; 11 effects; a mixer; transport controls; and three different samplers. The devices are all presented in analog style with knobs, sliders and buttons for you to move with the mouse. The rack is theoretically endless, so you can load up as many of these devices as your computer can handle.

As for the three samplers: the NN19 is a sample player with basic keyboard zoning facilities and a simple set of filters and envelopes; NNXT is an expanded version of NN19, with more complex zoning and layering facilities and increased sound-shaping and external control toolkit; and then there's Dr Rex, which only plays back REX files created by Steinberg's slicing & looping software package, Recycle (which we'll talk more about in Chapter 6). The whole point of REX files is that they have been sliced up for resequencing, and Dr Rex lets you adjust settings for each slice; and it automatically creates MIDI files from REX data, placing it into a sequencer for resequencing.

Reason is not equipped for actual audio sampling, so it requires a separate piece of software for recording and editing samples. But it's a very clever and extremely impressive set-up. It's easy to see why it's so popular – it looks great and is really easy to use. The analog-style control surface is very appealing; the vast majority of controls are laid out before you, so it responds really well to semi-random experimentation with settings. At the same time it's also fairly sophisticated in terms of capabilities, so quite complex compositions can be put together with ease.

If there is a downside to Reason, it may be the simple fact that it's all made by one company. This may seem like an odd observation (after all, that's why everything works so smoothly together), but there is sense to it. If this were a real studio rack, most of the gear would be made by different manufacturers. The sounds each machine produced would be generated by slightly varying technologies and circuitry and would reflect the sonic vision and, crucially, aesthetic taste of a range of designers. Reason has a tendency to sound like Reason. It's a magnificent sound, but it is distinctive, and can perhaps get a bit samey, a bit lacking in textural variety. Indeed some people say you can spot instantly when a piece of music has been made with Reason. Strangely, it's not a sound you hear much on commercial recordings.

image **17**

Ableton Live

Live, made by German company Ableton, was designed as an audio sequencer, to specialise in using audio samples. It has MIDI capability – namely a rather extensive implementation of MIDI controller assignment, so it's well suited to control from a hardware control surface – but it doesn't feature a MIDI sequencer as such. It's essentially based around a standard block-style linear sequencer (as you can see here in image 18), but it's oriented towards live onstage performances.

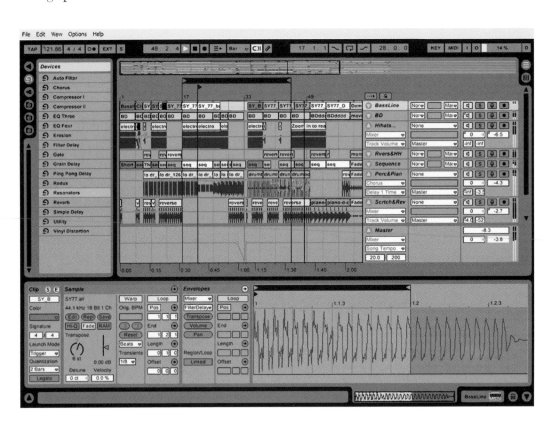

image **18**

Ableton Live is particularly good at automatically adjusting the tempo of audio files to match current song tempo (without affecting pitch). In fact it can tempo-adjust samples as you add them to a project without stopping playback. It's also able to rapidly change the song tempo in response to a numeric adjustment, or to a 'tempo tap' – again it does this on the fly without stopping.

To accompany these two particularly live/DJ-friendly facilities, it's also crammed with 'live sequencing' tools. For instance you can assign audio tracks to either the computer keyboard or incoming MIDI, so you can mute and un-mute individual audio files as the song plays.

There's plenty more to the software (like effects, full automation and so on), but as the name suggests, Ableton Live has acquired a very strong and devoted fanbase whose main interest is live performance, because it does things that the market-leading sequencers don't.

Making Waves

Making Waves, from the UK's Making Waves Audio, is also an audio sequencer, with some clear strengths that make it unique. It's been built from the ground up with audio sequencing in mind, so it uses a somewhat different sequencing environment to the other products mentioned here. Rather than the standard block audio+MIDI approach, it favours a much simplified 'dots on a grid' graphic (as you can see in image 19). The playback cursor still moves from left to right in the normal manner, but unlike a standard audio+MIDI sequencer, different audio files (samples) cannot share a track.

If you place a dot on the grid for a particular track, sample playback starts from the dot (in its relative location within the timeline). If you drag onwards into adjacent blocks on the grid, a line appears indicating an increased sample playback length. It's pretty straightforward and works incredibly well.

To create melodic sequences, you open a simple grid sequencer for each track with bars/beats on the horizontal axis and notes on the vertical. By placing blocks in the grid you can create melodies. Unlike most standard systems, this note grid extends for the entire length of the song, encouraging you to treat the entire arrangement for each track as a single sequence.

When adding effects, the approach is equally canny. If you create an 'effect track' below an audio track, the effects are applied to the audio track above – if you want more than one effect on a particular track, you just create more effect tracks. The send level and various parameters for the effects can also be sequenced via another deadly simple grid-based sequencer.

Remember, this is all sequencing audio samples directly, not via MIDI, and this is one of the reasons Making Waves operates with an incredibly low system resource overhead (the software will run on very primitive computers and still deliver the goods). As it happens, the audio sequencing capabilities can be used to send MIDI note information too, so although it might lack some sophistication, Making Waves will serve as a MIDI sequencer too. It is VST compatible too, running VSTi and VST effects.

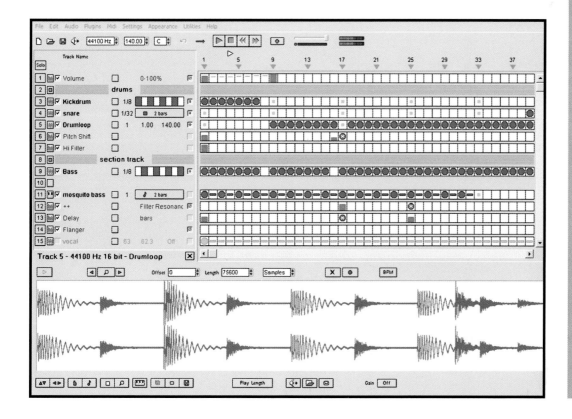

image **19**

1   5   9

Volume   0-100%

drums

Kickdrum   1/8   F

snare   1/32   2 bars   F

Drumloop   1   1.00   140.00   F

Pitch Shift

Hi Filter

section track

Bass   1/8   F

mosquito bass   1   2 bars

**   Filter Resonance

Delay   bars

Flanger

Track 5 - 44100 Hz 16 bit - Drumloop

Offset 0   Length 75800   Save

Play length

CHAPTER 3
setting up
& source
material

Once you've decided on which hardware and/or software sampler you want to use, you need to get some other bits of gear to connect it to, and some sounds to load into it…You have to think about your music-making environment too – how and where you set up your system. At its most basic level, this can make the difference between hearing a sound when you stab your keyboard or pulling your hair out because you hear nothing at all. But it goes deeper – a bit of old-fashioned homework, learning the basic rules, some forward-planning and attention to detail, can actually improve your music.

This chapter covers:

● Arranging your studio and positioning gear effectively.

● Using the right cables and connectors.

● Choosing source material – how and where to find samples, from the internet to your local shopping mall. Includes tips on DIY sound recording.

Where everything goes

There are a couple of very basic rules to follow when setting up any kind of music production studio (even if it's in your bedroom). It's all about connecting/operating your equipment efficiently, and being able to listen back to exactly what you're creating.

If you can't accurately hear what you're doing, you won't know what your music really sounds like, which kind of defeats the object. So a pair of decent studio reference monitors is essential. Too many aspiring producers ignore this basic fact, and then wonder why their music sounds all wrong when it's finished and played back in a club or on a demo CD. You can learn a lot about music production using hi-fi speakers, but trying to mix a record with them is pure guesswork, and the end result almost never sounds right outside of your own home studio. At the very least invest in a pair of studio reference headphones.

When you're using monitor speakers, place them at least two metres apart, the same height off the ground as each other, preferably not less than 2m from a wall. In an ideal world you, the listener, should sit at the point of a triangle, 2m from each speaker. The speakers should be angled in by about 45 degrees so they point directly at you – and you really shouldn't be less than 2m from the back wall of the room either. In the real world, your average bedroom is unlikely to be so accommodating, but if you get as near to the ideal as you can, it'll be worth it. If it's not possible all the time, at least try to make sure you'll be as close to the ideal listening position as possible while working on the final mix of your music.

Even if you have monitor speakers, it's worth having a decent pair of headphones – some small sonic details are easier to hear on 'cans', and they can be useful for recording audio, when using speakers can cause feedback (or just minimising neighbour-provoking noise).

It helps a lot if you can reach everything from a single seated position. This is obviously easily achievable if you're working with an entirely computer-based system or with a single hardware workstation – just place your system between the speakers and get on with it.

With a hardware-based or modular studio, things tend to spread out, and the more equipment you have the less likely you are to be able to reach everything. So things should be grouped according to what they're used for: in other words, keep the writing tools together – ie the sequencer (almost certainly running on your computer), your sampler, main keyboard, sound modules, etc. Then place the mixing tools together – the mixer itself, racked effect processors, etc.

It's a good idea to plan the layout of your studio on paper before you start setting up.

Getting connected

Have a think about what sort of sounds you're going to want to sample and how you're going to get them into your sampler, and position all of your equipment accordingly – before you begin plugging in cables. This is particularly important in a basic studio without a patchbay (an audio cable junction-box), or if you're planning to use microphones.

Make sure you buy cables that are long enough to reach the desired equipment, and try to avoid ending up with messy tangles of wires. If you can steer clear of bunching cables together, and particularly if you keep audio leads away from power cables, you will end up with less hum.

Connect all power cables first, then all the control cables (MIDI, SCSI, USB, Firewire, or mLAN). Then connect your audio cables – but think about it first. If you're working with a limited set-up, are there going to be things you'll need to constantly re-plug?

SIGNAL
The flow of sound (or electrical impulses) down a wire or through a circuit.

For example, let's say you have a small mixing desk with just enough inputs and outputs to accommodate your sampler, synthesiser, effects units etc, and this set-up uses all of your available power outlets. A guitarist and a friend with an old synth come round to work on a track. You will need to find power sockets for their equipment, and a way of connecting their audio outputs. You'll almost certainly need to disconnect some of your gear to accommodate them – and if you haven't planned for this, you could find yourself pulling half your set-up apart to achieve this apparently simple task. I know it sounds pedantic, but it can be very frustrating. Once you've set your studio up you don't want to be squeezing into corners, dragging stuff about and making a mess – chances are you'll accidentally disturb other connections, and cause yourself problems that may be tricky to trace.

Know Your Wires

There are two basic types of audio connection, balanced and unbalanced. Balanced cables contain three wires rather than two. Why is that better? Well, as Spinal Tap might put it, it's *one more*, isn't it?

The thing to bear in mind about audio cables is that, although you hear music at the output, what's travelling along those cables is actually electrical impulses, and electricity always needs to flow in a circuit. All cables need a minimum of two separate wires to complete a circuit.

An unbalanced cable has the minimum two wires inside – but if you look at them you'll see they're not the same as each other (you could say they're 'unbalanced'). One is a regular 'signal' wire, but the other is a braided metal mesh, which has the twin role of acting as a screen or shield against external noise interference (from nearby electrical cables and equipment, lighting or radio signals), which it diverts to earth/ground, as well as, crucially, carrying the returning signal. This kind of arrangement may be adequate for short cable runs, but the longer an unbalanced cable is, the more vulnerable it is to noise interference.

A balanced cable, in contrast, contains three wires – two to carry the signal, plus a separate screen/shield which can get on with its job in peace. The two signal wires also contribute to an improved sound in another way, because in a balanced circuit the version of the signal each wire carries is deliberately set out-of-phase with its twin. (We'll look at phase-shifting and cancellation in more detail in Chapter 6) In effect this means that, when the signals are put back in phase at their destination – at a balanced socket on a sampler, mixing desk etc – any interference picked up by the two wires along the way will cancel itself out. The result is a stronger, cleaner signal.

Balanced and unbalanced cables tend to use different types of plugs. There are three kinds commonly used for unbalanced cables: first the 'quarter-inch' or TS (tip-sleeve) plug, known in the UK as a jackplug, and in the US as a phone plug. It's widely used to carry mono signals, for instance connecting guitars to amplifiers, synthesisers to mixing desks, and with patchbays. It shouldn't be confused with the stereo version of the quarter-inch plug, known as a TRS (tip-ring-sleeve) – identifiable by the two dark rings around the shaft.

Then there's RCA/phono plugs – used in pairs to carry stereo signals, as in hi-fi set-ups. Similar plugs are used for S/PDIF connections (it stands for Sony/Philips Digital Interface), which carry digital signals between suitably equipped pieces of equipment. But digital transfer cables are different to normal RCA-equipped audio cables, so it's best to make sure you use the correct type for digital purposes.

The third sort of plug, sometimes used in budget recording set-ups, is the 'mini-jack' or 'mini-phone' plug. This is essentially a smaller version of the TRS quarter-inch plug, and is found mostly on budget computer soundcards and personal stereos.

For balanced audio connection there are two main types of plug – the sturdy, industry-standard three-pinned XLR, or the increasingly popular alternative, the TRS quarter-inch jack/phone plug, mentioned already. The latter is also used for 'insert' sockets in mixing consoles, which are designed to divert the signal from the mixer, take it off for processing, before returning it to the mixer channel – I'll be looking at this process in more detail later.

One of the best pieces of advice you'll ever get about plugs is "never force it". A plug should just slide into the right type of socket nice and smoothly. If you have to push or pull hard on a plug, there's something wrong. You're either trying to put the wrong plug in the wrong hole, or else something is broken. If you are sloppy and leave your cables lying around on the floor, sooner or later you, or someone else, will stand on them, and they bend fairly easily. Trying to use broken stuff can only cause more damage in the long run.

Signals and levels

Different types of equipment operate at different sound levels, so it helps to know which is which, and follow a few rules. Essentially there are two groups:

- Big signals, technically known as line level, are produced by things like samplers, synthesisers, sound modules, hardware effects units etc.
- Small signals, which might be either microphone or instrument level.

Line-level signals can be plugged into line input sockets on mixing consoles or amplifiers. As long as you have a cable with the correct type of plug, you should be OK. Well, almost… There are in fact two different line-level standards, operating at different voltage levels. Lower-cost 'consumer' and semi-pro gear tends to use –10dBV (or about 0.3 volts), while higher-cost, professional systems tend to operate at +4dBu (or about 1.2V – roughly four times the voltage). Generally, the higher the signal voltage, the less you need to boost the gain/volume, which helps to keep down background noise levels. Add to this the fact that the +4dBu gear also tends to use balanced connections, and you can see why this is preferred by audio professionals.

Some microphones produce very low-powered signals, sometimes as little as 0.2mV (a thousand times less than the 'consumer' line level). So they need to be boosted, usually via a mixer, or a dedicated mike preamp, to compete with line-level signals.

Guitars and basses produce 'instrument' level signals, which are usually pretty small too. The usual solution is to feed them through a DI (direct injection) unit – a little box that converts an instrument level signal to a line-level one.

Luckily, most mixing consoles and decent quality computer soundcards can cope with all of these standards. The role of a mixer, of course, is to mix together all of the signals from your instruments, microphones etc, so it's essential your mixer can accommodate all of your different sound sources with their

---

DECIBELS

Strictly speaking, the decibel (dB) is used to compare relative levels of sound, or voltage etc, so it's meaningless by itself. But adding a suffix after the dB gives it a particular reference point – for instance:

dB SPL ('sound pressure level') is the scale commonly quoted when measuring 'noise' levels, where 0dB SPL is the lowest threshold of human hearing, and 130dB SPL is ear-destroyingly loud. It rises in a logarithmic scale – every 6dB rise in SPLs is a doubling in sound pressure; every 20dB means getting ten times louder…

dBu generally relates to signal, voltage or impedance levels, and is most often used with pro gear.

dBV is similar, but based on a different reference scale, for some reason used more with non-pro gear.

various types of connection and signal level. Many mixers use the same physical sockets for all the different signal input levels and give you a 'gain' control with which to adjust the level of the incoming signal appropriately. Some also use a button to switch between mike and line-level input signals.

One rule is universal, though. If you connect a sound source that produces a 'big' signal to an input designed to accept a 'small' signal, the sound will end up distorted (and you may well damage the equipment on the receiving end). If you do it the other way around, you won't hear much at all. It pays to check before you go connecting things up.

MIDI connections

MIDI, as mentioned already, is the means by which electronic musical instruments communicate with each other, and as such it's central to the use of samplers as they exist today. MIDI can do more for you than most producers even scratch the surface of. Hopefully you'll get an insight into some of that mysterious hidden depth from this book – see Chapter 5 on 'creating sampler instruments' and Chapter 7 on 'using controllers'.

As for MIDI connections, if you're using a single computer running a software sampler within a host sequencer, the MIDI connection between the sampler and the sequencer is made automatically during the installation process. If you're using an all-in-one hardware sampler+sequencer, like the Yamaha RS7000, Roland MC-909, Korg Triton or Akai MPC3000 etc, then your MIDI connection is also made internally.

If you've got a hardware sampler, and a separate software sequencer, then you need to connect your sampler to your computer using a MIDI cable. MIDI cables always have a round five-pin 'DIN'-type plug on each end, which only fits in the MIDI socket if the plug is the right way up. Note that, although the plugs used are physically identical to the now almost extinct five-pin DIN audio cable, the internal wiring used is very different – so if your grandad hands you his old five-pin DIN audio cables, it's not worth trying to use them as MIDI cables. They could even do some damage.

Most samplers (and other MIDI-compatible gear) will have three MIDI sockets, labelled In, Out and Thru. If you're using a computer to run a sequencer, you'll need to have a MIDI interface attached to your computer to use any MIDI hardware. The computer MIDI interface will have at least one set of In and Out sockets. Connect a cable from the Out of the interface to the In of the sampler.

Many MIDI interfaces will have more than one set of In/Out sockets – four of each is fairly common, some have as

PREAMPS & MIXER CHANNELS

A preamp will take a small signal, from a microphone or guitar, and boost it to match a line-level signal. Very expensive preamps are supposed to give pristine, 100 per cent accurate results, and you work your way down the scale from there. By the time you get down to entry-level preamps, you'll be working with a circuit that very noticeably boosts some frequencies more than others, and will not produce a clinical result. But just because a circuit has a distinctive sound, that doesn't make it bad – it just gives it character… which may or may not be exactly what you want.

A breed of rack-mounting, usually relatively high-class and appropriately higher-priced 'recording channels' has evolved that offer all the features and components of a top-quality mixing desk, including a good preamp, but in a single-channel format. It's basically like a standalone, single channel strip from a mixer. Standout examples are made by Focusrite, TL Audio and Joe Meek. If you have the cash, one of these and a good vocal mike will get you 70 per cent of the way to a great recording.

AUDIO INTERFACES

For computer-based musicians, there are a number of audio interfaces available for connecting your microphones, instruments and/or mixing desk to your PC or Mac (via a USB or Firewire cable), at the same time solving the problems of preamplification and monitoring. Companies like M-Audio, RME, Edirol, Emagic (and many others) offer compact interfaces providing anything from one or two mike preamplifiers and basic headphone monitoring facilities to larger multi-in & out audio and MIDI interface solutions. Most of the large technology manufacturers are moving towards development and production of hybrid digital mixers/audio interfaces – a shining example would be the 01x from Yamaha.

FOLLOWING RULES... & BREAKING THEM

When you're setting up gear, or installing software, always read the manual, and especially the 'Read Me' file supplied with computer programs. They're there for a good reason. Having said that... once you've learned how it should be done, don't be afraid to experiment. Many producers get the best sounds by purposely connecting things up the wrong way round. The key to it all is, break the rules by all means, as long as it doesn't break your gear. If you know the theory behind how your equipment works, your experimentation will be less random, more systematic and potentially more creative.

many as eight. This allows several MIDI instruments to be linked easily to a computer at one time. Most people use a MIDI keyboard as the main means of recording notes into the computer sequencer, so we obviously need to have the MIDI Out from the keyboard connected to a MIDI In on the interface. Some of the newer hardware samplers and sound modules feature knobs and sliders that transmit MIDI control data, so we can have all the joys of twiddling knobs with the luxury of being able to record our twiddlings into our sequencer. To do this we need to have a cable connecting the MIDI Out from our sampler (or MIDI control surface or whatever) to a MIDI In on our computer. So having several MIDI In sockets is very handy.

If your computer/soundcard only has one MIDI Out socket, you'll need to connect a MIDI cable from the Thru socket on the sampler back to the In socket on your synthesiser and, if necessary, repeat the process from the Thru socket of the synth to your sound module, and so on. You can usually get away with stringing together four or five MIDI instruments using Thru sockets in this way – beyond that you can start to lose notes and things can begin to go wrong. Hence the need for multiple Out sockets on computer MIDI interfaces in larger studios.

If you've opted for a set-up where you have one computer running your audio+MIDI sequencer and a separate computer running a software sampler, like Kontakt or Gigasampler, you'll need a MIDI interface for each computer, connecting them in the same way you would a hardware sampler.

CHOOSING SOURCE MATERIAL

Next thing you need is some samples… For all the enormous potential power and versatility of a sampler, it's only as good as the samples you load into it – it can only play back what you feed it. To illustrate this, take one of the most widely used instruments in music, the piano.

Scenario 1: You load up a massive, factory-prepared 'multisample' of a beautiful-sounding, perfectly tuned concert grand piano. There are a few around, like the Gigastudio Grand Piano (which needs a staggering 1GB of RAM to play back properly). It will produce awesome, extremely high-quality, very convincing, professional standard piano sounds. It will fool a lot of people into thinking it's a real piano sound. If you hit a key softly, it will play back a lovely gentle tone; hit the same key hard and it will produce a loud and tonally very different sound (I'll explain later why this happens, when we're looking at how to create multisamples).

Scenario 2: You take a poor-quality microphone, walk up to an out-of-tune, nasty-sounding piano and record a three-second sample of a single key strike of middle C. Then you spread that sample across your MIDI keyboard and try to play it like a piano. You'll have a piano sound that occupies a mere 0.5MB of RAM, and it will be an out-of-tune, nasty-sounding, completely unconvincing, one-dimensional piano sound. Then again, you might decide you like it, especially if you're making music that suits a bit of nastiness – it could be very impressive in the right musical context.

Both sounds are equally valid, and can be used to create music. But they are suited to creating fundamentally different kinds of music. The underlying message is that you need to find the sounds that suit you and the music you want to make.

The other point to bear in mind is that you could, if you really wish, deliberately degrade the high-quality grand piano sample, using various filters and processors, to create a scuzzy-sounding bar-room piano tone (just about) – but there's no way you could do the reverse, and make that thin, nasty piano sample sound like a concert grand.

Samples can be obtained in two main ways: 1) in pre-recorded form, from a variety of sources; such as sample library collections; or 2) created from scratch using a microphone.

Manufacturer sample libraries

All samplers currently on the market are supplied with a library of samples. These samples have already been 'layered and zoned' into MIDI instruments and, usually, the instruments are in categorised banks. The idea is that you have MIDI-responsive instruments at your fingertips and ready to work with.

The quality and quantity of such pre-recorded sounds can vary, though bear in mind they'll generally be intended to please a very broad spectrum of users, so you won't necessarily like or want to use all of the supplied sounds. But they will provide you with at least a few examples of most of the traditional instrument types, plus some breakbeats, vocal samples etc.

The manufacturer-supplied library should be sufficient to get you started, and will always be there as a convenient back-up, but it will probably not sustain you for long, and you'll go looking for new sounds.

By the way, if you're buying a secondhand hardware sampler, it's worth checking that the original sample library is intact and included in the deal.

Sample CDs

One of the most popular sources of additional material is the commercially-produced sample CD set. The format is simple and highly effective: each CD contains up to 700MB of samples, and sometimes other types of data, like format-specific key-range data, or MIDI files. (Some drum/percussion sample CDs will contain 'beat-sliced' loop-type material accompanied by extracted MIDI files containing the rhythmic imprint of the samples.)

The samples themselves will usually have been played and recorded by professional musicians and experienced sound engineers, and purchasing the CD itself normally grants you a licence to use those samples as and when you wish.

There are literally hundreds of titles available, offering a wide range of different instruments played in a variety of ways, suitable for any number of musical genres.

At one end of the spectrum are 'construction kit' libraries full of complete tempo and key-matched loops, usually divided by musical genre and aimed at entry-level game-style software users. Users of Reason, eJay or Acid will find several collections of ready-made loop

ZONING, MAPPING & LAYERING
Zoning and mapping essentially determine which key or group of keys on a MIDI keyboard (or other control surface) will make a sample play, as well as things like how loud and how long the sound will be; layering determines how many samples will play on top of each other. These terms will all be explained more fully in Chapter 7.

BEAT SLICE
'Beat slice' commonly describes the process of chopping a sample up into relatively short sections, each of which contains an audio 'event'. The most obvious example would be a sample of a drum pattern where each slice would contain an individual drum hit. The idea is that once you have your sample chopped into slices in this way (often a semi-automated process), it becomes easier to manipulate both the tempo and rhythm of the sampled material. The technology was developed by Propellerhead Software in their Recycle application, but is now widespread in both hardware and software sampling systems. (See Chapter 4.)

and instrument samples in their own proprietary sample formats (which means they can't easily be used with other products).

Those seeking more professional, realistic, traditional instrument emulations will find plenty of outstanding, fully layered/zoned multisamples of everything from entire orchestras to every single type of ethnic instrument you can imagine. Such collections of multisample instruments are of a quality and scale that's way beyond the facilities of not only home studio owners but most serious professional establishments too. And crucially they're often also far superior to the supplied manufacturer libraries.

Among the most popular types of sample CD are the drum and percussion collections – featuring both loops/breaks and individual hits – largely because of the difficulties involved in capturing great drum/percussion sounds for yourself.

SAMPLE CD SUPPLIERS

Here's a short list of web addresses for some of the main current sample CD manufacturers:

www.bestservice.de
www.bigfishaudio.com
www.eastwestsamples.com
www.e-lab.se
www.powerfx.com
www.sonicimplants.com
www.soundburst.com
www.spectrasonics.net
www.timespace.com
www.ueberschall.de
www.wizoo.com
www.zero-g.co.uk

Alongside the traditional (mostly acoustic) instrument libraries, you will find CDs offering almost every vintage synthesiser ever made, plus bass guitar, electric guitars, organs, atmospheric soundscapes, vocals... Or how about miscellaneous collections of really quite random titbits from famous producers – offering a little bit of everything from 'a name you can trust'... The list is endless. If it exists as recorded sound, you can probably get it on a sample CD. As such, they represent the sampling musician's second-best friend (after the sampler, of course) because they're such a convenient source of sounds.

One of the only notable drawbacks of sample CDs, which may or may not matter to you, is that anybody and everybody else who's bought a copy will be using the same samples in their music. Sure, the samples can be reprocessed and personalised, but the fact is that someone somewhere will be using the same sounds, drum breaks, guitar riffs, brass stabs as you are.

Most sample CDs have one other killer advantage – they are copyright cleared. When you buy a sample CD you're not only paying to acquire sounds you might otherwise have difficulty obtaining, you're also buying the right to use them within your own recordings. Be careful though, this is not true of all sample CDs. There are some companies who only grant you a 'personal use' licence, which means that if you use the sample commercially you are supposed to make another payment to them. Make sure you check first, and if you're planning to use the samples in a commercial release (if there's any danger of you making any money from their use), and it's not possible to acquire a full licence, best look elsewhere.

Of course if the samples are delivered to you on a promotional compilation (as with the second attached disc with this book, CD2), it's an ideal source of free samples – with the proviso that, if the track(s) you create from them start to generate some revenue, you really ought to purchase a full copy of the original CD, just to be legally secure.

The actual sample data you'll find on sample CDs almost always takes two forms: the first is straight WAV audio files (because this is a format that can be imported into most audio production systems); the second is some form of proprietary sampler format, which contains not only the raw sample data but the key and velocity zone information that turns them into playable sampler instruments. These are often provided on two different CDs, with WAV files on one and the duplicate sample format files on the other.

The most common proprietary sample format is the good old Akai S1000/S3000 one, because it's effectively more or less universal – during the period when the sample CD rose to popularity (the mid to late 1990s), the Akai S series of hardware samplers were the de facto industry standard. As the whole host of different sampler platforms we see today evolved and eclipsed the S Series, each one adopted Akai-compatibility as an industry standard.

Music production magazines run regular reviews of sample CDs, so it's best to check there for the latest releases and recommendations. In fact, some music tech magazines are themselves fantastic sources of free samples – many mags provide covermount CDs each issue with a modest selection of free samples on each, and after a few years this can build into quite a library. Those same magazines may also operate ongoing download areas online.

If you're looking for professional sound design materials, or recordings of everyday noises, check out www.sound-ideas.com for the world's leading library. It's not free, or even cheap, but it is incredible.

And of course, don't forget to check out the sample disc attached to this book (CD2), with over 500MB of samples drawn from the extensive Zero-G catalogue.

The internet

The internet, as you know, is astoundingly huge and even more astoundingly strange. Just as with any other subject, there are novel and exciting samples to be discovered out there, often for free, but there's an awful lot of dross to wade through too.

Perhaps the best way to approach this is to hunt specifically for free demo samples being offered as 'try before you buy' purchase incentives by commercial sample CD producers online. The other route is the user exchange: one of the best things about the web is the way Johnny Anonymous from the mid-Antarctic can share his ideas, music and samples with other aspiring musicians around the world. The law of averages suggests the occasional one will be really good, and it can be a heap of fun hunting for those gems. But be warned, the vast majority of material being exchanged for free is unmitigated rubbish, so expect something like a 20 to 1 disappointment rate, and a lot of time online hunting.

There will of course be practical help and advice on tap on the web too – the trouble is, if you tap in a question you will almost certainly get six different answers. All you have to do is figure out which (if any) of them is correct. The best places to go for useful information are manufacturers' resource areas and popular user forums – if you can follow a thread with a number of different users agreeing on a decent answer to a problem, they may be onto something. The most reliable user forums tend to found either within manufacturers' websites or on sites belonging to long-established print magazines – which tend to be the best sources of all-round music-making information on the net.

A word about MP3 files

There is another serious problem with internet music downloads, and that's the widespread use of MP3 files. As a way of compressing audio to speed up downloads, it's great – but it's not at all ideal in terms of sonic quality. The MP3 format is based on what's known as perceptual coding – the idea that people usually 'skim-listen', a bit like skim-reading, where we only really pick out and

MORE WEBSITES

By no means a comprehensive list, or anything like it, but these few handy sites might kick-start your search for samples on the web:

www.google.com
www.samplenet.co.uk
www.synthzone.com
www.harmony-central.com
www.computermusic.co.uk
www.futuremusic.co.uk
www.soundonsound.com
www.keyboardmag.com
www.sonicstate.com

Sampler/software manufacturers:

www.ableton.com
www.akaipro.com
www.bias-inc.com
www.bitheadz.com
www.bitshiftaudio.com
www.cakewalk.com
www.clavia.se
www.creative.com
www.cycling74.com
www.digidesign.com

focus on the most significant bits of what we hear. The theory is that, in terms of the frequency range, we don't hear half the music we listen to because there's just too much going on in it; and so, it should follow, we wouldn't notice if some of the less important frequencies weren't there at all. So perceptual coding chops out and discards what it considers to be the least essential stuff in the hope we won't miss them.

Any discerning audio professional will point out, in response to this, that just because we don't actively listen to the subtle details of sound, that doesn't mean we don't hear them at all. We most definitely notice when they're not there. This is backed up by the pro audio industry's recent adoption of the higher digital recording resolution of 24-bit/96kHz as the new professional standard over the so-called CD quality consumer standard of 16-bit/44.1kHz – precisely because capturing the details of sound is so important to the perceived quality of the recording.

With MP3, the higher the bit rate at which an audio file is encoded, the fewer chunks are discarded, so the better the audio quality. At the maximum 320kbps (kilobits per second) it doesn't sound too bad, but still by no means perfect. Lower the bit rate, and things get worse.

Again the rule is, if you start trying to make music with low-grade material, you get low-grade end results, whether you want it or not. Particularly if you start slowing the sound down, reprocessing it and doing all the things you do with a sampler… then things can get very bad indeed. This is a subjective view, of course: try it and make up your own minds.

The internet is also a good place to find secondhand or rare music technology, thanks to sites like ebay. When it comes to shopping for samples, though, it's probably wise to visit a few of the online magazine sites, check out some reviews of specific sample CDs, and then look for the best prices at some mail order online retail sites.

Records

This is where things start to get dangerous. Sampling from someone else's work, without their permission, is illegal. Not that this seems to stop people doing it, which is why we can't ignore it here. Indeed it would be historically nonsensical to omit this whole area of sampling – even though the record industry might prefer to deny its importance, and even its continuing existence…

It really is a legal can of worms – and just because everyone probably knows someone who does it all the time, and seems to get away with it, it still can't honestly be recommended. To give you an idea why, read our section on copyright in Chapter 8 and see if you can find a way through the often convoluted, contradictory, and even anti-creative mess of legal restriction, and avoid getting yourself sued. It's taken about 15 years, but the legislation, and more crucially the enforcement, has got closer to catching up with the reality of how vast numbers of people choose to make music nowadays.

The undeniable fact is that your own record collection may well be the most inspiring, exciting library of samples you could ever wish to lay your hands on. Add to that all of your friends' collections, and those found in music libraries, and everything that's played on the radio, or TV, and we are really starting to cook in terms of sheer quantity of amazing samples. It's all out there, a whole world of music… and the sampler was, quite frankly, built to steal it. The technology, and the creative impulse, says yes; the lawyers say no.

In order to deal with the practicalities of this type of sampling, let's assume here that the sample you want to use is either: a) fully cleared with the relevant songwriter/publisher and record label, or b) entirely in the public domain. (See Chapter 8 for more details on these circumstances.) Right, let's get on…

Choosing exactly what to sample from a record is something of an art. It's easiest to work with and process samples of individual sounds, but it's rare to come across instruments playing 'solo' in a track, which would be ideal for letting you grab an isolated section. 'A cappella' voices are slightly more common, but still not the norm.

The best you're likely to get is a sparse intro (song introduction) or a 'breakdown' in the middle of the track, where the bulk of the instrumentation drops away for a few bars, perhaps leaving just the drums, or a guitar or bass riff. If you sample a breakdown you may find that you can employ filters and EQ (see Chapter 6 on 'Customising Sounds') to remove yet more of the instrumentation, to extract the individual sounds you want.

Part of the art of sampling – among its more creative possibilities – involves finding samples that will sound completely different out-of-context, in either a rhythmic or tonal sense. For instance, looping two thirds of a single four-beat bar (or a short snippet from an irregular-length bar of jazz) may produce a very interesting effect if it's re-employed in another rhythmic setting.

There's also a knack to knowing what type of material will transform well through processing. As soon as you begin attempting to sample sections of records with a view to isolation, re-contextualisation and transformation into new things, something else begins to become apparent. The most unexpected things often make great samples.

This is what makes people search through their grandparents' record collection, or stacks of children's music. It's a long, slippery slope to where many hip-hop devotees and sample maniacs end up… in junk shops, at flea markets, hunting down music they wouldn't sit and listen to as 'music'. They buy records that just might yield interesting and unique samples. Besides which, if the record's old enough, it just might be out of copyright. But be careful here too – the music might be out of copyright, but the recording itself might not be.

The aim of sampling is to find sounds and rhythms that are not easily created with the rest of the electronic musician's toolkit. Electronic instruments are fantastic at producing pristine, clean sounds and mechanised, precise rhythmic sequencing. Non-electronic music, on the other hand, is a great source of interesting quirky rhythms and happy accidents. That's why so many old jazz and funk records are the target of the sampler – they are not mechanised, as they generally pre-date electronic music-making. In short, they're more *human*.

Movies & TV

Here we go again… Sampling from these sources is very definitely illegal. Movie and TV soundtracks are copyright protected, and the companies that own them can be ruthless in their pursuit of infringement. Yet the temptation is obviously strong – the sheer quality of the sound you can find in movies can be breathtaking… and therefore seductively dangerous to the audiophile sample freak. Not to mention the appeal of those uncluttered instrumental passages, incidental sounds, and especially bits of speech, which can be very effective when cut and pasted into a music environment. Just trawl through the early days of house music or hip-hop and you'll find dozens of great examples of instantly-recognisable cultural references. Mostly unauthorised, of course – and sadly the illegality has all but removed this rich cultural seam from electronic music production, except perhaps in anonymous bootlegs.

Out in the real world – recording your own samples

With access to tens of thousands of professionally prepared, ready-made samples, it can be easy to go through your entire musical career without recording a single sample of your own. This is a real shame, because the whole process can be a lot of fun, and generate genuinely useful and, more importantly, unique results.

It might be anything from making your own breakbeats, or creating vocal or instrument loops, to producing original multisamples of traditional instruments. Even just reprocessing existing samples by playing them back through a speaker and recording the results with a microphone is not quite as mad an idea as it might sound, as I'll explain at the end of the chapter. And for the more experimental musician, there's also the process of capturing location sound for use as sound effects and atmospherics.

The first thing to try is recording real instruments played by musicians. It's probably not worth the time and effort attempting to produce your own serious, full-spectrum multisamples (like that 1GB grand piano sample I talked about earlier), but an octave's-worth of notes could be very useful. And it's extremely valuable to create your own loops and breakbeats, of more or less any instrument.

It can also be very worthwhile creating something like a hybrid between a multisample and a beat-sliced loop, where you get a musician to play short snippets of riffs or beats, runs of a few isolated notes, intended to be placed into a zoned sampler instrument for MIDI playback. This can be a great way for musicians to exceed their existing skill level, because you may find that a player can sustain only a few notes at a time of a particularly complex passage – they know what they're trying to play but can't quite get their fingers around it. Thanks to sampling, this complex part can be played in pieces and repeated. This also applies to skilled musicians who want to exceed the boundaries of what can be physically played.

The recording process

There's a vast array of recording equipment available, and literally dozens of good books presenting different approaches to the recording process, so I'm not going to attempt to go into every detail of that huge subject here. But there are a few underlying ideas that should help get you started. If you're already familiar enough with audio recording techniques – or if you really have no intention of creating your own samples from scratch – you can probably skip this next section and proceed to Chapter 4.

Still here? OK, the first rule of recording is an old favourite: 'There are no rules'. Or at least very few. As long as it doesn't make your equipment explode, if it sounds good to you, it's probably right. Certainly there are a few basic things you'll need in order to make recording a physical possibility, as we'll see, but beyond that, the choice of specific items and how you use them is totally open to personal taste. Good recording is all about getting the best out of the equipment available to you, and the environment in which you're working.

With all recording, the most important factor is the quality of the original sound you're recording. It may seem obvious, but most musicians taking their first recording steps tend to overlook this. It's all too common to find people believing that a poor sound can be made into a good sound through the recording process. Recording does what it says it does – it records whatever you present to the microphone. A good recording of a bad sound will sound like a nicely audible *bad* sound. Even a bad recording of a good sound might sound better.

The location in which you record can have a big influence on the sound. In the sections on reverb and echo in Chapter 6 we'll look at how different spaces have different acoustic properties, but suffice to say that the size, shape and construction materials of a room will boost some frequencies and suppress others, as well as affecting natural reverberation. The trouble is that it can be quite difficult to remedy fundamental acoustic 'flaws' in a recording by using EQ and other studio processing tools. These acoustic factors become particularly important when choosing where to record.

If you have access to a purpose-built recording facility, you are a lucky soul. But if you're recording in a large, makeshift space – like an old warehouse or church hall – you'll probably find it has a lot of natural reverb and unpredictable 'resonant' frequencies, which may vary in different areas of the room. Try making a number of short test recordings first, placing your microphone at a variety of locations in the space, before deciding where to set up to make your final recording.

If you're at home, the main difference is that the rooms will probably be smaller, with more soft furnishings – so there will be less reverb (apart from in a tiled bathroom or kitchen), and even more unpredictable resonances. Stairwells in particular tend to have very interesting acoustic properties. Again, try making test recordings in each area to see what result each produces on tape/disc. You might be surprised at how some instruments just seem to sound better in certain areas.

Choosing the right combination of equipment to use is down to trial and error. Each microphone design sounds slightly different, as does each preamp, and there are hundreds of permutations of the two – all of which may produce unique results in specific settings – so there are endless subtle variations in tonal response to be achieved. Even professional recording studios each have their own characteristics, which is why certain artists and producers keep going back to studios they like.

Microphones

Microphones can very broadly be divided into those designed for use in the studio and those designed for the stage. Stage mikes tend to be of more rugged 'bash-proof' construction, they reproduce very high sound pressure levels (SPLs) without distortion, and are less susceptible to handling noise (the rumbling sounds you get when you pick up a mike to use it). A stage mike design will often compromise its frequency response and the clarity and detail it can reproduce to prioritise these things. A studio mike, by contrast, prioritises capturing every little detail, but they can be fragile (particularly valve/tube models), are very susceptible to handling noise and, crucially, are fairly costly.

Stage mikes are comparatively inexpensive. They tend to employ a so-called 'dynamic' capsule design that doesn't require either batteries or an external power supply. Mikes intended for use by vocalists tend to have a tailored frequency response curve that rolls off a little very low bass and emphasises particular mid frequencies to produce a thick, punchy sound. Instrument mikes, used for anything from guitars to bass to brass etc, need to be a little more versatile and have a somewhat 'flatter' frequency response, although many will have an increased upper-mid presence.

DYNAMIC & CONDENSER MIKES

The most important thing to bear in mind about these words is that they are simply electronic distinctions – they don't signify anything at all about the tonal quality, or loudness, of the sound the mikes produce. So a 'dynamic' mike is no more 'dynamic-sounding' than a condenser mike (if anything, the opposite is often the case), and a condenser mike has no kind of 'condensing' or compressing effect on the sound. A better way to distinguish them is to think of dynamic mikes as being more suited to dynamic situations, like stage performances, or recording drum kits, while condenser mikes are useful for capturing the subtler musical details, like vocal nuances, and quieter or non-electric instruments.

If you're on a tight budget, you can use a stage mike in the studio for recording more or less anything – only experimentation will tell you if it sounds good in context. Stage mikes can yield strong sounds with distinctive character, and deliver very usable results.

The market leaders in stage mikes are: Shure (the well-worn 'industry standard' tag has been applied to their SM57 instrument mike and SM58 vocal mike for as long as anyone can remember); Sennheiser (especially their increasingly popular Evolution series); plus AKG and Audio Technica. But there are many more that are worthy of investigation, and may even offer similar results at a lower cost.

Choosing a studio mike is a big subject, one we can only scratch the surface of here. The most important difference between stage mikes and studio recording mikes is the latter's use of large diaphragm condenser-type designs. And of course condenser mikes require a power supply, either from batteries, a dedicated power supply, or more often a 'phantom power' feed from an appropriately equipped mixing desk or preamp.

The improvement in dynamic range, clarity, evenness of frequency response and all-round quality when you go from a mid-price stage mike to a serious studio condenser can be quite stunning. At the top of the heap we have the industry-standard Neumann U87 (daughter of an inspirational forebear, the classic valve U47), which sounds incredible and is so versatile that it could genuinely be the only microphone you'll ever need – well OK, it's not an ideal kick-drum mike. But it comes with a hefty price tag. There are now some very notable budget alternatives, such as the outstanding Samson CO1 (unbelievable value, basic condenser performance for £60/$80); the particularly strong SE Electronics condensers; the excellent Rode range; and valiant offerings from the likes of M-audio and Blue.

Instruments that cover extremes of frequency or volume level often need specialist microphones that can cope with the job. Top-class studio mikes are probably a little too sensitive for the high SPLs produced by drums, for instance, although most instrument mikes should manage OK. The exception is the kick drum, which requires something suited to capturing and emphasising very low frequencies at very high sound levels. The AKG D112 has long enjoyed industry-standard status in this role, although there are now some good competitors available. When it comes to overhead mikes, used for capturing cymbals and/or the entire kit, most engineers favour a pair of relatively directional, condenser-type mikes. These will have a broad dynamic range and are easier to focus on particular areas of the kit.

Most of the leading mike makers now produce dedicated drum mike kits, at various costs and performance levels – they'll include between three and seven mikes with specially-tailored frequency response curves that suit particular drums, and are well worth the modest investment if you do a lot of drum recording. As well as the big names already mentioned, check out mike kits from Superlux and Samson.

Microphone positioning

Mike placement is all about positioning microphones relative to the sound source – be it a guitar amplifier, drum kit, or a vocalist.

Mike placement is undeniably an art, and it takes good ears and plenty of experience to become really good at it. But we can break it down into two basic approaches: close-miking and ambient miking. With close-miking the idea is to get right up near a sound source, isolating it as much as possible from any other sounds around. This can produce a distinctive sound – and not necessarily what you might be used to hearing.

For example, when we listen to an acoustic guitar from a couple of metres away or more, much of what we hear is emanating from the body of the guitar – which acts as a natural amplifier and projects the sound – and also some reverberation from nearby walls and objects. Get up really close to the guitar (within a few centimetres) and you can now hear the detail of fingers sliding on strings and scraping on the fretboard.

Ambient miking gives a much broader picture, which includes the reflected sound and acoustic response of the recording environment.

Whichever method you choose – or it may be a combination of both techniques – depends on circumstances and desired results. Experiment with both approaches.

Recording vocals

You might think this would be simple enough: stick a mike in front of a singer and press Record. But getting a voice to sound full and natural on a recording is actually very tricky to achieve without good-quality equipment.

It's pretty easy to get a 'messed-up' vocal sound, whether it's deliberately distorted in a Strokes/Muse kind of way, or weirdly pitch-shifted or 'vocoded' etc. Just record the vocal as best you can – budget recording tools and minimal technique will suffice – and then experiment with adding effects, or removing certain frequencies with EQ, until you find a sound you like.

But let's say you want a voice to sound like a real voice. The human voice occupies a very broad range of frequencies, which not only makes it difficult to reproduce, it's also particularly susceptible to resonant room frequencies, which in some contexts can make it sound 'unnatural' before you even start. Sadly, most domestic spaces don't sound great with vocals – try the bathroom (if you like reverb), or the garden, if your garden is quiet and it's not a windy day.

Use the best quality vocal mike you can get your hands on, and put it on a stand about 30cm/one foot from the singer – though a good vocalist may well employ their own mike technique, moving closer for quiet passages and backing off for loud bits. Using a 'pop shield' – a piece of stretched fabric suspended between the singer and the mike – can reduce explosive consonants and sibilance; and a little gentle compression on the input channel can help smooth out differences in volume. You may find that getting the vocalist to move closer to or further away from the mike will improve the sound. You might find that getting a better vocalist will improve the sound too…

Recording instruments

Recording drums is a bit of a tricky thing to get right. A good sound source is essential: if your drummer has a decent drum kit, that will help, but if your drummer knows how to tune that kit properly and can play it well, then your job is considerably easier. Although we can't cover the intricacies of drum recording here, let's look at a few basic principles.

RESPONSE PATTERNS

Some microphones are designed to respond better to sounds from certain directions, and this is represented in their specifications by what's called 'polar patterns'. For instance, a directional mike – one that records sound from directly in front, where the mike is pointing, cutting out most sound coming from the sides and rear – is referred to as cardioid, or perhaps super-cardioid or hyper-cardioid, because the relevant polar pattern is heart-shaped (think of cardiology). Most dynamic stage mikes are fairly directional. An omni-directional (or 'omni') mike records sound arriving from every angle, so its polar pattern is almost spherical. Mikes with omni polar patterns are rarely used live, because of sound spillage, but can be useful as studio 'ambient' mikes, picking up the big sonic picture in one hit.

Sitting roughly between these two are 'bi-polar' mikes, sometimes known as figure-of-eight mikes, because that's the shape of their response pattern. These are usually studio condenser mikes with a large-diaphragm (the diaphragm is the bit that vibrates when the sound hits it) and the ability to capture sound equally from either side of the mike capsule. This can be used for recording two singers simultaneously, face-to-face, or to capture one close-mike signal on one side and some room ambience from the other.

Some very fancy mikes will have selectable polar patterns, so by turning a dial or flicking a switch they'll operate as directional, bi-polar or even omni – which is very useful. The classic AKG C414 is a popular example.

Most engineers favour close-miking drum kits. The idea is to get as close as you can to each drum (say 5-10cm from the skin), but without getting in the way of the drummer or flailing drumsticks. With the snare and toms, this is achieved by using a boom mike-stand (one with a moveable arm) to position the mike above the drum, by the rim, a few centimetres up from the surface, angled slightly down towards the centre of the skin.

With the kick drum, the microphone should really go inside the drum, so you'll either need a hole in the front skin (the one that doesn't get hit) or to remove it completely. You'll need to use a cushion or special damping pillow to deaden the sound somewhat, or the recording will be ringy and lack definition. The kick drum mike should be placed, either resting on the cushion or on a stand, about 5cm away from the batter head (the skin that gets hit), and pointing slightly off to one side of the spot where the beater strikes.

With hi-hats, place a mike above the top cymbal, pointing towards the rim. Avoid pointing directly at the raised 'bell' area, or being too close to the rush of air that's pushed out from between the two cymbals as they close. With overhead cymbals, because they ring so loudly, the most common solution is to employ a stereo pair of condenser mikes above and to either side, at the front of the kit, pointing in and down towards the drummer. This should capture the sound of the whole kit, including the cymbals, in a stereo image. Later, in the mix, you can EQ-out the low frequencies if you want to zone in on the cymbals. Alternatively, you could close-mike cymbals in much the same way as the hi-hats.

Recording amplified guitars and bass guitars is pretty straightforward. Close-mike the speaker cabinet by placing a directional microphone about 10cm in front of the speaker (or one of the speakers), with the mike pointing at the centre of the speaker cone. For guitars, any instrument mike is worth a try, but for bass you will probably get best results from a similar mike to the one used for kick drum recording.

There are too many other types of instrument to go into details on recording them all. Best results are often achieved after some experimentation with mikes and positions, but as a rule it helps to identify where most of the sound of an instrument emanates from. With many instruments, like some woodwind and other orchestral instruments, it's more or less essential to use two mikes at once – pointing one at the 'bell' or open end, and another at the keys or valves, and perhaps even a third at the mouthpiece. The player should be able to help in this regard. Some instruments even come with their own specialist mikes, often clipped-on, to allow the player to move around a bit without detriment to the sound levels etc.

Remember, only use compression, or any other effects, sparingly during recording, or preferably not at all – you can always add some later, but you can't remove it once recorded. The exception is guitar effects, like distortion, which sound best through a guitar amp, rather than added in the mix.

Location recording

Capturing the sounds from streets, bars, markets, factories and any number of other places can generate lots of atmospheric samples and textures. Close-miking everyday domestic or industrial machinery can produce excellent rhythmic material. You might be surprised at how

HIRING GEAR

If you can't afford to buy the particular piece of equipment you want to use for a specific recording, why not hire it for a day or two? If you live in or near a major city you may well find a specialist pro-audio hire centre that can rent you almost any studio item you want. Hiring is also an ideal way of gaining essential learning experience with particular pieces of gear – and you can find out whether it does what you want and expect before you commit yourself to buying.

different (and interesting) the world sounds when it's recorded and played back out of context. Sounds you take for granted suddenly take on a whole new nature.

There are quite a lot of professional location-recording systems in existence, thanks to the film and broadcast industries. Such professional equipment yields extremely high-quality professional results – but it can be costly. If you're on a budget, using a recordable Minidisc Walkman can achieve some very impressive results, at a relatively low cost. Sony's mini stereo recording mikes work really well, as do mikes from Beyerdynamic and other professional manufacturers. (Personally, I use a $49, stereo, single-point T-mike from Sound Professionals.)

Another solution is using a video camera – many low-cost home video cameras have decent-quality stereo mikes built-in. Using a camera seems to have another, unexpected advantage. If you're trying to record on the streets, one of the biggest challenges is remaining unobtrusive. Seeing someone with a microphone seems to make people nervous – or worse, inquisitive. Having people constantly ask what you're doing can seriously impair an ambient street sound recording... But for some weird reason, a camera doesn't have the same effect. People might pull faces at you, but that won't ruin your audio recording. I also sometimes work with a pair of miniature lapel mikes attached to a hidden Walkman for stealth recording.

The main problems with location recording are handling noise and gusts of wind. The only way to combat the former is to keep very still, or not actually touch your mike, hanging it up or lying it down somewhere safe – which is not always possible. You can stand dead still in the middle of a shopping mall, or set up mikes in public places, but it's not exactly inconspicuous, and might even attract some unwanted attention from the police.

The thing about wind noise is you might not even be aware it's having an effect, unless you're monitoring through headphones as you record. A small amount of wind is often overcome by using a 'wind shield', a foam or fluffy cover for your microphone. Large amounts of wind will ruin a recording, and is impossible to beat. So if you want to record outdoors, choose a calm day.

Re-recording

Only a few years ago this was one of the most popular professional 'insider' tricks. The technique involves playing a sample back through an amplifier and speaker cabinet, using a microphone to re-record the result. (The same rules apply, with regards to mike placement, as they would with any other instrument.)

Guitar or bass amplifiers and cabinets are the usual choice, because they're designed for specific jobs: guitar amps are built to make the thin, twangy sound of vibrating guitar strings sound huge and wonderful; while bass gear will obviously make bassy signals sound good in the low-end department. Valve amplifiers are particularly admired for adding warmth and natural compression, with a hint of smooth distortion. (Bear in mind that guitar and bass amps are designed to accept instrument-level signals rather than line-level, so it's wise to begin with the input gain and output volume kept low, or use a low-level signal from your sampler/mixer.)

The downside is it's only worth doing if you have the right equipment on hand. Most commercial recording facilities have a stock of lovely-sounding guitar or bass amplifiers and speaker cabinets available for use. Or you could always hire something appropriate.

Modern software-based effects and amplifier modelling systems have made this method somewhat redundant, but it's still worth experimenting with, if you have the wherewithal.

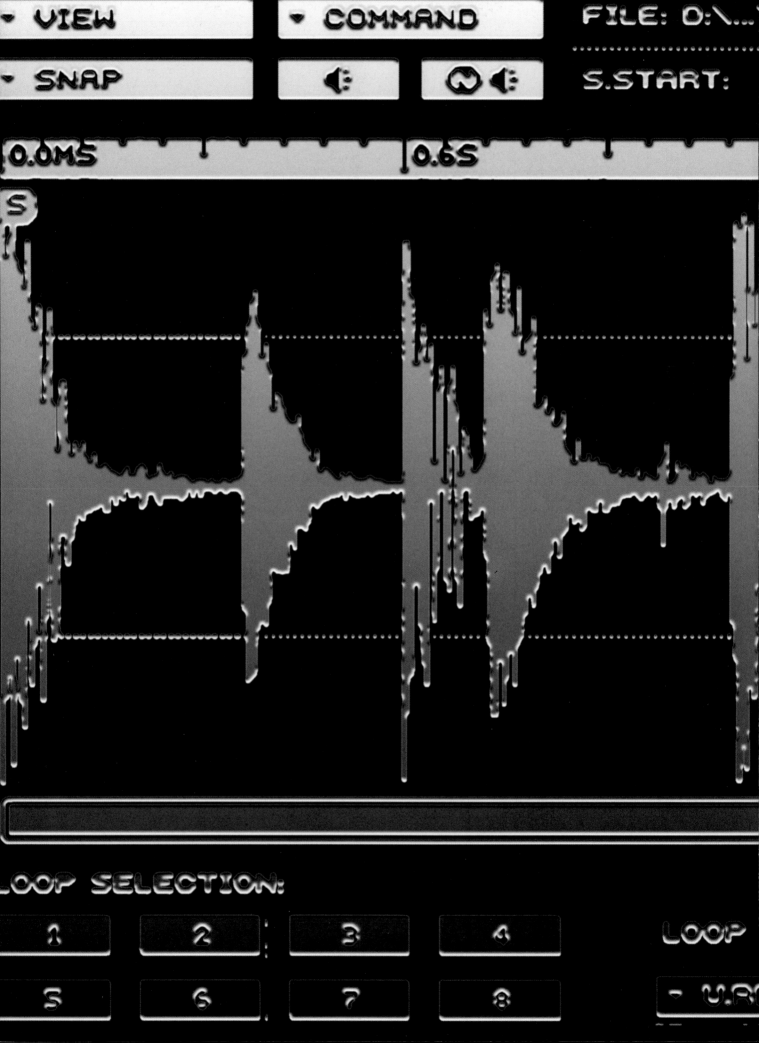

CHAPTER 4

loading & editing samples

Once you've chosen your samples – whether you've recorded them yourself or selected them from a sample CD – the next step is to transfer them into your sampler, where they can be manipulated and processed as required. This chapter looks at:

- Loading/capturing samples, normalising, topping & tailing, using zero crossings.

- Selecting and editing loops.

- Altering tempo and pitch, timestretch, and beat slicing.

Loading pre-recorded samples

There are two basic approaches to getting pre-recorded samples into your sampler: if you're using a software sampler (or a screen editor for a hardware machine) it's usually a matter of locating the desired sample in an 'explorer'-style window or folder and then using standard drag & drop procedure to move the sample into an open project window. If you're using just a hardware machine, it's a case of going to the File menu and hitting Open when the appropriate sample name appears.

The only possible niggle is file formats. Each manufacturer has its own proprietary format – so, for instance, a sample in E-mu or Korg format may not load directly into an Akai Sampler, etc. But there are a few basic formats that are very widely used. The standard PC audio file format is the WAV file (.WAV suffix), and these can be opened by all current samplers. Although WAV is a dependable format for transferring audio between different machines, it doesn't cater for any subtleties like loop points or envelope settings etc.

Most machines can open samples in Akai format, mainly because there's a huge number of commercial sample libraries available in this format. You'll find each sampler will be able to read a slightly different selection of file formats, so the sensible policy is to check which ones your own machine can deal with before attempting to acquire pre-recorded samples.

Specialised audio editing software like Spark, Sound Forge, Wavelab, Cool Edit, Peak and many others can all import audio files stored in .CDA (the standard music CD file format) directly from CD. This is usually done via an Import Audio command in the File menu. Once imported, the sound files can be edited or stored as normal samples.

Loading your own recordings

The basic rules of recording samples are very simple and apply to all digital audio recording. Place your sampler or software in record-standby mode by pressing the Record button – this will bring up a window that contains a set of level meters and an input level control slider.

Set the recording level as high as possible without it distorting. The meter should peak as close to the zero mark as possible. Do a 'dry-run' in standby mode, then begin the actual recording process when your levels are correct.

The better the quality of an initial recording the less work you will have to do on it later. Ensure there are no dodgy cables involved or anything causing background hum or hiss. If you are recording through a mixing desk, it's often a good plan to 'solo' the sound you are recording to cut down background noise from the other instruments in your set-up – low-cost hardware effect units in particular tend to be quite noisy.

Have a listen to how much background noise your studio really makes – simply stop a song playing and listen carefully with the monitoring level up fairly high. All budget studios, and quite a lot of supposedly professional ones, create an inherent amount of background noise – it's known as a noise floor. You may even think this is tolerable, but consider this: every time you record a sample you'll be recording and amplifying an extra copy of that noise. If every sample you record has a copy of the background noise in it, you will end up with perhaps 20 times as much noise in your final mix. Careful,

SONG OR PROJECT

Obviously not everything created using a sequencer or in a studio set-up is a 'song' – for example you might be adding sound effects or doing sound design work for TV or a video game. The word 'project' is used to mean all of the elements that go together to form either the song or piece of work you are creating.

SOLO

In the context of a recording or mixing console, the solo switch simply turns off all the channels other than the one you want to listen to. Almost all hardware desks, and software equivalents, have a button on each channel that does this.

systematic elimination of noise when sampling/recording can dramatically improve the clarity of a final mix.

If you've never worked with digital audio before, you might be astounded at just quite how much disk space it devours. At standard CD-level format, one minute of audio requires approximately 10MB of disk space – that's 1MB for every six seconds of sound. A ten-second sample would be too big to fit on a standard floppy disk. Don't even think about anything less than a Zip drive for archiving or backup storage, but you'd be far better off going straight for at least a CD burner, and ideally a DVD burner, where you can store at least 4GB per disk. As for hard disk space, the more gigabytes the better: 40, 80, 160GB – whatever you can afford. (The same rule applies to RAM memory, by the way: for music work, buy as much as you can afford – 512MB should be an absolute minimum, and preferably go for twice that amount. The good thing about RAM is you can generally add more as your work demands it.)

The amount of storage space you have – either on your hard drive(s) or on CD or DVD archives – will have a bearing on how many and what size of samples you can deal with at any one time. You can control the size of each sample by determining the bit rate, recording frequency, and whether it's to be stereo or mono (with some systems these things are set up in the global 'preferences'). Standard CD quality is 16-bit/stereo/44.1kHz, so these settings should produce a sample that sounds reasonable yet doesn't consume too much data storage/retrieval capacity. It's what we are all used to hearing as a standard audio recording fidelity benchmark, so it should be fine for most needs.

If you have enough storage space – and if your computer or sampler is powerful enough to cope with high levels of data throughput, and your soundcard/recording hardware will let you – you may even wish to record at a higher resolution. If you can, it's at least worthwhile increasing the quality of your standard configuration to 24-bit/48kHz, as this does deliver an improved quality of recording/reproduction. A configuration of 24-bit/stereo/192kHz should produce an absolutely top-quality recording, but will require a very powerful system – and you may not always notice the extra benefits. (If your music is going to end up on a CD anyway, obviously it will be converted back to 16-bit/44.1kHz at some point – although audio pros insist it's still worth using the higher resolution until that point.) Conversely, if your system is desperately short of power, you may wish to consider recording in mono, or reducing the bit rate to 12-bit or the frequency to 32kHz, but you will notice a drop in quality.

Automating sample capture

With some systems it's possible to automate the sample recording process. You set up your sampler so that when it detects a sound arriving at its input, it begins recording. When it detects that the sound is no longer there, it stops recording. You're provided with threshold controls, which allow you to set how loud the sound needs to be to trigger the recording, and the level the sound needs to drop below to cease recording. With the correct type of sound, this works extremely well – it effectively edits the start and end of the sample for you. But it needs to be something like drums, which have a sharp attack at the start; it isn't so great with sounds that fade up gradually, or indeed fade out gently. In those cases it's often quicker and easier to stick to manual recording rather than spend time fiddling with the threshold.

One area where automated sample capture can be invaluable is when you have large quantities of fairly similar sounds to sample. A good example of this would be systematically sampling all of the sounds from a drum machine.

EDITING SAMPLES

Before we start to explore editing, it's worth making the point that the changes you make when editing samples don't immediately affect the stored copy of your sample on your hard disk. This is what's known as 'non-destructive' editing. Changes only become permanent when you save the new version of the sample.

It's important to be aware of this. It means the changes you make to start and end points, or to tone etc, are temporary, and the sample only changes irreversibly when you press Save. Crucially, this means you can change your mind, and undo what you've done if you don't like it. Or you can choose to create many alternative versions of the same sample, saving them each under different names (using the 'Save As' command), and keeping the original or previous version intact, if you wish. It's usually a good idea to keep a backup copy of the original sample anyway, just in case you need to refer or even revert to it.

On the downside, it also means that if you don't remember to save your alterations, and you quit the application, or (perish the thought) the system crashes, those changes, and all that added work, will be lost.

Normalising

Normalising is the first thing I'd do to a sample once it's loaded into the sampler, before any editing or processing is carried out. It's an automated, digital method of making sure you have the highest-level signal possible with the minimum amount of unwanted background noise.

The sample editor examines the content of the sample, looking for the loudest point. From this level, it knows precisely how much the volume of the entire sample could be increased to bring that loudest point up to the optimum 'zero dB' level. If the loudest point of a sample falls short of the optimum level, the only thing that can be lurking in the gap is unwanted noise. By increasing the volume through normalisation, much of the noise is eliminated.

Simply select the entire sample in your sample editor, find the normalise function (probably lurking in one of the pull-down menus), ensure that the 'optimum level' setting is at 0dB, and hit the Process button. It's worth getting into the habit of normalising your samples early on in the production process, before you go applying any EQ or effects.

The only thing to be wary of with normalising concerns longer passages of recorded live material such as vocals. A good vocal performance will have a fairly broad dynamic range, meaning some sections of the recording will be deliberately louder than others. Whispered sections followed by belting vocals are desirable for dramatic effect, indeed good vocalists will have spent a considerable amount of time and effort perfecting their ability to use their voice effectively over a wide dynamic range. In these instances it's always best to normalise the entire vocal track as a single piece. If you chop the vocal performance into sections first and then normalise the individual pieces, you will remove those carefully honed dynamics by bringing all the sections up to the same volume.

Topping & tailing – editing start and end points

When you load a sound into a computer-based edit system, the sample is presented in its own window with a wonderfully large graphic image of the sound in the middle of it. If you press Play, the sample will start at the beginning and play though to its end. But let's say we want the sample to start or finish at some other points, perhaps because the sample has a slight pause at the start, which throws out the timing, or an unwanted extra beat at the end.

First you need to drag-select the desired area with the mouse – simply click on the point where you want it to start, hold the mouse button down and drag to the new end point. When you release the button, an area of the sample will be highlighted. If you now press Play, you should hear just the selected area. You can then repeat and refine the process until you get it just exactly as you want it. You will probably find that your sample editor has functions that allow you to set up whether the sample plays just the selected section (for instance with Wavelab, if you press Control on your computer keyboard while hitting Play, it does this) or plays on through to the end of the sample.

When you move your mouse pointer back over either edge of the highlighted area, a couple of little connected arrows will appear. This symbol means that if you now click, hold and drag you will move the edge of the selected area. Moving the left-hand edge adjusts the start point of the sample; moving the right hand edge adjusts the end point. In other words you are changing the playback length of the sample – temporarily, remember, at least until you save it. If you wish to keep only the selected area and discard the rest, you will need to use the Truncate function and then save the edited sample. This command is usually found in one of the pull-down menus or assigned to an onscreen button.

The image or 'view' of the sample can be zoomed right in so you can see the waveform in minute detail. This is usually done in one of several ways. You should find a little handle icon somewhere around the edge of the sample waveform display (often the bottom right-hand corner). Sliding the handle to the right usually magnifies the waveform, so more detail can be seen. Sliding the handle to the left zooms out, giving you a better overview of the whole sample. It doesn't take much practice to get an idea of the relationship between what a waveform display looks like and what it will sound like.

It's important to be quite fussy about the details when it comes to start and end points of a sample, particularly a rhythmic one like a drum part. You need to ensure that when you hit a key on a keyboard, the sample starts playing at the right moment. It's not always clear to the uninitiated just how much effect the 'fine-editing' of the start point can influence the musical feel, and particularly the timing, of a sample. Try taking a factory-produced library sound that's working perfectly, and experiment with editing the start point – you'll soon hear how easily even a small adjustment can make things sound wrong.

Hardware editing

If you're using an older hardware sampler you may not have a graphic sample editing system of this kind. With such machines, editing start and end points is done numerically. When you navigate your way to the sample edit window you should see the word 'start' and the word 'end' and each will have a number beside it. Initially the start point might be 00000 and the end point will be a much larger number. By moving your cursor to the appropriate number (so it's highlighted) and using either the data wheel or value buttons, you can adjust the positions of the two points. If you increase the value of the start point and audition the sample you should be able to hear that it starts to play back from slightly further into the sample. You may

ALTERING NUMERICALLY

As far as a sampler or computer is concerned, a sample is basically a digitised piece of sound made entirely of measurements expressed as numbers. Literally every aspect of a sample and its associated sampler instrument can be expressed as a number. In the early days of sampling, all editing functions and playback parameters, like volume, pan, filter and envelope settings, were done solely by altering these numbers – simply highlighting the relevant digits on the LCD screen and typing in new values.

Even using a software sampler, with its massive graphic user interface, there are times when altering things numerically is considerably simpler – perhaps to quickly give several samples the same matching values.

have to move the point by 100 ticks or more before you hear an obvious difference, because a single increment adjustment is very small. If you decrease the value of the end point setting, the sample playback length will be reduced.

Some entry-level hardware samplers don't provide graphic waveform editing *or* numeric editing. With this type of machine you have to adjust start and end point settings purely by ear. You need to make adjustments and listen to whether you're achieving what you want.

Avoiding clicks and pops

The next thing to be sure of is that the sample starts and stops at a point when the waveform is crossing the zero line – the vertical midpoint of the wave, where it's neither above nor below the horizontal centre line. Since the waveform that you see represents the volume level (amplitude) of the signal, and as loud signals produce the more extreme peaks and troughs, it follows that a flat line equates to silence. So whenever the waves cross that zero line (however briefly), the signal level at that moment is zero. That's where you want to make your edits. Otherwise you'll be cutting a signal in mid flow, and at best you'll get some unnatural leaps, at worst some nasty clicks or pops.

It's not as tricky as it sounds, because in almost all instances you can simply activate the 'snap to zero crossings' control (or 'search for zero crossings'), within your editor. This sets the editor so it can only place start/end points at zero crossings. You still have sufficient control of where you place your points, the software simply takes care of the very fine detail for you.

If you do find you really must place a start or end point somewhere other than where your editor is putting it, you can switch the function off. Computer-based editors will allow you to zoom the graphic sample display right in to microscopic detail, so you can manually attempt to find a point that achieves the musical result you're after without causing clicks.

Looping or sequencing?

The word 'loop' is generally being used here to mean a repeated section of sound, like a breakbeat – but it doesn't specifically refer to using the actual loop mechanism on a sampler. (The use of loops when creating your own sampler instruments is covered in Chapter 5.)

Looping in general has always been central to the art of making music with samplers. Over the past 20 years or so, the musical importance and impact of repeating small sections of borrowed sound to create new pieces of music has been consistent and undeniable, especially in rhythm-centred genres like hip-hop, drum & bass, and many popular forms of four-to-the-floor dance music, from techno to garage. Throughout the early evolution of these styles, loop-making was a vital tool in the producer's box.

But the use of the loop facility within a sampler itself, once the commonest way of repeating a small section of a sampled sound, has fallen out of favour. Many of the production techniques that historically required the use of loops have been superseded by ever-more sophisticated, computer-based MIDI sequencing and audio manipulation software. It's now easier, quicker and more musically versatile to chop up a sample into pieces and sequence new patterns, using repeated MIDI notes to re-trigger the sample to create the same effects.

TRIGGERING

In the context of sampling, to trigger means to play back a sample using a MIDI note-on message. The roots of the word come from the very early days of sampling drum machines like the Linn LM1, which only played back their samples in 'one-shot' playback mode. When the sampler receives a note-on message it simply ignores the note-off message and plays the sound right through to the end of the sample. This means users would have no control over note length. These days it often specifies one-shot mode of playback.

The reasons for the change are clear. Until the mid 1990s, many MIDI sequencers were limited to 16 or 24 tracks and, even worse, they were hardware-based, which meant working numerically on a tiny little LCD display. This made MIDI sequencing a chore – so setting loop points was often the easier solution.

Early samplers were also much more limited in terms of sample capacity, multi-timbrality and polyphony, which meant that using lots of separate samples was less feasible. Plus, the very act of cutting up samples was done numerically, without the aid of graphic displays of sample waveforms, which made it much more laborious. All in all, it was much easier to loop the same short sample.

The upshot of all this is that, although this next section looks at the theory of creating and using loops within a sampler to produce interesting rhythms and musical effects, I can't honestly say you should bother. It's easier instead to extract and manipulate rhythmic material in conjunction with your sequencer to achieve the beats and feel you're after.

How to create a loop using 'loop points'

Although most sample editing software has facilities that let you set traditional-style 'loop points', there's usually a quick and easy way to hear in advance how a sample or a section of a sample will sound looped. In the section on 'topping and tailing' I talked about drag-selecting a section of a sample so you can edit the start and end points. Most sample editors that work in this way also have a 'looped playback' mode. In this mode the editor will play the highlighted section as though it were a loop. In fact, most of them have an additional 'shortcut' command that enables you to 'Set Loop To Current Selection' – which does as it says, creating loop start and end points in the same locations as the current positions of the start and end Points.

MULTI-TIMBRAL
Most modern samplers or other MIDI sound sources can play back a different sound responding to each of the available 16 MIDI channels. Such machines are said to be multi-timbral (literally 'many-toned') – meaning they can play several different sounds at once. When an instrument is said to be 32-part multi-timbral, it means it uses two 16-channel MIDI ports; the maximum is generally 128-part multi-timbral (ie eight MIDI ports).

The actual process of editing loop points is practically identical to editing start and end points of any sample. With hardware samplers you'll need to navigate yourself to the 'loop edit' window in much the same way that you go to the 'sample edit' window. With software samplers the approach varies, but the basic principle remains consistent: you'll need to actually create or activate a loop, usually via a pull-down menu.

By default, a start point and end point will be created for you by the sampler, either at the start and end of the selected sample or, if you have drag-selected a portion of a sample, the selected section will usually be used. You then move these loop points in exactly the same way you move the start and end points of a sample. With a hardware system this will be numeric; with a software system you usually get to choose whether you work numerically or graphically. With the graphic approach, a pair of little arrows will appear as you move the cursor over either the start or end of the selected area. When the arrows appear, click and drag to move the start or end point.

Looping offers several options regarding playback modes. Assuming that you are triggering your sample via MIDI, when you strike a key the sample begins to play from the start point of the sample. Without a loop in place it simply plays through to the end point and stops; but if you have a loop enabled, playback starts at the beginning, continues until it reaches the loop end point, then returns to the loop start point and repeats that section.

How playback ends is down to you – it will usually continue for as long as you hold down a

POLYPHONIC

A Greek-derived word that can be translated as something very similar to multi-timbral (many-toned), but it might help to differentiate the two by thinking of polyphony as meaning 'lots of sound'. In music technology terms, polyphony specifies how many simultaneous sounds can be made by a piece of musical equipment – not necessarily different sounds, just sounds. If you start holding down notes on an electronic keyboard, one key then two then three, four, five etc (until you're using your arm to hold them down), at some point the first notes you played will be cut out and replaced by the new ones. That's when you've reached the limit of the keyboard's polyphony – if indeed you can reach its limit, because nowadays this may well be higher than the standard keyboard's 88 notes. Certainly 16-note (or '16-voice') polyphony would be an entry-level minimum, but it won't get you far – some new mobile phones have 32-note polyphonic ringtones. Higher-quality gear is more likely to have at least 64-note, or 128-note polyphony, or more. Extra polyphony is useful for multi-timbral instruments, because if each note is triggering more than one sound, that uses up the available polyphony more quickly. A monophonic instrument can only play one note at a time – ie it can't play chords – but that single note could still trigger multiple sounds. In other words, a monophonic instrument could still be multi-timbral.

MIDI note. The sample can be set to either stop playing the moment the note is released, or continue to the sample end point – this is determined by a loop playback or loop mode setting, usually found in a pull-down menu. Some loop playback modes include a reverse setting that causes the loop to be played first forwards, then backwards, then forwards, etc...

The simplest form of loop places the start and end points in the same locations as the actual sample start and end points, and so repeats the entire sample. But it's common to loop one or more smaller sections of a larger sample.

In image 20 (a loop editor screen from Kontakt), you can see a drum sample with three different loops defined by three highlighted areas. The playback procedure of such a multi-loop situation follows a couple of simple rules. When you strike a key the sample plays from the sample start point, continues until it reaches the end point of the first loop, then jumps back to the start point of that first loop and begins to repeat.

The number of repeats is determined by a 'count' parameter: a count of 0 usually repeats the loop indefinitely; a count of 1 will repeat the looped section once and then continue to play onwards through the sample; a count of 2 repeats the loop twice, and so on. Once the first loop has been repeated the specified number of times it carries on playing past the loop end point, until it either encounters another loop (in which case it repeats this second loop for the specified count), or it reaches the end of the sample.

Many software samplers allow for multiple loops to be defined within a single larger sample in this way. This will vary from system to system and can become quite complex. Kontakt, for example, allows you to set up to 128 consecutive loops within a single sample, then even alter the order in which they're played – each of the 128 loops is numbered, so you place the numbers into a list that specifies the order in which they're played.

Creating loops also comes in very handy for producing sustained notes from short samples when creating sampler instruments – there's more about this in Chapter 5.

Audio illustration – rhythmic looping

Listen to CD1 Track 1 and you'll hear a breakbeat, as supplied by drummer/producer Shaun Lee. This is what you can see in image 20 – the three highlighted zones represent loops I've created within the single one-bar breakbeat. Now listen to CD1 Track 2, and you can hear a somewhat different version of the breakbeat. The same original sample was used, but now it has a very different rhythm and structure, ready to be placed in a completely new context. This was done by 'rhythmic looping'.

I'll explain how those changes were made, transforming the sample in Track 1 to the one in Track 2, step-by-step... (Remember you need to zoom right in on the waveform display to make precise settings to loop start and end points. Even small adjustments can dramatically

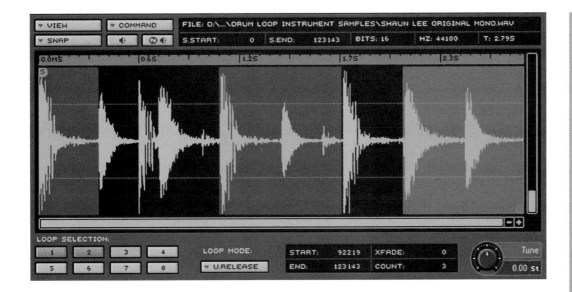

affect timing. If you want to see the actual sample manipulation in closer detail, you can load the relevant audio tracks from CD1 into your own sampler, as we discuss the process, and zoom in on them onscreen.)

I started by creating a loop that only contained the very first kick drum beat of the break, and set the count for this to 1. The original break only has a single kick drum beat at the start, but I fancied enhancing the rhythm with a double beat. With Kontakt the procedure entailed using the Loop Mode menu to activate loop number one. Because the kick drum is right at the start of our breakbeat, I didn't need to alter the loop start point for loop number one, but I did need to drag the loop end point to just a few ticks before the first hi-hat.

Next, the second loop. This one contains a combination of a kick drum and a hi-hat beat, and I set the count for it to 1 as well. I did this because I like the effect created by repeating such a disjointed section of rhythmic material. For the third loop I chose to use the snare beat at the end of the bar and the little vocal 'ah' that sneaks in at the finish. I set the count to 3 because it repeats the snare, and this is going to be useful in the next step of the process.

If you listen to CD1 Track 3 you can hear the three new loops in action. But this doesn't really sound very good, does it? The new rhythm no longer really hangs together. That's because the creation of our loops has actually messed up the original rhythm of the break, and changed the overall length.

But it's just an example of the stages you have to go through as part of the musical composition process. Very few aspects of sampling exist in isolation – things occur to you as you go along that might be worth incorporating, and tracks are often built from a lot of trial and error. For instance, when I was choosing which sections of this breakbeat to loop, I was playing them via MIDI using a keyboard. While I was experimenting by triggering the sample from different keys on the keyboard, two things became apparent.

The first was that I rather liked the tonal and rhythmic qualities of the breakbeat when it was transposed up by five semitones, so rather than using its 'root note' – its original key, in this instance C – I played it using the F key. It comes out faster, and at a higher musical pitch (we'll look at this in more detail later under 'Altering Tempo', and also in Chapter 5, under 'Keyboard Mapping'). The initial transposed result can be heard on CD1 Track 4.

The second thing I noticed was that a better rhythm was created when I repeated the first half of the newly looped sample. And also that the second half of the new loop (with just the snare in it) makes a good rhythmic variation or 'fill'. So I created a sequence in Cubase (any sequencer would do) to make it play back that way: first I had to find the correct tempo for the newly transposed break (see 'Guess The Tempo'), then I created a MIDI part and entered two one-bar notes followed by a two-bar note.

The final result (as heard in CD1 Track 2) is that we get the first part of our new beat repeated three times, followed by the snare fill.

WHY LOOPS AT ALL?

Why, you might wonder, should you bother with sample loops, and the inherent hassle of finding, recording, editing and storing them… not to mention worrying about the legal issues? Surely, for electronic music at least, it would be simpler just to use a pre-sampled drum machine pattern? Perhaps there's a psychological element to the answer – an illicit thrill in taking some sounds intended for another purpose and moulding them to your own, or just the basic appeal of the 'hunt and capture' aspect of sampling. But in purely musical terms, the attraction is simply in acquiring the feel of a spontaneous human performance, in what can otherwise become a mechanistic digital domain – without the bother of finding a suitably skilled and like-minded real drummer. However, sampling and reusing an entire performance (even if it were technically feasible) wouldn't necessarily be desirable. Using short clips gives you more control, not only over song structure, but over timing too. The fact is, a lot of samples originate from old recordings, from the days before drummers habitually played along to 'click-tracks' in the studio to help keep a perfect rhythm – and so it wasn't unusual for songs to drift out of time, sometimes almost imperceptibly, over the course of a track. Often the bpms would speed up as the song progressed, as the players' excitement would build. If you sample just a small section of such a track, and then loop it, this won't be a problem.

Getting the same results by sequencing

If the desired start point of your loop is the same as the start point of your sample, and you intend to trigger the loop using a MIDI sequencer, there's very little point in setting up loop points at all. You would need to record a MIDI note to cause playback to start from the correct song position anyway (regardless of loop point settings). By shortening the length of the MIDI note to determine the playback end point of the sample, and then re-triggering the start of the sample at the right moment (with another MIDI note), you have effectively looped the playback of the sample, regardless of loop point settings.

Under such circumstances, if you were to use a loop, the loop points would almost certainly be exactly the same as the start and end locations of the relevant MIDI notes, so you'd be wasting your time. Inputting MIDI notes on a sequencer is easier, quicker and more versatile than messing about with loop points in a sampler.

If the section you wish to repeat is not at the start of the sample, you're better off chopping up the sample and sequencing. The process of cutting up the sample in a graphic-based editor and then sequencing in a modern sequencer will probably take about as long to set up as the loop (and an accompanying MIDI sequence) would. But once you have a series of short sections of sample and a MIDI sequence running, the creative possibilities are far greater than the more rigidly fixed process of working with the looped version.

How to pick out a loop

Regardless of whether you intend to use a traditional loop mechanism on a sampler, or 'looped playback mode', or simply fake looped playback using a MIDI sequencer, the aesthetic rules concerning what to loop are the same. The first principle of sampling applies here just as with everything else that's subjective and not strictly to do with pressing buttons, namely 'anything goes'. There really are no fixed rules – if *you* happen to like the way a thing sounds, it's probably fine for *your* music.

But if you're trying to capture something predictable like a drum break, it does help to bear a few things in mind. First, count the beats and bars of the material you're trying to sample. Try to identify the first and last beats of the bar. Then sample an entire bar. Try experimenting by sampling from somewhere obviously wrong, perhaps the first snare beat. You'll find that, in isolation from other musical material, as long as you sample a length of time equivalent to a whole bar, the result should loop quite well. Even if playback starts from the snare, after the first cycle of the loop your ear/brain is liable to re-adjust to identifying the kick drum at the start of the bar as the most important focus and start re-counting normally.

It's an interesting phenomenon, and a good illustration of the way the brain likes to keep things in a recognisable order, and is quite prone to deceiving us to make us feel more comfortable. It's also a valuable lesson to learn if you come to try and loop material you've taken from music that was originally in awkward or unusual musical timings (jazz or various types of ethnic music). Although your lovely loop might sound great on its own, you may encounter problems when trying to place more familiar ¼ time signature material alongside it (we'll look at time signatures shortly).

The advantages of editing 'in context'

Finding the correct start, end or loop points is not always as easy as it looks. And often the way a sample sounds playing back on its own will be very different to how it's going to work alongside other elements of a song – especially if the new sampled material has a different inherent tempo. The answer is to actually edit a sample within the context of the piece of music where you want to use it.

In practice, editing a sample 'in context' is simply a case of adjusting the start point so it's 'nearly' right, importing the sample into a sampler instrument, and then using an appropriate MIDI sequence to play the sample back alongside other elements of your music. Some samplers will allow you to adjust start, loop and end points during playback, others will not. Sometimes you might have to try listening to a sample in context, stopping playback, making adjustments, then re-import it to a sampler instrument to hear the results. Just a little experimentation can often make it much easier to find a setting that works for you.

When setting start points, the general area in which we want a sample to start playing is usually pretty obvious, because it's relatively easy to identify the beginning of a sound. This is particularly true of individual hit samples like drum sounds, which have loud and short start or attack. There are times though when there is some room for manoeuvre with the finer details of the position of a Start Point. This is especially true with any instrument that has a slower attack characteristic – for instance a stringed instrument like a violin – which starts more gently. Triggering it via MIDI can be very helpful for fine adjustment so the attack of the sample fits rhythmically with the tempo and feel of a specific piece of music. You may find that samples you use in several different pieces of music benefit from slight adjustment of their start point in context for each different song.

Editing in context is especially helpful when it comes to rhythmic material. When a musician plays there tend to be very subtle errors or nuances of timing that provide a pleasing overall feel to the finished result. Musicians tend to be sensitive to these timing nuances and can often play along to other musicians and match the feel of their own playing to that. If you've ever witnessed a 200-piece Brazilian samba band in action, you'll know just how incredible this can be, as 199 musicians lock onto the timing nuances of a single player. Within a more traditional band, the drummer is often delegated as the musician that all the other players take their timing from. If the drummer decides to play one of the snare beats slightly early or slightly late, everybody else will follow. So a drummer can start playing and a percussionist etc can join in, and all will be groovy.

But if you sample two musicians playing just *reasonably* similar rhythms, at *broadly* similar tempos, the chances are they will be using slightly different nuances of timing. So if you are halfway through a composition and decide you want to incorporate a sample taken from a heavily rhythmic source, things can be tricky – in many cases almost impossible. There are many producers who wouldn't even bother trying. If you're determined, though, editing in context can help a little. As those little timing nuances are all about placing particular beats slightly before or after the metronomic timing, adjusting the start points of your samples in context may be able to pull or push the subtle differences in timing back together till they fit.

Editing in context will also show you where the end of the sample is. When triggering a sample via MIDI, from within a sequencer, the end of the MIDI note usually determines when the sample stops playing. In fact you quickly realise that, in this musical context, you often don't need to crop the end off the sample at all – the MIDI note-off message does that for you. This can be beneficial: it can be useful with some kinds of source material to leave an extra bit of sample at the end in case you decide to slow down the song at a later date. But it's a double-edged sword because, with most systems, when a sample is loaded for playback it's stored in RAM, so any unused sections of sample you leave lying about will be using up that precious RAM. So once you have edited your sample 'in context' like this, think about going back and chopping off most of the unwanted end section. If you do have plenty of RAM, and you do want to leave an 'extra bit', then a mere second at most should suffice for an adjustment of a bpm or two later.

The role of tempo when using loops

When it comes to trying to get a sample to loop correctly, even tiny adjustments in timing can make a great difference. Try experimenting with very small alterations to a 'factory-prepared' simple drum loop from the library that shipped with your sampler. By starting with a loop that's functioning correctly, you can soon see how easy it is to make the rhythm drift out of time by messing with the loop length. This process should help you get a feel for how to make your own loops repeat correctly.

The secret to getting the timing of loops right is, as with so many musical matters, just to listen. Once you have the start and end points in approximately the right locations, you need to start making small adjustments and listening closely to the result. You can't always guess the right adjustments before you begin, you just have to try something and see what happens. If you move a point and the timing of the loop sounds better, you're probably heading in the right direction; if the change makes the loop sound more out-of-time, you're probably moving it the wrong way.

Every piece of music has tempo. The tempo can of course change within the course of an arrangement – jazz and experimental musicians might even create music that's constantly changing tempo. But 95 per cent of popular music maintains a regular tempo throughout a song, or at least within each section of a song.

Any rhythmic sample (like a drumbeat) will have an inherent tempo. The crucial point is that any particular rhythm or melody will sound very different played at different tempos.

As a general rule, if you want to blend two samples of distinctly rhythmic material, the contents will at least need to be at the same tempo

TEMPO

Tempo is the musical terminology for the speed of a piece of music. It's expressed in beats-per-minute, usually abbreviated to bpm. A piece of music with a tempo of 80bpm is half the speed of one with a tempo of 160bpm. The other point to keep in mind is if you play a sample back an octave below its root pitch (triggered an octave lower on a MIDI keyboard, for instance), it plays back at half the musical tempo – that's assuming you're not using timestretch, which is something we'll be looking at shortly.

to fit together pleasingly. There are exceptions, but they are mathematically complex, and by the time you encounter them you'll no doubt appreciate that, ultimately, if it sounds OK, it is OK.

There's also the complication of time signature. You'll usually need to ensure that all your samples are in the same time signature, or are at least mathematically compatible – again, there are exceptions, and you will know when you've found one (see 'Blending Rhythms' over the page).

Each audio+MIDI sequencer song or project will have a playback tempo and a time signature, and it's essential that the inherent tempos/ tempi of the samples (or audio recordings) you are using match the tempo of your project. Whether you choose to adjust the tempo of your sequencer to match a sample, or whether you set about adjusting the inherent tempo of a sample to match the playback tempo of the sequencer, depends on what stage of the writing process you're at, and a few aesthetic decisions. As a general rule, once you decide upon a tempo for a song, it's often best to adjust the tempo of each sample you add to match the song tempo. The time signature setting of your sequencer determines the nature of bar lengths, quantise and edit grid settings, etc.

Finding out the tempo of a sample

One of the advantages of using material from sample CDs (besides the ease of copyright clearance) is that the tempo of each sample should be listed for you on the CD sleeve – or, in the case of our very own sample CD2, listed at the back of the book.

If you choose not to go down the CD route, working out the tempo of a sample for yourself can be trickier. The good news is there are a number of sample editors that do a pretty good job of finding the tempo of a sample automatically. Most of them simply presume that the sample is four beats (one bar) in length and that it's in $\frac{4}{4}$ time signature, and then use a mathematical equation to calculate the tempo. You simply isolate a four-beat chunk of sound, locate the relevant function within your application and hit Calculate. Programs with this facility include Sound Forge, Spark, Peak, Cubase SX, Logic Audio, Acid, and Propellerhead's classic Recycle.

If you don't have access to any of these, and you need to figure out the tempo of a particular sample for yourself, the simplest solution is mathematical. Basically you'd use the same equation employed by the auto-detection systems, which is this: 60 divided by the length of the sample (in seconds), multiplied by the number of beats.

Here's how it works in practice. With your sample loaded into your sample editor, you should be able to see the length of the sample, in seconds. You should also be able to count the number of beats in your sample (easy enough in a straight four-to-the-floor rhythm). Get

TIME SIGNATURE

In traditional musical notation, this is a shorthand way of describing the rhythmic properties or 'timing' of musical phrases. Most dance and rock-based forms of music are in what's called $\frac{4}{4}$ timing, which tells you there are four beats in each bar.

All music is divided into bars. You can picture it best in a straightforward dance tune, where the kick drum is pounding out every single beat in an incessant, regular rhythm (informally known as 'four-to-the-floor'). Start counting out loud to the bass drum beats: *1,2,3,4*, then when you get to four, go back to one, so it's *1,2,3,4,1,2,3,4, 1,2,3,4*, and so on. For every four beats of the kick drum you are counting, you're listening to a single bar of the music. One of the beats might be clearly emphasised to stand out from the others – usually the first beat of the bar (the 'one').

In fact, it's the first (or upper) digit in $\frac{4}{4}$ that tells you there are four beats per bar. The second (or bottom) 4 tells you that the measuring scale is quarter-notes (more old-fashionedly known as crotchets). If that number was an 8, it would mean the fundamental note-length is shorter (measured in eighth-notes rather than quarter-notes), so there are twice as many potential pulses between each emphasis – ie eight per bar instead of four. A common eighth-note rhythm might be something like a regular steady hi-hat strike. A 16th-note rhythm would be more like a fast hi-hat shuffle pattern. This still wouldn't tell you the overall speed of the track, of course – that depends on the tempo, or bpms.

The time signature of $\frac{3}{4}$ would describe a piece of music that's counted *1,2,3,1,2,3, 1,2,3* etc. Most classical waltzes are in $\frac{3}{4}$ time. Jazz has a habit of being in really weird time signatures – one of the slightly more common is $\frac{5}{4}$, or five beats in the bar, which you would count *1,2,3,4,5,1,2,3,4,5, 1,2,3,4,5* etc. Jazz-oriented tracks may also suddenly change time signature in the course of a tune or arrangement.

a calculator, key in 60, hit the divide button, enter the length of the sample, hit the multiply key, enter the number of beats, hit the equals key.

For instance, let's say you have a four-beat sample that's 2.526 seconds long. 60 ÷ 2.526 = 23.753. And then 23.753 x 4 = 95.012. So the sample is running at 95bpm.

It is possible to have a very abstract sample that's an irregular length but you can play in a way that sounds good. Perhaps the sample works rhythmically if you play it all the way through and then leave a small silence before you re-trigger it. You might not know how many beats long it is – it could be three-and-a-half beats, perhaps. The solution is to use a sequencer, and trust your ears.

BLENDING RHYTHMS

Imagine you were to sample two rhythms, both at precisely the same tempo, but one is in 4/4 time and the other is in 3/4. If you try to overlay them, weird stuff happens. Assuming you start both rhythms at the first beat in the bar, at exactly the same time, the two rhythms will very quickly go out of time with each other. But they'll briefly coincide again every 12 beats – which of course happens to be after three bars of four beats as well as four bars of three beats. Chances are this will sound dreadful, but it's just possible it will create a musically interesting effect.

If you were to try the same experiment with two rhythms recorded at different *tempos*, it's extremely unlikely to sound anything other than horrendous from the very first beat. Unless of course the tempo of one rhythm is exactly half, or some other fraction, of the other.

Get the sample set up in your sampler so you can trigger it from the sequencer. Create a one-bar long MIDI part, and enter one long MIDI note in your new part, ensuring the note runs right from the start to the end. Also make sure the note you create corresponds to the root note your sample has been assigned to within your sampler, and you have your MIDI channels set correctly. (If you're confused by all this, flick forward to Chapter 5 and read up about 'keyboard mapping'.)

Now hit Play on your sequencer. If what you hear doesn't sound right, you need to adjust the playback tempo of your sequencer – try increasing or decreasing it till what you hear sounds OK. At that point, you'll have found the tempo of your sample.

I should point out that this only works for samples that are played from the start right through to the end. It's not a method for finding the tempo of a riff you've just made up. If you are actually playing a rhythm by repeatedly hitting your keyboard several times within the length of a bar, the solution is to use a metronome or audible click from your sequencer and play along to it. Adjust the tempo of your click until the rhythm you are playing fits with it. Then record your performance into the sequencer.

Altering the tempo of a sample by changing pitch

The most primitive method of altering the tempo of a sample is done via pitch alteration. As I'll explore in more detail in the next chapter, a sample that's mapped to play across the length of a MIDI keyboard can be played back either very slowly or very quickly, depending on which key/note you press on the keyboard. Playing back a sample at an octave below its root note on your keyboard will not only reduce the musical pitch of the sampled material by an octave, it will also halve its inherent tempo.

Altering pitch is a crucial tool when it comes to purposeful, creative manipulation of the nature of sound. But when it comes to trying to get rhythmic material to fit the tempo of a project, it's often not the most desirable solution. The following two methods are more appropriate for altering tempo without altering pitch.

Altering tempo using timestretch

Digital timestretching can make your sample longer, slowing down the tempo, spreading out the beats and notes, but without lowering the pitch – so the original key and tuning is preserved. It can also, of course, go the other way and speed up a sample, compressing the length of a piece of audio, increasing the tempo, but again without affecting pitch. Try it – it's an audio miracle in action. Yet it's a fairly straightforward job for a sample editor to perform.

Just select your sample and open the timestretch function page in your sample editor. You'll be presented with two sets of numbers: one tells you how long (or what tempo) your sample is at present; the other is to tell you how long it will be after processing. Between the two is a third figure showing the percentage by which the sample will need to be slowed down or sped up to reach the destination. You can either simply alter the percentage, which will automatically alter the figure in the destinations pane, or you can enter the figures for the desired new sample length in the destination window, which will automatically alter the percentage.

Each editing system deals with timestretching slightly differently, so produce varying results. If you have access to more than one editor, try timestretching the same sample in two or more systems and you will notice the results have their own distinctive musical characters.

In general, though, the more stretching you apply, the more unnatural the outcome will be. Extreme timestretching produces the famous drum & bass 'zipper' vocal sound that turns human voices into slowed-down demented robots. If you slow the tempo (ie increase the sample length) within five per cent of the original, the results usually tend to be quite impressively natural, or 'transparent'. When speeding up tempo (decreasing sample length) it can be impressive over much greater percentages.

What timestretch actually does is quite clever. It chops a sound into hundreds of short slices, and then, to make the sound longer, it pulls those slices apart from each other, adding a small amount of silence between each slice. At small percentages of tempo adjustment you don't really hear the silence, because your ear does a little conjuring trick and puts the sound back together as you listen. As the lengths of silence get bigger, the ear can no longer compensate and you start to perceive the slices as hard-edged individual events – hence the typical timestretch buzzing or zipper sounds.

As a creative effect, timestretching can come up with some interesting and quite musical results, but its sound is often instantly recognisable, so it should be approached with caution on longer samples. It can certainly add some very welcome zing to percussion sounds: try elongating a snare sound until it starts to rattle nicely – it will of course now be a bit unnaturally long for a snare sound, so you might need to cut it back again to near the original length, adjusting any applied effects accordingly (we'll look at this in detail in Chapter 6).

Altering tempo by beat slicing

Beat slicing has revolutionised the way many musicians and producers operate, especially with breakbeats and drum programming (because that's where beat slicing works best). It uses the same basic concept as timestretching, except instead of chopping the sample into hundreds of tiny slices, beat slicing chops it into just a few pieces, each of which contains a whole, single instrument hit, note or beat.

With drums, it means you can isolate the different drum beats (kicks, snare, hats etc), then control the tempo by either putting longer spaces between them to slow the tempo, or shorter spaces to speed things up, all without affecting the pitch, tone or playing nuances of the beats themselves. And you can do it over a much bigger range of tempos than you can with timestretching.

The beat-slicing technique was pioneered by Propellerhead Software in one of their first (and still current) products, the innovative Recycle. Recycle works by finding the loudest or most significant peaks within a sample and attaching a marker to each one. Once you've loaded up your sample, you move a little handle marked Sensitivity a small amount from left to right and you see some markers appear. The first to appear are attached to the biggest, loudest events (usually the kick drums). Slide the handle further to the right and more markers appear, attached to the next loudest events (the snares). The next events to be identified would probably be the hi-hats. By the time the slider gets all the way to the right, the software will be adding markers to any significant elements of background noise.

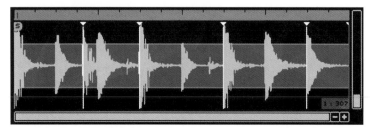

image **21**

In the File menu you'll find a command that will then chop the sample up into chunks that run from marker to marker. Recycle will also create a MIDI file, the same length as your sample, containing a note in the location of each marker. The idea is if you then load all the slices into a sampler and the MIDI file into a sequencer, you can use the sequencer to play back the slices of sample one after another. If the sequencer is set to the right tempo, it should sound exactly the same as the original sample (though sometimes with a slight change in feel).

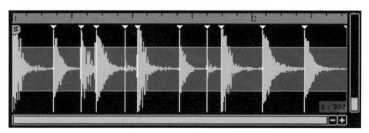

image **22**

Recycle may have been the first to do this, but it's far from the only current application with built-in slicing facilities. I've used NI's Intakt, a dedicated beat slicing and manipulating sampler instrument, as an illustration here. Images 21-23 are Intakt screengrabs, showing the familiar drum sample from Track 1 of CD1, with added beat-slicing markers responding to different sensitivity settings: the low-sensitivity setting results in markers only at the high-amplitude kick drum beats (as in image 21); medium-sensitivity adds a couple more (image 22); while a high-sensitivity setting shows markers on all of the events (see image 23).

image **23**

Altering the rhythm of a sample

The second common use for slicing up breaks is that you can then use your sequencer to create new rhythms with the individual sounds from your sample. Because the low-sensitivity setting produces fewer sections, each section will probably contain a sequence of events – such as a kick drum followed by snare and hi-hat hits. If you simply re-arrange the order in which you play back the chunks (without altering the sequencer tempo), you can create dynamic new rhythms that retain the all-important human feel of a real drummer.

When real musicians play, their performances aren't completely perfect, regardless of how proficient they are. There are tiny little variations in timing that would take a lot of fiddly programming to reproduce with a sequencer (if you could do it at all). By keeping a few hits or notes of the human performance together in chunks, you get to alter the overall rhythm while retaining the little imperfections in timing that give the original beat some of its groove.

This is illustrated by Track 5, which is a straight re-ordering of the sections of our Shaun

Lee rhythm sample (Track 1). In this instance you're hearing slice 2, slice 1, then slice 3.

I've deliberately kept things simple for Track 5, but by chopping the break into more pieces and rearranging the bits, you can produce quite complex results. This can even be done randomly by some machines. CD1 Track 6 is an example of this: I used the medium-sensitivity beat slice example (from image 22) and employed the Intakt 'Randomize Slice Order' command. It decided to play the five slices in the following order: 1, 4, 2, 3, 5, space, 3 (it randomly adds spaces too).

Transient trouble

There is a bit of a hitch with all this chopping up and playing around with recordings of real drummers (or any other loop of a real instrument sound). It's to do with how musical sounds interact and overlap in the real world. This is where it helps if you have a background in using, or especially recording, real instruments.

Take drums, for example. Attempting to record a drummer playing an acoustic drum kit is a battle of control for a recording engineer. As described in the 'Recording Your Own Samples' section in Chapter 3, the idea of close-miking is to isolate each drum sound so EQ and effects can be applied individually to the sounds within the kit, and the relative levels can be adjusted to achieve a good balance. Basically the aim is to 'take control' of the overall drum kit sound. To some extent, of course, this is an impossible task...

If you stand in a venue and listen to the glories of a cool drummer bashing out a funky beat, there is a bit of magic going on. All of the individual sounds flow into each other and merge to form a single sonic image. The ringing tails of a snare hit, or cymbal crash, will be resonating over several bars of the beat, subtly influencing the tone and character of the subsequent sounds. A drum kit is a single instrument that is far more than the sum of its individual parts. Close-miking is an attempt to get the best of both worlds – a good engineer accepts that all the mikes will, inevitably, pick up at least a little of all the other drums in the kit too. But the main aim is to achieve the best overall 'kit' sound, rather than getting too caught up in the individual sounds of each drum in isolation.

So, here's the relevance to beat slicing... If the ringing tones of that snare are carrying across a whole bar then, logically, if you chop that bar up into pieces and re-order the beats, you will, at some point, be putting the ringing, harmonic, reverberating tail of the snare sound before the actual hit that created it. You're putting the cart before the horse, as it were.

This may not seem too important, but listen closely to the detail of CD1 Track 3 and you can hear it in action – it's subtle, but it does have an effect. In some cases this can sound OK, sometimes not so OK. But if you're chopping up a beat with a fair bit of reverb on it, you can end up with some pretty weird and unnatural-sounding results. You might actually like the musical effect, but if you're after a finished product that convinces people it's a real drummer supplying a funky beat, you may be in trouble.

CD1 Track 6 provides another example of what can happen when re-ordering events. In this case there is a stray snippet of sound – a tiny, almost subliminal click – at the end of the sample... an unwanted blip of noise technically known as a 'transient'. In context, when this sample is played as a loop, you don't really notice the click because it's actually a part of the beat, but let the sample play through to the end and it becomes annoyingly audible.

I'm going to look at how to remove this blip by replacing it with a bit of silence. In image 24 you'll see I've opened the sample in a waveform editor (in this case Wavelab) and zoomed

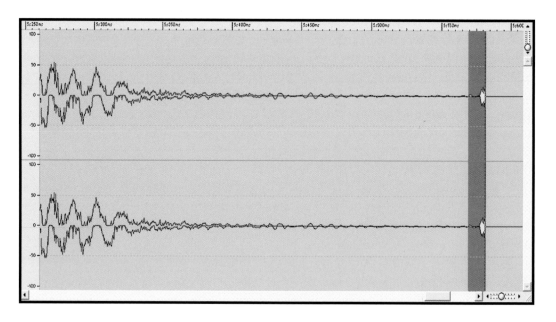

image **24**

in on the very end part, where I've highlighted the offending 'transient' sound. I then used the Silence command in Wavelab's File menu to remove it. Notice that you don't simply chop it off, because that would alter the overall length of the sample, and so upset the timing.

If your sampler doesn't have a Silence command, it will almost certainly have a Change Gain command, which you can use to turn the volume of the offending section down to zero.

The other point to note here is that this sample consists of two repeated bars of the same rhythm, and because the blip is only a problem when the sample plays through to its end, I've not altered it the first time it appears, at the end of the first bar. You can hear the final result in CD1 Track 7.

Copying the rhythm from a sample

This technique is another contentious sampling issue that can't be condoned, as it strays into the legal minefield of copyright infringement... but it does happen to be an undeniable fact of modern musical life, which is why it's being mentioned here.

When you ask most electronic-based music producers how they start a new track, the vast majority give the same answer. They start with a sample of one of their favourite records. They get it looped-up and running in a sequencer and then start adding layers of their own sounds to it. By the time a few layers are added, it's possible to switch off the original sample and, hey presto, you've got yourself a new track. By copying the rhythm of a record you know works, and has a good feel, you get a rhythm you know is right, but with a very different tonal character thanks to the new sounds.

As I've said, this procedure is technically illegal as far as the record industry is concerned – despite the fact that there's nothing from the original recording left in your new track, or that rhythms themselves can't be copyrighted, or even that it's been a common practice for many years. You're still not allowed to do it – or at least without first getting permission and paying a royalty to the copyright holder(s). So let's say you've gone through the legal hoops with the relevant artists/publishers/record labels, and the original record has been cleared for this kind of use. Well done. Now we can get on with the musical techniques involved...

Producers who work this way often start by sampling between one and four bars, which they think will work well as a repeated loop. Then once the loop is running in a sequencer, they start to meticulously replicate what's going on in the sample.

For instance, say there's a standard drumbeat that consists of the usual kick, snare, open hi-hat, closed hi-hat and a cymbal crash. The first thing they'd do is find some new drum sounds, which might be from a drum machine, a bank of sounds that shipped with the sampler, or a lovingly crafted collection of individual samples from other sources. These will need to be mapped and set up to respond to MIDI. They get the loop running perfectly in their sequencer, create a MIDI part on a track, and open the grid-style MIDI editor for their newly created part.

With the original sample loop playing, they'd place a kick drum sound on the grid. For 99 per cent of dance music it'll go on the first beat of the first bar. Then they place a kick drum on top of each existing kick drum in turn through the loop. When they're done with the kicks, they'd move on to the snares, then the hi-hats etc. It's crucial that these occur absolutely, precisely in time with the sounds playing in the sampled loop. *Almost* right won't do.

This precision really comes into its own when trying to copy a sample of a real 'human' performance – something with a very unpredictable groove, like a 'funky drummer'-style break, for instance. All of the major sequencing packages have a List editor where you can literally move the start point of your MIDI notes by hundredths of a second, experimenting with positions until it sounds absolutely right.

In fact, no matter how hard you try you'd probably not be able to replicate the beat you've sampled precisely. What you will gain, though, is an invaluable insight into how your favourite music hangs together, which can prove to be an inspirational springboard in itself.

Storing samples

You need to get organised about storing samples, and music projects in general. If you're working on a computer, use a single folder per project or song. Keep everything concerned with the relevant project in there – which includes the song files when you save them in your sequencer, any audio tracks you record, any samples you use (if you use a factory sample or one from a CD, move a copy of it into this folder), effects settings, patches for virtual instruments... *everything*. The idea is that if you take the project to another studio to work on it, you will have everything you need at hand to get it up and running on somebody else's set-up.

Even more importantly, by keeping it all together in a labelled folder you'll still be able to find everything you need should you decide to return to a song months or years later to re-work it – whether or not your studio set-up has evolved in the intervening period.

If you use a hardware sampler, apply the same rules about keeping a single song or project disk. If you have the facility to do so, it's a good idea to transfer copies of samples to the 'project' folder on your computer when you finish the track.

Similarly, if you're using external hardware like synthesisers within a song, sample off the sounds you're using (or record them as audio tracks on hard disk) and store them in the project folder. You'll kick yourself if you return to a track to remix it and one of the major sound elements is no longer available to you because the synth you used is now broken, or you've sold it, or you can't store the sounds on it, or whatever.

If you can't do any of the above, at least make notes in a text file about where all of your sounds were came from, and store that file in your project folder too.

Just a little time spent doing boring, organisational stuff means more time for fun in the end.

Program 2

Program 3

+20

CHAPTER 5

creating sampler instruments

The aim of this section is to show how to arrange the samples inside your sampler in the most useable manner. You want to create a situation where hitting keys on a MIDI keyboard will play back the right samples in the right way, and have them respond correctly to MIDI information from your sequencer. To do this you need to create what's called sampler 'instruments'. Processes involved include:

● Keyboard mapping/zoning, velocity mapping, crossfades, layering.

● Using envelopes.

● Building your own multisamples... if you think it's worth the trouble.

Program 27

What is a sampler instrument?

A textbook answer to this question would be that it's a collection of samples grouped together for processing and/or responding to MIDI messages. The name itself can be misleading: a sampler 'instrument' can either be a simple, single-sample sound, or it can be a very complex thing with a lot of different samples and processes going on within it. There can be so much going on, in fact, that we may have different types of instrument for different uses. (As I mentioned before, some manufacturers, such as Steinberg, call this kind of 'instrument' a program.)

Creating sampler instruments, by the way, is one of the areas where using a computer-based sample editing system really comes in to its own. With older, hardware-based samplers, most things are set numerically. With a computer-based system you're helped by the effortless simplicity of large graphic representations of what you're doing.

There are two basic uses for, and therefore types of, sampler instrument: the first use is creating and playing multisamples, and the second is for the creation and playback of MIDI 'drum kits'.

Multisamples

With a real instrument, like a piano, you can play a whole range of notes, right across the frequency spectrum. With an eight-octave piano this would be 96 individual notes. If you sample the sound of the piano being played at middle C and play it back (at the right pitch/speed), it should sound pretty good. If you want to play a note at two octaves below middle C, on a real piano this sounds every bit as good as the first note, just at a different musical pitch. But if you were simply to slow down your sample by 200 per cent, in order to get it to play at the desired new pitch, it's liable to sound quite unconvincing.

In fact, your original sample will sound progressively worse the lower or higher it's played, as it gets further away from its original pitch and speed. Generally, once a sample is transposed (the proper musical word for changing pitch) by more than two or three notes, it stops sounding natural.

The way to get around this is to take another sample of the piano played at your chosen note, in this case two octaves below middle C. When you play back this second sample, it will sound good at this pitch.

The way to get a sampler to sound like a real, eight-octave piano is to take a sample of the sound of each and every key on the keyboard – so you end up with 96 individual samples. This system of taking multiple samples of an instrument playing different notes is central to the success of replicating 'real' instruments using samplers. The resulting collection of samples is known as a 'multisample'.

If you want to be even more thorough, you would then record the instrument played softly (producing another 96 samples) and then played quite hard (another 96). A particularly complex, professionally prepared multisample of an acoustic instrument may consist of hundreds of individual samples. Later in this chapter we'll look at how that might be done – and maybe why it's worth leaving such a job to the professionals.

In the dark early days of sampling, those first machines barely had enough ROM or RAM to hold even one short sample. To produce a piano sound, a brief single sample was used in conjunction with traditional synthesis tools like envelopes. The sample would be slowed down or sped up by three or four octaves to hit those low or high notes. As you will spot immediately if you ever get your hands on a vintage sampler, it sounded dreadful by today's standards.

As sampler memory capacity improved from the humble 128kB beginnings to the joys of a gigabyte of RAM (and high-definition streaming), so developers have produced ever-larger and more sophisticated multisamples. The Kontakt grand piano sample, for instance, weighs in at a whopping 203MB.

MIDI drum kit

A MIDI drum kit is simply the name given to a sampler instrument that's used for playing back a collection of drum sounds, rather than a multisample. A real drum kit consists of an average of five drums and three cymbals, so eight samples would give you a whole kit. With a sampler instrument you're lucky enough to be able to assign a sample to each note – so you can assign a different drum sound to each of the available notes on a MIDI keyboard.

Most producers tend to take advantage of this and build up large collections of drum sounds that can all be loaded at the same time into one instrument. Because the instrument responds to a single MIDI channel, all of the individual drum samples can either be played from a single keyboard or sequenced from a single part in a sequencer. The advantage of this is it gives swift access to a broad palette of sounds to work from, and makes it easy to compare how different combinations of sounds work together.

Controlling with MIDI

Before you can configure a set of samples as an effective MIDI instrument, you'll need to understand a few basics about MIDI itself. As mentioned in Chapter 1, MIDI stands for Musical Instrument Digital Interface, and it's the language electronic instruments use to communicate with each other.

When you hit a key on a MIDI keyboard it sends a series of messages down your MIDI cable. The messages happen in order, one after another: the first message says a note has been struck (this is called note-on); then it says which note has been hit (note value); the next message says how hard you've hit the key (known as note velocity); and when you let go of the key it sends another message saying you've released it (note-off).

A sampler can play back hundreds of samples at once, so we need a way of defining which of those sounds you want to respond when you hit the keyboard (or play a note from your sequencer). We do this by using a MIDI channel. Each instrument in a sampler, synthesiser etc can be set to respond to a specific MIDI channel. There are usually 16 of these. A hardware sampler may have two different MIDI In ports (labelled A & B) so it can effectively respond to 32 different MIDI Channels (A1-16 and B1-16). You can load multiple copies of a software sampler into your audio+MIDI sequencer to achieve the effect of multiple MIDI ports.

As well as the standard role of MIDI, which concerns note transmission, we use MIDI for two other important purposes. The first concerns tempo and synchronisation. All MIDI instruments employ what's called MIDI time code, which they use to keep a steady tempo for recording and playback. MIDI time code (or MTC) can be used to make one machine (perhaps a sequencer) play in time with another (perhaps a drum machine). Most people use the MTC from their sequencer as a master to keep all the other machines in the studio – including effects, synthesisers and samplers – in time with each other, as slaves.

The other job MIDI performs is automation. For a few years now many leading hardware manufacturers have been producing what are commonly (mis)named virtual analog instruments. They're called virtual because they use digital modelling of analog components to produce sound. One of the common features of these machines is that they look and operate just like their analog counterparts, in that you turn knobs and push sliders to make stuff happen. But the sound is created by a digital model, which has one clear advantage over analog systems.

When you turn these knobs they send out a steady stream of information that we call MIDI control change messages, which can then be recorded into a sequencer. When the sequence is played back the sounds produced by the physical knob and slider movements are recreated automatically. So you get to enjoy all of the intuitive immediacy of knob twiddling, with all of the obvious advantages of being able to record and play back your performance. Almost everything within these 'virtual' machines can be automated in this way. This extends to the latest generations of digital instruments, including samplers.

Obviously software instruments, by their nature, do not have any physical hardware controls. Hence the birth of little boxes covered in knobs, buttons and sliders, known as hardware control surfaces (HCS). These little boxes – such as the Phat Boy by Keyfax Hardware, to name but one – do not produce any sounds of their own, they're designed specifically to be used as controllers for software instruments running on a computer.

The whole process of using control change messages to automate and dynamically alter the various sound-shaping tools we'll need (envelopes, filters, LFOs etc, all of which we'll look at shortly) is becoming increasingly central to the music production process.

The sequencer-sampler-MIDI relationship

If you have a keyboard connected directly to your sampler, you need to match the receive channel of your instrument to the transmit channel of the keyboard. If you're using a computer-based MIDI sequencer you'll find it more convenient to simply set the receive channel of the sampler instrument to match the transmit channel of the selected track in the sequencer.

It helps to think of this set-up as using the keyboard to play the sequencer track. So the actual keyboard stays in Omni mode at all times, which means it sends out information on all MIDI channels at once. You then use the channel selection system on the track in the sequencer to determine which MIDI channel it will use to communicate with the sampler instrument. To make this work you'll probably need to ensure the MIDI Thru facility on your sequencer is switched off (which is usually the default setting).

With a traditional hardware sampler, or a separate second computer running a standalone software sampler, it's a two-stage process. First you need to ensure that you select the MIDI interface to which your sampler is attached for a standard MIDI track in the main arrange page of your sequencer. Emagic Logic users will need to have created an

ENVELOPE

Envelopes are among the tools that samplers have borrowed from synthesisers. They're used to control how various settings and processes change over time. It's all about what happens to a sample after you hit a key on a keyboard and playback begins. Envelopes are commonly used to control amplitude (ie volume) and filter cutoff.

FILTERS, AGAIN

Different filter types will change the signal flow in different ways – like changing the type of mesh in your coffee filter. The most common kinds of audio filter are the low-pass filter (LPF), which lets through low-frequency sounds, and the high-pass filter (HPF), which lets high-frequency sounds pass through. More in Chapter 6...

OSCILLATOR

Oscillate means vibrate, or move up and down, or backwards and forwards. In music technology terms, oscillators are devices that produce waveforms, at a wide range of frequencies. For instance in analog synthesisers, oscillators produce the basic waveforms that are then processed into the many different sounds and tones required by the instrument. Low-frequency oscillators (LFOs) can even be used for controlling operations such as filtering and modulation.

'Environment Multi-Instrument' for their sampler and then select this from the sequencer track. Then you need to set a MIDI channel for the sequencer track, and set the corresponding MIDI receive channel in the appropriate sampler instrument. Most hardware studio samplers and software samplers are multi-timbral, so they can load and play a number of instruments (often 16 or 32) at once.

With Emagic's EXS24 soft sampler you have to create an empty Audio Instrument track on the Logic main arrange page. Then go to the mixer window (double-click on the track), click and hold on the insert slot on the appropriate mixer channel, and select EXS24 from the menu that appears. Each instance, or installation, of EXS24 amounts to a single sampler instrument, so you don't need to worry about which MIDI channel you're using . If you want more instruments, you open more copies of EXS24 on new instrument tracks.

With Steinberg's Halion you need to open the VST instrument rack and select Halion for one of the slots. Halion is multi-timbral, so it provides 16 'programs' for each instance of Halion. Use the Channel/Program Page view (within Halion) to ensure that the MIDI channel selected in your sequencer track matches the instrument you wish to use.

If you're using a sampling workstation, all MIDI routing will be internal, but you'll still need to ensure you match the MIDI channel of the sampler instrument you want to use to a sequencer track.

BUILDING A SAMPLER INSTRUMENT

The first step is to create an empty instrument on your sampler, usually done by going to the File menu and choosing New and Instrument from the drop-down menu. You're then faced with a very versatile, and so potentially complicated, set of controls for developing sampler instruments. Luckily there are a few common concepts and terms used to simplify the whole issue.

First of all you're given a 'map' of the structure of our instrument – well, actually you're able to make up your own map. When you load a sample into an instrument you're invited to put it somewhere within the structure, on your imaginary map. The instrument map is centred on a virtual MIDI keyboard (as illustrated in the Halion screengrab in image 25). The keyboard offers two main mechanisms that we use to determine the sound that will be played: the key being struck (which comes under 'keyboard mapping'), and how hard it's being struck ('velocity mapping').

What is layering?

When creating instruments, it'll often be the case that you want several individual samples to play at once when you hit a single key, or you might want to set up complex multisamples, with dozens of samples assigned to play back according to which key you strike, or how hard you play it. The process of setting this up is described as 'layering'.

The tools and techniques used for layering will include key mapping, key crossfading, velocity mapping, and velocity crossfading. These can all be used to combine two or more sounds to create one new sound, or simulate convincing real-instrument multisamples.

LFO

A low-frequency oscillator (LFO) generates very low soundwaves – so low, in fact, that they're inaudible to the human ear (somewhat below 20Hz). But the rising and falling shapes/values of an oscillating waveform can be used to trigger and adjust other settings within a sampling (or synthesis) system. Because we can't hear the actual LFO, all we hear is the effect it's having on whatever we're adjusting. Using an LFO is like having an extra pair of hands – it's an artificial device that will sit there reliably turning up and down some setting or other, as predetermined by the user.

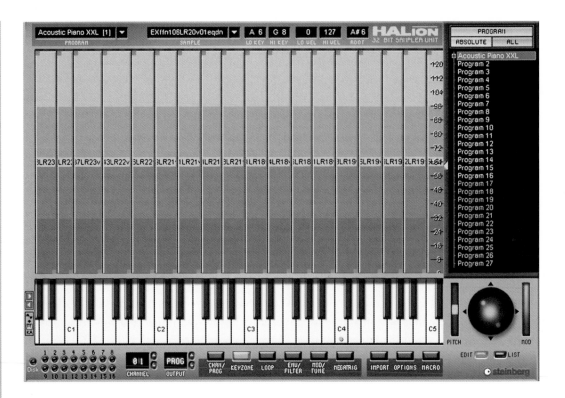

image **25**

The huge piano multisample I talked about a few pages back is a good illustration of layering, as it shows how using several samples of the same instrument, taken at different intensities, can be used to create more convincing instrument emulations.

Keyboard mapping (aka 'zoning')

There are two issues here: you have to ensure that the key you hit makes the right sample play, and that the sample plays back at the right speed.

The way to ensure that the right sample plays when you strike a certain key is to assign the desired sample to that note on your keyboard map. The secret to then controlling the

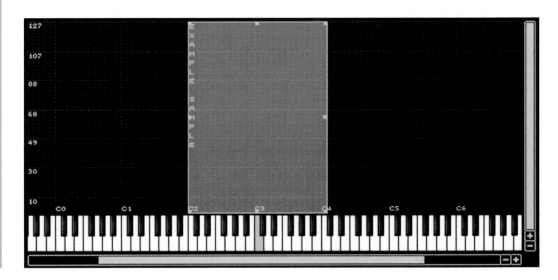

image **26**

speed/pitch at which the sample plays back is the location of what's called the 'root note'.

With all hardware samplers, when you first load a sample into an instrument, its root note is automatically placed on middle C (known as C3). This means when you hit the corresponding note on your keyboard (in this case C3), the sample will play back at the correct speed and pitch. Once the sample is loaded you can change this 'root note' to any note you fancy.

You can also decide what will be the lowest and highest MIDI note on your keyboard that the sample will respond to. This is known as setting the key range. Any notes played within this key range will alter the musical pitch and playback speed of your sample proportionately. Playing notes below the root note, within a key range, will cause samples to be played back more slowly and at a lower musical pitch. Notes above the root note within a key range will cause the sample to be played back faster and at a higher musical pitch.

Setting the root note and key range can be done in several ways. Suppose you want to set the root note to an octave below middle C, and set the highest playable note in the key range an octave up the keyboard, and the lowest note an octave below.

You can see from image 26 that software screen editors use a mapping screen consisting of two elements – a graphic representation of a keyboard and an editing area. The first step is to get samples out and onto the map. With many soft-samplers the process is simplified by the use of drag & drop from a standard explorer-style window (or folder). You locate the sample you want to use, drag it across to the mapping area, and drop it in the editing area above the appropriate key.

With some samplers, like Kontakt, if you drop the sample towards the bottom of the edit area, near the keyboard, it will be placed on a single key, represented by a narrow vertical bar. Drop it higher up the edit area and it will automatically be spread over a range of notes, as in image 26. Samplers that don't use drag & drop will have an Import Sample command, found within a menu or via a right-mouse click. If you place more than one sample on the same note, both (or all of) the samples will be played when you hit the note.

Once your sample is in the edit area you can adjust its mapping settings. Move the mouse over the vertical bar and little arrows will appear. If you're over one of the edges (sides, top or bottom) the arrows will point in two directions (left/right or up/down). If you're over the bar but not over any edge, a four-way arrow appears, and if you click while this is on show you can pick up and move the sample to any location on the keyboard.

In image 26 you can see that one of the keys on the keyboard is shaded to indicate this is the current root note. Moving the entire sample to a new location on the keyboard will alter its root note. If you grab the left edge of the bar and drag to the left, the range of notes and the width of the bar will increase as you spread the sample over a greater range of notes running down the keyboard. Grab the right handle and drag to the right and the width of the bar increases as you spread the sample up the keyboard. Image 26 shows the desired two-octave key range, with the root note set to C3 and the playable key range running from C2 up to C4.

KEY NOTES & NAMES

An octave consists of 12 notes. A complete, or 'chromatic' octave in C would be: C, C♯ (also called D♭), D, D♯/E♭, E, F, F♯/G♭, G, G♯/A♭, A, A♯/B♭, B. (The sharps/flats are the black notes on a piano.) Each octave is also given a number to locate its note's exact position on the keyboard. What's commonly called middle C (C is always just to the left of the two isolated black keys on a piano) is technically known as C3; the C above middle C is therefore C4, and the C an octave below is called C2, and so on. On a full-size keyboard, as you can see in image 26, the lowest C is actually called C0.

On MIDI devices, this same octave-referencing system is used – the range available from the edit pages of a sequencer usually runs from C1 up to C8 (this is in fact a greater range of notes than is playable from a standard MIDI keyboard, which normally only runs to C7). But MIDI also employs a separate numbering system to identify the keys on a keyboard: middle C is note number 63, and the rest of the keys are numbered in order.

Things are a little trickier with a hardware sampler. Perhaps the easiest method is to use a MIDI keyboard and a facility found within many samplers that's often called MIDI Learn. MIDI Learn can be used to quickly and easily set up a broad range of relationships between MIDI hardware, sequencers and sound sources, such as samplers.

Accessing this facility is slightly different for each brand of sampler, but all samplers (including soft-samplers) have a button you can hit that makes the sampler stop and wait for incoming MIDI messages from a keyboard or sequencer. The sampler will presume that the next notes it receives are the notes you wish to use – for instance it could take the first note you hit as the root note, the next you hit to be the lowest, and the third to set the highest note.

So, for this example, you would put the sampler into MIDI Learn mode, strike C3 (root), then C2, then C4. Once the three notes have been set, the sampler returns to normal playback mode.

If you're using a hardware sampler and you don't have a keyboard attached, the only option you have is to set the range numerically. You'll need to navigate to the correct edit screen, then highlight the parameter you want to change, and use the usual value buttons or slider etc to set the value.

ONSCREEN KEYBOARDS

The mapping screens of a software sampler feature a graphic representation of a piano-style keyboard. This style of on-screen keyboard appears in many contexts in different kinds of software instrument. You play it by clicking on individual notes with your mouse. In many cases, clicking higher up on a particular key will play the note softly (sending low-velocity messages), while clicking on the note further down its length will play the note much louder/brighter (by by sending higher-velocity messages).

Velocity mapping

Velocity means 'rate of motion', and in a musical context refers to how hard you strike a note. With a real instrument, if you hit a string or bang a drum softly it will make a quiet and often tonally gentle sound. Hit the instrument a little harder and the sound gets louder and/or more strident. Hit it really hard and we get a much more aggressive tone and dynamic sound. When creating sampler instruments, we can use velocity controls (in conjunction with multisampling, envelopes, filters and many other sound-shaping tools) to help emulate this tonal and volume range.

In MIDI terms it works like this: when you hit your keyboard gently, a low-velocity value is sent via MIDI from your keyboard to either your sequencer or a sound module, or your sampler or any MIDI device you have connected. If you hit it hard, a higher-velocity value is sent. MIDI note velocity can be mapped to almost any parameter within a sampler instrument (see Chapter 7, 'Hands-on Sampling', for more on this), but here we're concerned with the two most commonly used functions when setting up sampler instruments: choice of sample, and playback volume.

As we saw in the keyboard mapping section, you can set up the horizontal axis of your instrument map to establish a key range. You can do anything from spreading a single sample across a keyboard, to assigning a different sample to each individual note, or even assigning many samples to each note.

If you have a single sample assigned to respond to a particular note (or range of notes), MIDI note velocity is commonly used to control the playback volume. The range of velocity values available within MIDI is 0-127: low velocity values cause the sample to be played back very quietly (0 = silence), and 127 the loudest volume.

Velocity also has a vital role to play when it comes to assigning multiple samples to the same note. There are two reasons you might want to do this:

● 1: You might want to combine two sounds, something that's done a lot with drum samples. Let's say you have two different snare sounds, one has a rich, phat mid tone to it but lacks high-end ring, the other is all high-mid crack and harmonic ring. Together they combine to form the perfect snare sound. In this instance you would assign both samples to the same key range so they play back together, and then set the velocity range of both samples to the full range of 0-127. They will then respond to MIDI as though they're a single sample.

● 2: Within the piano multisample, you've seen that each note on the keyboard can have several samples, each with a slightly different tonal character assigned to it. You can use incoming MIDI note velocity to determine which of those samples will be played according to how hard you hit the key. Because the available velocity range within MIDI is 0-127, each note on the keyboard can be set to play up to 127 individual samples.

Editing velocity ranges

Once the sample is loaded, the velocity range can be edited in a number of ways.

Editing it manually with a software editor involves grabbing and dragging the little handles that appear in the corners at the top and bottom of an individual sample's vertical bar within the editing area. Dragging up or down adjusts the height of the bar, and thus the range of velocities the sample will respond to.

Velocity settings can also be set using MIDI Learn, in the same way as the key range was set. In this case, when you access MIDI Learn, the sampler will presume that the next velocity values it receives are the ones you wish to use: you hit the note at the velocity you wish to be the lowest at which the sample will play, then hit a key as hard as you wish to be the highest velocity at which the sample will play. Once the two values have been set, the sampler returns to normal playback mode.

Manually editing velocity range on a hardware sampler without a screen editor needs to be done numerically. You'll need to navigate to the correct edit screen, then highlight the parameter you want to change and use the usual value buttons, value slider or data wheel to set the correct value.

Crossfading

The polished sophistication of factory-prepared multisamples is due, to a large extent, to careful use of crossfading in keyboard and velocity mapping. The idea is that you can achieve smoother, subtler and therefore more realistic results if the transition from one sample to the next is gradual. With key range, crossfading can be used so that as you play successive notes on the keyboard the two samples can be layered, so one is faded out while the next is faded up. Crossfading can similarly be used for velocity, so as you progressively strike a key harder, one sample is faded out while the next is faded up.

Here's how it's done. Let's assume you have two samples, both with the same overall volume. In the usual scheme of things, if you play back both samples at the same time, the volume of the two samples will be added together and the result will be twice as loud as either of the individual samples. This is often not what we want – it might be preferable to have the combined result remain at the same volume as each sample. The obvious answer is to halve the volume of each sample as you combine them.

Conceptually it helps to think about 'overlapping' the two sounds. If you assign two samples to ranges that overlap, they will both play when notes (or velocities) within the overlap are played. In a crossfade operation an X will appear on the overlapping area, at the crossing point of which both samples are effectively halved in volume.

You can see an illustration of this in image 27. Move to either side of the centre spot and the proportionate blend of the two samples changes. In the middle each sample plays at 50 per cent of full volume; outside the overlap they play at 100 per cent of full volume. So at any point on the X the percentage will be reduced proportionately.

In most soft-samplers the X of the crossfade is not fixed, and can often be altered in two ways. With some samplers the spot at the crossing point of the X always represents the point at which each sample will play at half of full volume, but it can be moved. By dragging this point closer to either sample, you change how steeply the fade between each sample occurs. By moving the crossing point you inevitably cause one sample to be reduced in volume more quickly, and the other to be reduced more slowly within the rest of the overlap.

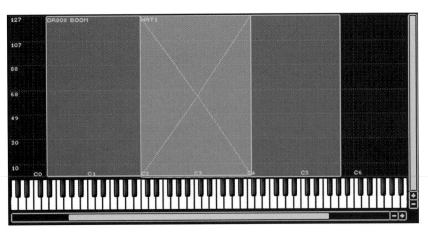

image **27**

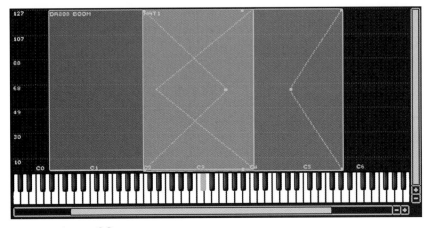

image **28**

With other samplers the process doesn't actually use an X at all, but rather two triangles set up individually. The peak of each triangle represents the spot at which the volume of the sample is reduced to 50 per cent, but the two points of the two triangles don't have to be in the same location – as you can see in image 28. In this example the result would be an increase in overall volume within the diamond shape produced by the two overlapping triangles.

Image 28 also shows that with this system you don't need to have two overlapping samples to set up a volume fade over a range, because we have pulled across the right edge of the right sample so it will fade to 50 per cent of full volume over the specified key range.

With some samplers you can set the key range of two adjacent samples so they overlap. You then select both or all of the samples you want to crossfade. Locate the 'Set Key Crossfade' function from the pull-down menus. An X will appear superimposed on the overlapping areas to illustrate the crossfade properties. You can then click on the crossing point and drag it to a new location. With Kontakt and some others you can grab the handle in the middle of either vertical bar edge and drag it to a new location to form a triangle whose point represents that 50 per cent volume cut.

With older hardware machines the process is not quite so intuitive, but it can be done. Again, although it's implemented slightly differently by each manufacturer, the procedure is essentially numeric: you locate the correct edit page and set overlapping key range values for adjacent samples, then set a numeric fade value. Usually, the higher the value the steeper the curve.

The procedure for setting up a velocity crossfade is essentially identical to establishing key-range crossfades.

Using groups

Groups are a handy way of speeding up the working process. As the name suggests, it's a way of gathering together a collection of samples so they can all be edited at once.

For example, going back to that piano multisample, there are 96 different notes of a piano being played, each note sampled three times, once played softly, once medium and once hard. So that's 288 individual samples to make one sampler instrument.

Let's say you want to set up a velocity crossfade between the softly-played samples and the medium samples, and then another velocity crossfade between the medium and hard samples. Rather than setting up 192 individual crossfades, you'd use groups. It works like this...

First you need to select all the individual samples you would like to have in your group – with screen editors this is done either by drag-selecting or by clicking on each sample in turn while holding down the Shift key on your keyboard. When you have all the desired samples highlighted, select Send To Group from the appropriate menu.

With hardware you will need to navigate your way to the group editing page and assign each individual sample to the same group number or group name. For our example we need to set up three groups, one each for soft, medium and hard samples. The next step is hitting Edit Group.

There's a range of things you can do to samples within groups but this varies between manufacturers and models. You can now adjust the velocity crossfade setting for all of the samples in the group.

Layering drum sounds

Probably the most common trick with layering – and one of the most impressive-sounding – is using it to create bigger, stronger, more dynamic drum sounds. If you listen carefully to a kick drum sound, for instance, you'll notice there are at least two distinct sonic elements within a single drum hit. There's the big bass frequency boom that gives the sound its wallop, and drives dance music along with its stomach-thumping oomph. Then there's a much higher-pitched element, in the mid register or above, which provides the thwack that makes a kick drum cut through the rest of a mix. An effective kick drum usually needs both elements to work well.

By finding a kick drum sample with the perfect amount of low-end power, and finding another sound with the perfect high-mid-range thwack, and combining the two, you can create your perfect kick sound. The same is true of more or less any drum sound (as well as other sounds such as bass guitar).

By using several samples, each with slightly different tonal properties, and carefully setting up a velocity map, you can add not only punch to your overall sound but also a sense of dynamic, realtime change as your music develops.

Audio illustration – key & velocity mapping, crossfades & layering

I've put together a step-by-step example that illustrates much of what's been covered so far in this chapter.

First I selected a collection of complementary drum samples, picking out four kick drums, three snares, two closed hi-hats and two open hi-hats. One of each drum type was used as the basis for a drum kit. The second step was to create a fresh sampler instrument and to place each of the samples on a note. I chose to place them so their root notes were C0, C1, C2 and C3 – which produced the map you can see in image 29.

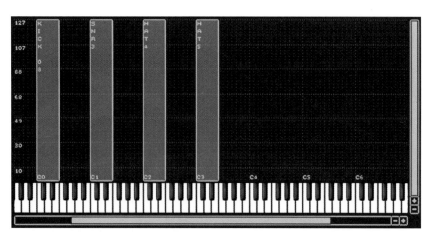

image **29**

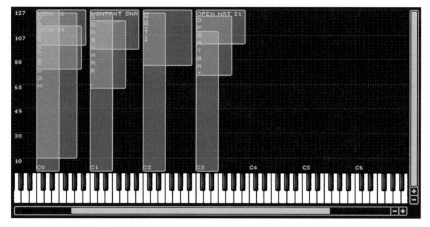

image **30**

Next job was to create a simple MIDI sequence with which to play them. I chose a very basic $^4_4$ techno-style beat, but gave it a twist. It's set up so the velocity of the notes in the pattern gradually increases: it starts at a velocity value of 65 for the first beat and then rises steadily and evenly until the very last beat has a value of 125. The simple one-bar drum pattern is repeated, so there are 40 bars of it, and our steady velocity increase happens over the duration of the entire 40 bars.

The result, so far, can be heard on CD1 Track 8. You can hear the samples get louder as the velocity values increase.

It sounds OK, but you'd probably want to add extra substance and more vibrant dynamic change, so next I added some more layers. I wanted extra sounds to be played in addition to our four foundation samples as the velocities increase. Image 30 shows that I've restricted the velocity range of each of the samples as I added them.

If you're wondering why I've set up the key range for each sample the way I have, the answer is it's for convenience. In this instance I'm only going to be triggering samples from the root notes, so they could all be restricted to a single-note key range and assigned to each root note. But having four samples piled up on the same note can make them tricky to select with the mouse. By spreading each one out across a slightly different range of notes in the way I have, a section of each one is left sticking out, so I can easily point at it and click on it when I want to edit it.

I've used two kick drums throughout almost the entire velocity range, because they sound bigger combined than our foundation kick does alone. The third kick drum is quite a full-bodied beast, which I've set up to only sound within a velocity range of 81-114, because I wanted it to add extra power as the velocities rise. The fourth kick drum has a nice distorted element that gives it lots of energy, so I wanted this to sound when the velocities are towards their highest values – it has a velocity range of 100-127.

I've applied a similar principle to the snares: the foundation snare is fairly gentle, so works well at lower velocities. The second snare is much grittier, so I wanted it to be added to our first snare and sound as the velocities rise (its velocity range is 66-115). The third snare has a lovely high-frequency ring that gives plenty of energy, so this is set to occupy the upper velocity ranges (its range is 97-127). The same goes for the two closed hi-hats and the three open hi-hats.

CD1 Track 9 lets you hear this new, improved instrument. You can hear that now the beat doesn't just get louder but changes tone as the velocity values rise too – but it doesn't really work all that well. This is because, as the velocities rise, each sample just jumps in suddenly, causing things to be lumpy and lack flow. What it needs is some velocity crossfading...

image **31**

If you look at image 31 you'll see the crossfades indicated by the triangles. Taking the kick drum as an example, you can see that the second kick now has a rather steep vertical triangle in place rising from the bottom edge. Towards the bottom of the triangle the sample playback volume will be almost zero, but by the time you reach the point of the triangle, playback volume will be dependant entirely on incoming note velocity.

I've set up velocity crossfades for all the samples in the map, and you might notice that the end results are not really mathematically regular. This is because it was done by trial and error, setting crossfades, listening to the effect, then adjusting the crossfades until I felt it sounded right. You can hear the result in CD1 Track 10 – it's not a polished, finished item by any means, but it gives an indication of the gradual smoothing that crossfading can achieve.

Layering synth sounds

Similar principles to those used for drum layering can be applied to other instruments. Let's look at synthesiser sounds... If you've ever programmed a synthesiser you'll know that when you create a sound it might only sound its best played within a particular octave, and loses something when played at other notes. The same basic sound can often be tweaked a little to work well when played at a different octave – but then of course it no longer works in the first. The answer is obviously to sample both versions of the sound and then set up a layered sampler instrument to combine your various samples. I decided to combine this idea with taking additional samples so I could create a key and velocity-responsive instrument.

The first step was to find a sound to use as a starting point. In this instance I used a vintage Roland Juno 6 analog synthesiser – this kind of keyboard is a prime candidate for sampling because as it's not MIDI responsive (assuming it's not been MIDI retro-fitted), the only way to use it effectively is either to play it live or sample it.

I created a sound that works well when played at C2 on the Juno keyboard, sampled this, and then tweaked the sound a little so that it sounded OK played at C1 on the Juno. Next I tweaked the sound again, so it worked at C3. I then moved on to creating three more versions of the sound, each working best played at C1, C2 and C3, but this time with higher filter resonance and envelopes applied on the Juno to create somewhat more aggressive versions of the sounds.

Then I created a fresh sampler instrument and placed the first C2 sample into it, with its root note at C2, and the sample spread across the entire key and velocity ranges. I used this basic sampler instrument to write a MIDI sequence with which to play back the instrument. You can hear this on CD1 Track 11. I employed the same technique as with the drum layering example to gradually increase the velocity of the notes within the sequence over 40 bars of the riff. You can hear it gradually gets louder as it progresses.

The next step was to add the next two samples (the ones tweaked to work well at C1 and C3) to C1 and C3 of our sampler instrument and spread them out to encompass a four-octave range. This creates the map you see in image 32, and you can hear what this sounds like in CD1 Track 12. Listen out for the change of tone in the low and higher notes within the sequence.

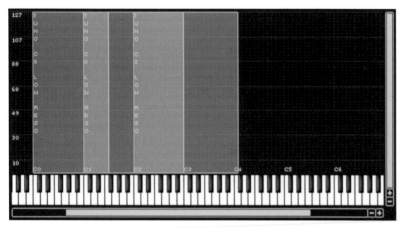

image **32**

Next I added the remaining three sampled variations of the sound. This time I used similar key ranges to the first samples, but restricted the additional trio to the upper velocity ranges, to produce the map in image 33, and the sequence you'll hear in CD1 Track 13 from our new instrument. You can hear that, as the velocities increase, the tone changes as well as the volume swelling.

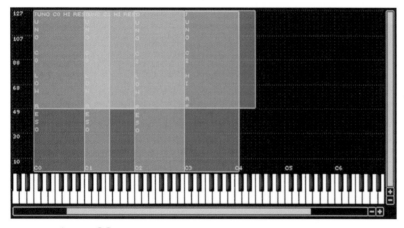

image **33**

The final step was to add crossfades to each of the six samples we now have in the instrument, so the transitions between samples become much smoother as the note velocities increase. This resulted in the map you can see in image 34, and hear in CD Track 14. Now the tone changes and the volume increases as the incoming velocities rise, and the whole transition is smooth.

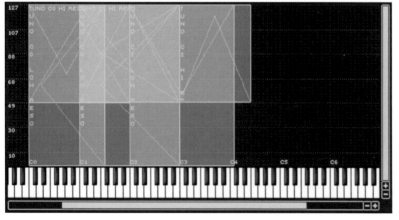

image **34**

ENVELOPES

As mentioned already, envelopes are used to control the changes to various settings over time, and are most often associated with amplitude (volume) or filter cutoff.

An amplitude envelope can change the 'attack' of notes, adding dynamics or generally making a sound more natural and flowing. Amplitude envelopes can also be tweaked to improve the way a sample fits into a particular melody line, or a song with a particular tempo. Shifting the rise and fall of the volume of a sound gives it a feeling of movement. As movement implies speed, and therefore tempo, and since timing is central to the way music works, even very subtle changes like this can make an enormous difference.

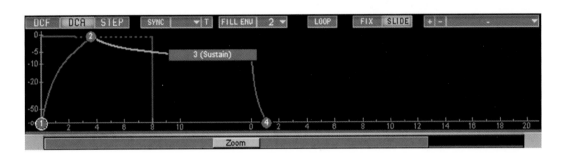

image 35

Let's examine an amplitude envelope in action. Take a look at image 35...
Here's what's happening in this image: right at the start of the sample (far left) you can see a line with a distinct curve to it, stretching between the dots numbered 1 and 2. This is the 'attack' stage of the envelope. Adjusting the attack allows you to make the sample fade up gradually rather than just banging in straight away at full volume when it responds to a note-on message.

Moving along the image you can see that the 'line' of the envelope goes from a peak at the end of the attack section into a downward curve, then it levels out for a while, represented by the rectangle marked '3 (Sustain)', and finally goes into a downward curve until it ends at the dot marked 4.

The little curve immediately after the attack (between dot 2 and the sustain stage) is the 'decay' stage. The point where attack meets decay can be said to be the loudest peak of the envelope; the decay control itself lets you set up a little volume curve that gets your sample from the attack to the 'sustain' section. The sustain is the volume at which the sample will play as long as the note coming from the keyboard is held down (or 'sustained').

The downward slope at the end of the envelope is called the 'release' section. Release lets you control how long the sample takes to fade out after the key is released and a note-off message arrives at the sampler instrument.

This four-stage envelope is a standard tool that appears in most synthesisers, samplers and many drum machines. The four stages – attack, decay, sustain and release – are often abbreviated to ADSR, which is why you'll hear the term 'ADSR envelope'.

A fifth envelope stage can be found on a few machines (like NI Kontakt). It's an additional facility called 'hold'. Hold allows you to maintain the peak level reached at the transition from the attack to the decay stage. It means you can set up a period of time for the sample to continue to play at this loudest level, before descending through the decay. This facility is offered by what's called an AHDSR envelope, because the order of events is Attack, Hold, Decay, Sustain, Release.

Editing envelopes

Basic editing of envelopes is done by clicking on the dots and dragging them around. But with many of the latest-generation software-based samplers, the simple envelope has evolved into a much more powerful beast. If you look at image 36 you can see that the lines of this ADSR envelope are curved rather than straight. This is because we've been given the ability to create far more complex multi-element curves at each stage of our envelope.

image **36**

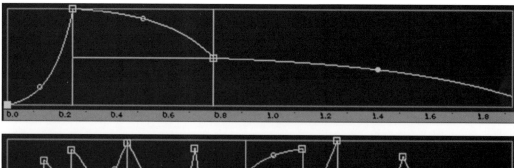

image **37**

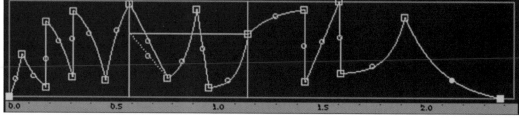

Image 36 shows the 'flexible envelope' from Kontakt. If you right-mouse click (control-click on a Mac) at any point along any of the lines of the envelope, an additional handle (known as a 'breakpoint') appears. By dragging these new handles, curves can be created.

An extra feature of this particular envelope is that the two vertical lines mark the boundaries of the sustain stage. Once three or more breakpoints have been created, the sustain stage acts as a loop for however long a sustained note is received. As you can see from image 37, this envelope allows you to add up to 32 breakpoints.

Although this is still essentially, theoretically, an ADSR envelope, the ability to animate the volume curves in these ways changes all the rules, and means you can make playback values increase or decrease within any stage of the envelope. To do this just aim your mouse at any point on the line of the envelope, click and drag – and a new curve appears. Try it and you'll get the idea. It can be used to create absolute audio mayhem, as you can see here.

BREAKPOINT

A breakpoint can be defined as a transitionary moment – a point where something changes – whether it be amplitude, filter setting, or pitch.

Filter cutoff envelopes

Filter envelopes are used for much the same reasons as amplitude envelopes – they add another layer to sounds, bringing an increased sense of depth as well as timing. They can also be manipulated in realtime as a riff is playing (often via a separate controller), adding the naturalistic and intriguing feel of a sound that's gradually changing, from bar to bar.

The actual functionality of the filter envelope is identical to an amplitude envelope, except that instead of the volume of the sample we're controlling filter cutoff settings. The attack stage takes the filter cutoff from a zero setting up to a level determined by the decay. The decay settings shape the alteration of the cutoff frequency from a peak setting to the frequency set by the sustain value. The release setting determines how long it takes for the cutoff frequency to return to zero.

DBD envelope

Some advanced software samplers include what's known as a DBD envelope, which is used to control sample pitch. DBD stands for decay-breakpoint-decay. A positive breakpoint setting causes the pitch of the sample to rise, and a negative setting causes the pitch to fall.

Decay 1 determines the time it takes for the sample pitch to rise (or fall) from a zero pitch setting (ie the pitch at which the sample arrives at the envelope) to the new pitch as set via the breakpoint. Decay 2 determines the time it takes for the sample pitch to return to the zero setting.

DBD envelopes can be used to great effect on drum sounds, and were found on several classic analog drum machines.

Envelope amount and delay

Having decided on the shape of your amplitude and filter envelopes, you're provided with two more controls that dictate exactly how much, and when, the envelopes will be applied – namely envelope amount and envelope delay.

With the envelope amount set at zero, a sample will effectively bypass the envelope. With the amount at maximum, all of the sample (in the case of an amplitude envelope) or all of the filtered sound (in the case of a filter envelope) will be passed through the envelope. The usual default setting is 50 per cent. It's a little like a level control for envelopes, but in practice operates more like an intensity control.

The reason there's an 'amount' control is that amplitude envelopes can have quite an extreme effect on sound – a little too extreme for many uses. The amplitude envelope is in fact commonly used to reduce the overall intensity of the action of the envelope on the sample being passed through it, to make the result a little subtler. Filter envelopes can be equally extreme, but again bring a very welcome extra layer of density and sense of movement to a sound.

Filters are often most effective when they are adjusted in realtime, as the sample plays, and this is where filter envelope amount really comes into its own. If you set up an extreme filter and then fade an envelope in and out over it gradually, you might recognise one of the classic dance music effects (we'll look at this in more detail under Filters Chapter 6).

Because messing about with the envelope amount in realtime sounds so cool, it's useful to assign it to a hardware controller (like a modulation wheel), as covered in more detail in 'Hands-On Sampling', Chapter 7. It can also be great as the target for an LFO.

The use of the word 'delay' in the context of envelopes has nothing to do with the echo-repeat effect of the same name (we'll come to that in Chapter 6). Adjusting the envelope delay

ENVELOPE FOLLOWER

The concept of the envelope can sort of be 'reverse engineered' through use of an envelope follower. As the characteristics of an envelope (attack, decay, sustain and release) exist in all sounds, an envelope follower is designed to look at a particular sound and identify its envelope. Once the envelope follower has analysed the envelope of an incoming sound, the characteristics of that sound can then be applied to another sound or sample, in much the same way as a standard envelope. That's the theory, anyway. They rarely actually do what you might expect, but they can produce some interesting results all the same.

value – which isn't found in all that many envelope pages – sets up a pause between a note-on message arriving (thus triggering the start of a sample playback) and the moment when the envelope begins to have an effect. The greater the delay setting, the longer the pause before the attack setting of the envelope begins to affect the sample.

It can be useful for adding some additional dynamics to synthesised 'pad'-type sounds. For example, you might want to create a situation where a sample plays normally for three seconds and then has the decay, sustain and release sections of an envelope applied, to add some interest. To achieve this you'd set a delay time of three seconds, set a 'vertical' attack curve (ie one that has no effect) so the sample passes straight to the decay stage and onwards to the sustain and then release portions of the envelope. A delay parameter is essential if you want several envelopes to be applied consecutively.

MAKING YOUR OWN MULTISAMPLES – OR NOT...

When you know what a multisample is, you realise just how much effort is involved in constructing one. Take our much-discussed piano sample as an illustration. The first consideration would be the equipment you'd need: a good piano, a good microphone and stand, an acoustically treated room to record in, a separate room to monitor the results in, speakers and headphones to hear what you're doing, and of course a sampler.

Then there's the actual recording process – knowing where to position the mike to achieve the best results for each key strike, and how to operate the recording equipment. Not to mention the need for a skilled pianist. You may think this is going too far... why not just play it yourself, after all it's only one note at a time? But consider this: how easy is it to strike a key on a piano at precisely the same velocity umpteen times in a row? You have to do this consistently, for all 96 keys, striking each key at three very distinct velocity levels, hard, medium and soft.

Presuming you've made it this far, you come to editing each individual sample: setting start and end points, assigning each sample to the correct location in a keyboard map, setting up velocity maps, crossfades, envelopes, filters etc. Even if you had all the right equipment and skills, it would take days of meticulous work to get right. Lucky for us, then, that professional engineers and musicians sit in top-quality studios doing it for us, recording their labours onto sample CDs.

And a piano is by no means the hardest instrument from which to make a multisample. Trying to record a cello or a clarinet or trumpet is far more complex, as there's much more of a human element involved in the playing – breath control, embouchure, fingering etc. Attempting to create multisamples of string ensembles, or brass sections, or any part of a proper orchestra, becomes a truly monumental undertaking – how likely are you to be able to get hold of the Royal Albert Hall for a couple of weeks?.

So it's not surprising that sample-using musicians tend to find it more conducive to the creative process to simply buy professional sound libraries of acoustic instruments on CD or DVD. It's also no surprise to find there are very few really good, comprehensive, orchestral sample collections around – and those that are available retail for around £300/$500.

I don't mean to seem pessimistic here, but you might want to think twice before you bother attempting to capture any such complex instruments using the step-by-step, one-note-at-a-time multisample route. I have an alternative suggestion...

The easier option

Personal experience has led me to believe that, rather than recording individual notes, you're usually better off creating riff-based samples to use as loops for specific tracks.

In the time it might take you to build one half-decent multisample, you could construct 20 inspirationally diverse loop-riffs to base songs around. I'd suggest it could well be more productive, if you have a musician on-hand for a day, just to get them to perform some stuff for you and sample the results. Get a percussionist to play a selection of patterns, or a keyboard player to improvise a selection of melodies, or guitarist to play some licks or riffs, or bass player to lay down a load of basslines. Not only will this give you access to the sounds, you'll get the human feel of their performance too. You can always slice up what they've played at a later date, using snippets of their riffs to create single notes, tones, or drum hits, which can then be rearranged into new patterns as you require.

Another argument against DIY multisampling is beautifully illustrated by the notion of sampling vintage analog synthesisers. Much of the attraction of analog synths lies in their ability to create sounds and textures that change and evolve over time – it's this sonic variation that makes them great for realtime tweaking. For instance an LFO can be set up to create subtle changes in the sound, rising, falling or repeating over a bar or many bars or even minutes. When this occurs through a performance it adds to the musical dynamics – the kind of subtle variation that also comes with real musicians playing, rather than repetitive sequencing.

But when it comes to sampling such an instrument, how are you going to ensure you'll catch the particular note at the correct part of the LFO cycle? The answer is you can't. Each sample will most likely be slightly tonally different from all the others. The result will probably be chaotic, disjointed and almost certainly not sound like the same instrument being played across the range of the keyboard.

This is why multisamples of analog synths rarely sound as good as the real thing – they're dull and lifeless in comparison. You can always try to compensate by applying processing tools within your sampler (as outlined in Chapter 6, 'Customising Sounds'), which can work, but it won't be quite the same. If you listen to multisamples of vintage analog synths on commercial sample CDs with this in mind, you'll hear the distinct lack of sounds that evolve over time without the aid of processing tools. If the professionals can't find a way around it, there quite possibly isn't one.

Sampling riffs is often the answer – perhaps getting a few slightly varying versions of the same riff. This can be a superb way to capture the range of subtle options an analog synthesiser can offer. The idea is to emulate what happens when you tweak the controls of an analog synth while a riff plays.

If you have any hard disk or multi-track recording system at your disposal, it makes sense to record several entire song-length performances, including the tweaks. If you're working solely with a sampler, you can achieve good results by first sampling a bar (or four bars, or even more if you have the capacity) with a particular combination of settings. Then alter the sound and sample another four bars and repeat the process a few times.

You can then sequence the different variations to emulate the effect of realtime tweaking. Sampling a few bars of an evolving riff, in a variety of ways, works well as a compromise, and you can then add more layers of processing within your sampler to homogenise the overall effect.

Still want to make your own multisamples?

Having said all of that... DIY multisamples can still be an excellent idea for percussion sounds. As I suggested earlier, taking several different samples of a single snare drum hit and weaving them back together into a carefully layered construction can work extremely well. This is because a snare drum is a relatively simple sound. Taking, say, seven samples of a one-note instrument like a snare is easy enough to plan and keep track of, and not too time-consuming to do. You wouldn't dream of attempting a multisample of a piano that's seven layers deep on every key.

So... if you are adventurous/crazy enough to attempt the process of creating complex multisamples yourself, here are a few tips that might help you along the way.

● Be systematic – both in the way you capture the sounds and in how you store and organise the resulting samples.

● Pay particular attention to unwanted noise – if at all possible set up a 'noise gate' (see the 'Studio Toolkit' in Chapter 6) to completely cut all background noise during the recording process. Most vintage instruments create dreadful amounts of residual noise, and you don't want to multiply it. Set the controls of the gate so it's closed when the sound source is not playing, but with a fairly low threshold so the gate is opened relatively easily.

Subtle use of a low-pass shelving filter or EQ to remove high-level hiss can sometimes be worthwhile too. Similarly a high-pass filter or EQ can be used to remove low-end rumble. But always use these things sparingly, and only if strictly necessary when confronted with very noisy source material. Remember that any filter or EQ is also altering the musical sounds themselves, which may not be desirable.

● Use some gentle compression during recording to make the overall volume more consistent. Otherwise you will find it very difficult to achieve consistent performance results; with electronic sounds particularly, you'll find that some frequencies will seem much louder than others. Be sure not to over do the compression, though, you don't want to hear it 'pumping' – it may sound OK at one frequency, but will become inconsistent at others. (There's more on using compression in Chapter 6.)

● Using electronic instruments, the process can be simpler if you employ MIDI to consistently trigger sounds at constant velocities. Using a sequencer emitting different notes to play the sounds can even eliminate the necessity of using a skilled musician to play the parts.

● For older, non-MIDI analog synthesisers, use an arpeggiator to play sequences of notes for you – it can create a similarly consistent result to using MIDI. Set up the arpeggiator to play a series of notes and then strike several keys at the same time and hold them down, while sampling the results. The arpeggiator will probably alternate between playing each of the notes you're holding at a consistent velocity, so if the keys are at opposite ends of the keyboard you'll get a good spread of notes. If you hold down as many notes as you can (get a friend to lend a hand or two if necessary) you'll get a better spread, and you can slice the resulting sample into individual notes afterwards. Slowing down the arpeggiator will give you longer individual notes, and speeding it up will produce shorter notes.

● It's often the case with analog synths that one particular combination of settings will work very well sonically for one particular range of notes... but that same combination of settings will not sound nearly as impressive in another range. Bass can be particularly susceptible to this, as can any sound that uses filtering with large amounts of boosted resonance to form the tonal character of the sound (see the Filter section in Chapter 6).

This often occurs because the frequency at which you set the filter cutoff dominates the tonal character of the sound. As the filter cutoff frequency corresponds to a particular musical note or small range of notes, the secret is to adjust the cutoff frequency to match the range of notes you're trying to play the riff within. Then take samples of the riff with different cutoff frequencies for different note ranges.

● Pay attention to level metering (volume levels are usually gauged by bar-type meters), and try to ensure you've captured the varying volume relationships between different samples.

A great illustration of this is using the kind of close-miking techniques we looked at earlier. It applies to all instruments, but we'll stick to the piano illustration. Stand in a concert hall or any good-sized room and listen carefully to a piano being played, from a few metres away. You should hear a consistent, natural spread of notes across the note range. A significant part of this comes from the way in which the sounds bounce back at you from the walls of the room... the bigger the room the more pronounced the reverberations.

If you place a microphone at your listening position it will capture that same consistency, but it will not necessarily capture all the detail of the piano sound. Placing a mike right inside the piano will solve the detail problem, and deliver a stronger signal for recording too. But the strings of a full-size piano are spread across about two metres: if you put the mike in the middle, logically you'll get stronger, louder mid notes and weaker, quieter bass and treble notes.

When close-miking for a live performance you'd have to try and find a compromise position that would give the most consistent result across the note range – probably fairly central and between 1m and 2m away. But when close-miking a piano to create a multisample, you have the luxury of being able to move the microphone around between recordings to get the best results. So you'd place it close to the bass end to record the bass notes, and then progressively move it along the strings to capture the rest of the notes. Obviously you need to try and be consistent with the distance between the mike and the piano strings to maintain an even recording.

This raises the thorny issue of perceived relative volume of notes within different tonal registers – ignoring for the moment the complications added by the actual construction of acoustic instrument enclosures. High-pitched sounds are more piercing and so always, as far as the human ear is concerned, seem to be louder than lower notes. This is despite the fact that, in terms of level metering and scientific measurement of sound, lower notes are actually louder (and travel further). This is a vital piece of knowledge for each step of the whole music production process, and means you often have to set the lower frequencies (kick drum etc) at a higher physical volume than the high-register sounds (hi-hats etc).

When it comes to creating good multisamples, though, it's best to record all of the notes across the range at the same metered level. That way you achieve the best signal-to-noise (S/N) levels, and can be confident you've captured all the detail within each note. Then when it comes to the mapping stage of the process, you set the relative perceived level of each note by simply setting the correct playback volume for each sample. (I did warn you this wasn't going to be easy.)

Here's another close-miking dilemma. I've said already that, for a good piano multisample, you'd have to take at least three samples of each note, played hard, medium and soft. But would the same distance between microphone and strings be appropriate for all three samples? If you decide it's not, and that to maintain our perfect S/N ratio and level of detail you need to get the mike closer to record the softer key strikes, you're obviously committing to a lot more time and effort. Experiment and make your own decisions with each instrument.

● When it comes to mapping, you really do need to be very organised about naming and storing each sample. Each ought to be named according to its final destination within the keyboard map.

An appropriate name for a piano sample, for instance, might be the note itself (say C1) followed by an indication of layer (m for medium, h for hard, or s for soft). That way when you look at a sample named G♯3s you immediately know you need to place it on note G♯3 and set its velocity range to respond to low-velocity value note messages.

You may also find it beneficial to use sub-folders if you're working on a computer. Most modern samplers will allow you to use a folder called, for example, Piano Multisample, and then place three more folders within it called Hard, Medium and Soft, so you can store the sample for each layer separately. The value of this will become apparent if you decide to perform a 'batch process' on all the samples within a layer.

Meticulous forward-planning is the key to creating good multisamples. Listen meticulously to the instrument you're trying to record. Talk to the musician who will be playing it, and try to find out how many different types of sound the instrument can produce, how the musician gets those sounds out of the instrument, and in what musical context those variations of tonal character might be best used.

Let's take the conga as an example: it looks like a simple hand drum, and the uninitiated might think all you have to do is slap it with your hand. But the conga can produce a massive range of sounds, depending on a great many factors, including the shape of the hand when striking – is it flat or cupped, striking with the fingers or the heel of the hand, turning the hand sideways... not to mention where on the conga skin any of these techniques is used; and also whether the other hand is being used to damp the skin at the same time; and how hard any of this is done. And that's just part of the story.

Once you're aware of all this you can begin to make decisions about which range of sounds you want to capture, how they might go together in a keyboard map, and how you might wish to use them in a composition.

Personally, I have to admit that I've never ever encountered a multisample of a conga that even comes close to the sound of the real instrument in the hands of an experienced player...

But by understanding the complexity of the issues involved and appreciating that compromises will probably need to be made, you can choose where those compromises are going to be. This is better than getting halfway through and then being forced to make the wrong compromises.

BATCH PROCESS

It's quite likely that at some point you'll want to perform some process or other on a large number of samples together. The most obvious case would be to change a file format for use on different platforms – for instance from the primarily PC-based WAV audio file format to the primarily Mac-based AIFF format – or perhaps to change a large number of samples from 24-bit/48KHz sample rate to 16-bit/ 44.1KHz. A more musical example would be applying a low-pass filter to a whole set of samples. Rather than opening each file in turn, performing the operation and then saving the result, most computer-based samplers have a Batch Process facility, which allows you to automate such repetitive, laborious procedures. Automating tasks like this can save an awful lot of time and trouble.

You'll usually find a Batch Process command within the File menu. You just compile a list of samples to be processed (or specify a source location if you want all samples within a particular folder to be altered), set up the tasks to be performed, then specify where you'd like the resulting edited files to be saved. Hit Perform, sit back and wait.

Audio illustration – creating sustained sounds using loops

Percussive sounds are usually fairly short, so even if you want to capture the natural decay of a drum sound it doesn't demand too much sample time and memory capacity. But if you want to sample an instrument that produces much longer sustained notes, it can be a little more troublesome.

A traditional stringed instrument like the cello is a perfect example, because pulling the bow repeatedly back and forth across a string can theoretically produce an endless note. Many wind instruments, like the flute (or for that matter the human voice), also produce long sustained notes, though at least their length might be limited by lung capacity and breath technique.

When you bear in mind that every minute of CD-quality audio requires 10MB of memory, you'll appreciate why reproducing endless sustained notes with a sampler might require a little trickery.

Image 38 shows a zoomed-in picture of a very short sample containing just one cycle of a sine wave, which can be heard on CD1 Track 60. You may even find it's too short to be recognised by a CD player or basic computer audio file player, but load it into a sampler and you should be able to hear a brief blip. Now loop the entire length of the sample and play it. Each subsequent repetition of the sine wave sounds precisely like the original sample and is indistinguishable, so you will find that it happily repeats to form a smooth sustained note, until you decide to stop it. The effect can be heard in Track 61.

This principle can be applied to almost any other short sound. (There's an extreme example on the web called 'Canned', where a melodic track is made (using Reason) solely from the sound of two Coke cans being hit with a stick – see www.gwydi.com.)

Image 39 shows a brief sample of a cello, which can be heard on CD1 Track 62. (I downloaded this sample from www.fitchsounds.com, where you will find lots more wonderful and free cello samples.) At the beginning of the sample you can see the louder bulge of the 'attack' stage of the sound. After this you can see the sample settle down into a more repetitive pattern. There's an additional bulge at the end of the sample where the bow is removed from the string and the sound then decays.

I loaded the sample into a sampler and selected a short section of the sustained part, as shown in image 40. The plan is to make this highlighted area the basis for a loop – creating a long, smooth sustained cello note from this short snippet.

Deciding which section to loop is not always straightforward, but zooming in on the waveform can help pinpoint an appropriate area. In the zoomed image below (41) you can see that the sustained note of a cello is itself essentially a repeated pattern – though obviously a far more complex one than the simple sine wave we just looked. The aim now is to choose one or more complete waveform cycles, and repeat it.

In the end I chose a section to loop by trial and error. I simply selected a portion of the sustained note and listened to how it sounded when looped. By gradually adjusting the loop start and end points, and experimenting with different sections of the sample, I finally arrived at a selection that looped relatively smoothly.

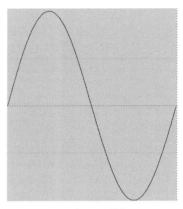

image **38**

SINE WAVE

A sine wave is the purest form of sound. Seen onscreen (as in image 38), it's a smooth, curved, repetitive waveform where the positive and negative cycles of the wave are equal but opposite. The amplitude (volume) of the wave determines the height of the wave above and below the zero line. The frequency of the wave determines the gradient of the slopes of the curves – how steep and close together they are. If you visit the website www.udel.edu/idsardi/sinewave/sinewave.html you'll find an interactively adjustable waveform (by Prof Idsardi at the University of Delaware), which shows the way soundwaves combine to produce more complex waveforms.

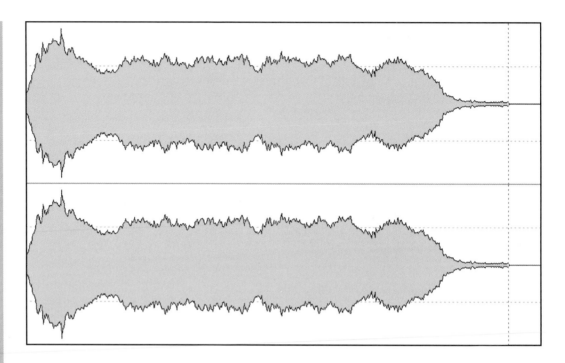

image **39**

Listen to Track 63 on CD1 and you'll hear the result. When the sample starts you'll hear the original attack portion, then the sustain section I chose to loop is repeated for as long as I held down the key. When the key was released, the sampler continued to play on through the end of the loop, through the decay portion, to the end of the sample.

This basic technique can be applied to a broad range of instruments, with varying degrees of success, depending largely on the nature of the source material. The result here is musically fairly convincing – it might sit OK in a busy mix, but listening to it in isolation you can still clearly identify the looped section. With some material this is unavoidable, but the point is that you'll have managed to effectively create an endlessly sustainable sound from a relatively short sample.

You can take this process a step further and attempt to mimic the natural fluctuation of acoustic instrument sounds by employing LFOs... but if you're going to mimic acoustic instruments, you need to understand them. So let's briefly investigate why acoustic instruments shift in volume and tonal character over time.

Almost all electronic instruments (like synthesisers) use a similar principle of repeating short cycles of electricity or digital data (models or samples) to create sustained notes. So sampling them and creating sustained notes tends to produce results that sound a lot like the real thing. Most acoustic instrument sounds, on the other hand, involve one crucial factor that complicates proceedings: the player. Humans are almost never mechanically repetitive.

Using the cello as an example, the variation in the speed and force with which the bow is pulled and pushed will produce subtle variations in the volume of the sustained note – indeed a cello player deliberately uses bow control to change volume. Pitch can wobble slightly too, either unintentionally, through tiny inaccuracies in fingering, or deliberately through use of vibrato technique. Wind instrument players use their breath to control volume, and the different-shaped holes on the instrument to control pitch. In both instances there can also be a very slight fluctuation in musical pitch because of natural harmonics.

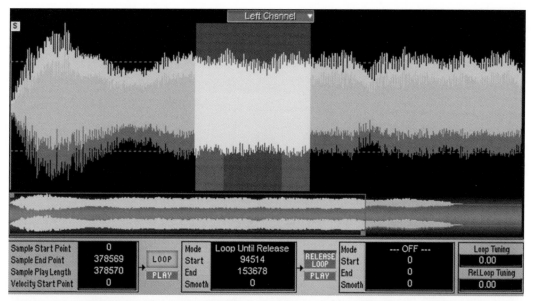

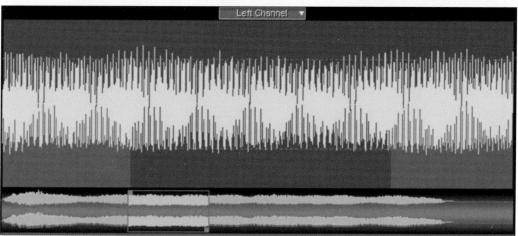

Here's a brief description of how the LFOs on your sampler can be subtly used to replicate this 'human' variation in your sustained sample sound.

● Assign an LFO to control the amplitude (volume) envelope of the sample.

● Set the LFO to its very slowest rate – the one I used for the cello was at 50Hz.

● Set up an LFO delay, so the LFO doesn't begin to take hold until after the looped section of the sample has repeated a few times. In the cello example I used the maximum delay of three seconds.

● Once I'd set up the speed and delay for the LFO, I reduced the envelope amount so its effect on the volume of the sample is very slight.

Track 64 on CD1 illustrates the effect of just such an LFO applied to the cello sample. Yes, it's a subtle effect, but it is there...

You might want to experiment with assigning another LFO to the pitch of the sample. In fact you can try the same thing with pan, filter cutoff, EQ, or anything else. The basic principle remains the same – you're trying to disguise the repetitive nature of the looped sustained note by introducing other, more irregular variations that distract the listener.

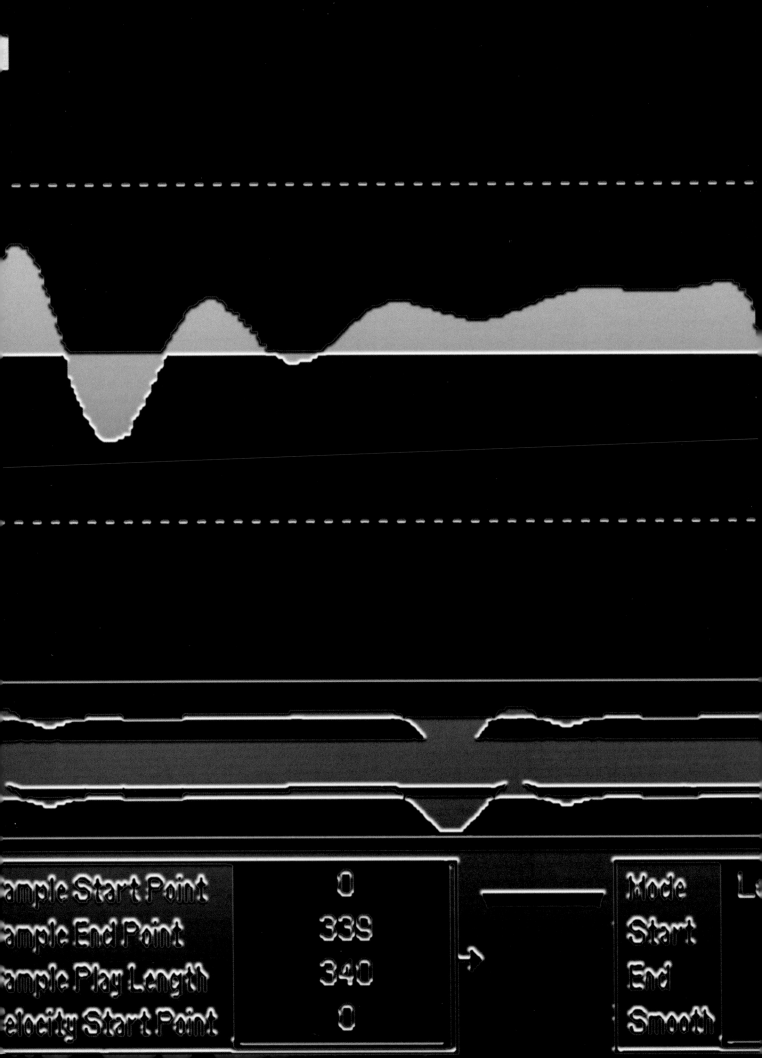

CHAPTER 6
customising
sounds

The sampler is arguably the most sonically diverse musical instrument ever created. Not only can it reproduce almost any sound, you can also alter and adapt your chosen sample in a variety of ways to create a virtually unlimited sound palette.

This is a long chapter, but it's the heart of the book. Sampling is as much about what you do to your sounds, once you've imported them and cut them to size, as it is about anything else. This is where a lot of modern music producers make their unique mark, and let their creativity have free rein.

- Using processors – from frequency analysis, filtering and EQ to compressors, limiters, reverb, modulation, distortion… any 'effects' you can think of.

- Sampling & synthesis – incorporating samples into a synthesis environment (including modular systems and granular synthesis), which opens up a new world of sonic possibilities, some of them pretty strange…

- Resampling – making the results of the various processes permanent.

Until Release

0

170

0

RELEASE
LOOP

Start

End

Smooth

Continuous

169

339

0

Do you know what it is yet?

The sampling musician is often engaged in a kind of game with the listener, playing with the element of recognition. This notion is central to much of the mythology and kudos of sampling for some musicians. For many hip-hop-producing vinyl junkies, finding effective samples that are rare enough to be considered unique is a holy grail. But another, very popular way of playing with recognition is where producers employ effects to carefully veil the samples they've taken, transforming them to a point where their original form or identity is no longer obvious. An example would be taking a drum pattern and distorting it, through effects processing and/or synthesis, so it might end up sounding more like a bassline or guitar riff. A lot of fun can then be had by gradually lifting the veils of layered effects to see how long it takes for recognition to return – the point where the listener says, "Ah, *that's* what it is…"

DIGITAL MODELLING

Sometimes referred to (for marketing reasons perhaps) as the process of creating "virtual" instruments, the jury is still out on the effectiveness of digital modelling. The reason is that, despite the best efforts of instrument designers and software engineers, it's still not actually possible to predict and mimic nature 100 per cent accurately. Designers are required to mark out the boundaries of their set-up, to categorically define the way the various elements interact. They can embrace chaos theory and try to build in random elements (the best do), but ultimately they are designing an enclosed system with fixed parameters. Nature doesn't suffer from the same constriction – nor, oddly enough, did early analog synthesisers, to a great extent. When the early synth designers like Robert Moog built their first machines, the only components they could lay their hands on were basically unreliable. A box of components that were theoretically identical could not really be relied on to behave in exactly the same way. So each machine could have a slightly different tonal quality. Even as manufacturing improved through the 1970s, synthesisers were prone to drifts in tuning and shifts in tone due to temperature, humidity, inconsistency of power supply and failing components. All of which actually added to their appeal, because they inadvertently had that slightly random, unpredictability of nature. Digital modellers are definitely getting closer… you decide whether or not they've made it yet

Once you step beyond the boundary of simply taking a slice of sound and using it untreated, purely for the dramatic effect of placement or repetition in a new context, you enter a world of subterfuge. A world of textures and layers. Sampling musicians have an increasingly vast arsenal of tools at their disposal with which to corrupt, mask and sonically manipulate – in fact one tool on its own is rarely enough. A truly transformed sound may have gone through dozens of processes on its journey.

There is no definitive way to use these tools – no 'correct' order, no such thing as an incorrect sound (a sound might be inappropriate for the context, but that doesn't make it 'wrong'). So it's not possible – even if it were desirable – to tell you exactly how you should use these sound-shaping tools, but what I can do is take each tool out of the box, tell you what it does, how to plug it in, and what the controls do. I can also offer some examples of what to expect from them – separately and in combination.

Before going on to look in detail at that tool kit, it's worth a brief exploration of where all the tools came from. There are two primary sources: synthesisers and recording studios.

In traditional analog synthesis a wave pattern, generated by an oscillator, is used as the fundamental sonic building block. The pure waveforms from the oscillator are processed using a number of other electrical circuits designed to twist and shape the signals – originally in an attempt to mimic acoustic instrument sounds. This set of circuits gives us the first category of sample processing tools, which I've touched on already, namely filters, envelopes and LFOs.

In most modern sampling systems these analog synthesis tools have been 'digitally modelled' and their effects applied to samples as mathematical equations at the digital level, not simply electricity passing through circuits.

The second category of processing tools comes from the recording studio. EQ was originally developed to compensate for the inadequacies of recorded sound, which in its early years inevitably failed to sound 'equal' to the original sound source, largely because the existing technology didn't allow the full frequency range of music to be captured.

Reverberation has long been understood to make voices sound bigger, more powerful, even other-worldly... try visiting a few medieval cathedrals or mosques for proof of this. When close-miking of voices and instruments was introduced in the recording studio, detail improved but ambient reverberations were lost, so artificial reverb processors were developed to help give recorded sound back a more natural feel. Other artificial effects like echo, phasers, flangers, and many more, were created to either emulate the way sounds are heard naturally or simply to add extra depth. In recent years, the ever-increasing number of digital effects have perhaps become the most widely used sample processing tools.

image **42**

'MIXING' ON A SAMPLER

A hardware sampler takes the concept of the mixing console and employs it slightly differently. It gathers samples together into 'banks', 'programs' or 'patches' – the name varies according to manufacturer (some even have an actual mixer), but the principle is the same. There is always a central nervous system that makes it possible to connect everything together. Each sample or group of samples (once mapped on a keyboard and layered etc) can have its level and pan position adjusted, be EQ'd, and be sent off to an effect processor to be manipulated. Software samplers follow the same basic format, but often with even greater flexibility and ease of use.

Working with a mixer

As in an analog studio set-up, the main piece of equipment is the mixing console, or desk. Traditionally at the heart of any studio, the mixing console allows you to gather together a number of individual sounds (from two up to as many as the system can handle) and combine them so they can be played through a stereo monitoring system. It's like a funnel – a simple way of getting dozens of individual sounds and squashing them together so they come out as a cohesive single stereo signal (known as a stereo master). Mixing consoles are often simply called mixers, precisely because they mix together many sounds to form one new one.

Each individual sound runs through its own mixer channel, which allows it to be processed independently. The console channel itself provides many useful features – such as pan (or panorama) controls, for balancing the signal in the stereo image, and individual level-setting faders for sliding the volume up and down – though it usually only has one built-in sound processing tool, namely EQ.

But the console channel provides two other methods of passing sounds through processing tools: these are the insert socket and the send & return circuit. The whole business of setting up a path, or route, for the flow of sounds around the studio, passing through various pieces of equipment – hardware or virtual – is known as routing.

The insert

On a traditional analog mixing console, each channel usually has a single 1/4″ jack socket labelled 'Insert', located beside the other input connections. This socket accepts a specialised plug and cable that diverts the sound flowing through that channel, carrying it away to a signal processor – traditionally a gate or compressor – then back into the console channel (via the same socket), where the signal carries on its merry way through the rest of the channel controls and into the final mix. All before you even realise it's gone.

The insert idea has been borrowed extensively within software samplers and audio+MIDI sequencers. Image 42 shows the 'master' section of Wavelab, which I'm going to be using to illustrate the significance of inserts for sampling musicians.

At the top of the section you can see eight effect 'slots'. Clicking on the number to the right of the slot opens a pull-down menu that lets you choose from the effects currently installed on your system. Once loaded, the name of the effect appears. Each individual effect can be switched on/off with the button to the left, or listened to in isolation using the solo button. Solo temporarily switches off all the other effects in the rack so you can hear one particular effect on its own.

The effects work in series, so the sound passes through the first effect, then through the next and onwards through each in turn. This means that the order in which effects are loaded into the rack makes an enormous difference to the sonic results.

The same layout – a rack of empty slots into which different effects can be loaded – also appears in the track mixers of the leading audio+MIDI sequencing packages.

The two distinguishing and crucial factors about the insert are that it's generally intended for processing individual sounds (or channels), and the effects are always loaded in series.

Using the bus

The disadvantage of each channel being wired up to a separate processing device, via an insert cable, is that it requires a lot of available effects units if you want to cover every channel on a mixer. A traditional 'realworld' mixing console offers an alternative. It's possible instead to link one or two effects units to the mixer as a whole, via what's called an 'auxiliary' circuit. Each channel can then tap into this effect as much or as little as you think it needs to – the amount of effect used (if any) is controlled by an 'aux' level knob on each channel strip. By adjusting the level of this control you can increase or decrease the degree to which that channel is affected by that processor – effectively changing the wet/dry balance of the signal.

Each channel is linked to this 'auxiliary' effects circuit by an internal routing system called a bus, and the relevant sockets and level controls (at the mixer's master section) would likely be labelled Aux Send and Aux Return (or FX Send & Return).

This routing method is also useful if you want to pass a number of different sounds through the same processor, so that they're all treated by the same effect simultaneously. Obviously they couldn't all be plugged into the processor individually, so they're grouped together first inside using the bus system.

Software set-ups are often short of computer processing power, so the same rule of economy applies. The send & return/bus system means you can share the same 'virtual' effects unit between lots of different sounds.

You'll find that even lowest-budget mixers these days will have at least two auxiliary send circuits (and knobs) per channel, and a professional mixer may have six or even eight.

WET & DRY

A source sound, without any effects applied to it, is called 'dry'. When you feed a dry sound into an effect processor, what comes out the other side is called the 'wet sound. Most processors provide a control that sets the balance between whether we hear the wet sound, the dry sound, or a combination of the two. This is often expressed as a percentage: a setting of 50 per cent means we hear an equal mix of the wet and dry sound.

THE STUDIO TOOLKIT

In this section I'll look at the various technical ways you can sonically examine and re-shape the samples you have, finding out what sonic frequencies they contain, why and how you might adjust and alter those frequencies (using filters, EQ, compressors, gates etc), dabble in using synthesis tools and techniques, and revel in the sheer quantity and versatility of effect processors available nowadays to tweak your samples to your heart's content.

Audio analysis

One great advantage of a professional audio editing application, like Wavelab or Sound Forge, is the inclusion of advanced audio analysis tools, the type commonly found in professional mastering studios.

You could argue these are not crucial to the sampling musician, but they can be very beneficial to further your understanding of how sound really works, and help when it comes to using EQ and other processing tools to isolate, suppress or emphasise individual elements within samples.

If you can look at a graph and see instantly which frequencies are occupied by which musical elements and instruments within a sound, you'll know which frequencies you need to target with your EQ.

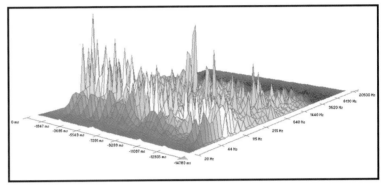

image **43**

The process of breaking sound down into its constituent waves is called a Fourier analysis, and the result can be represented graphically in several different ways.

By looking at thousands of individual consecutive slices within a specified period of time, a 'three-dimensional' map like the one in image 43 can be drawn up. In this image, time is running down the left edge (here a 1000ms slice of a song), frequency down the right, and the height of the spikes represents volume/sound level. (In an editing program like Wavelab you can rotate the graph to get different perspectives.)

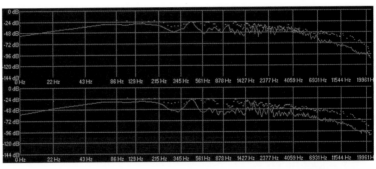

image **44**

The same information can also be shown in realtime, in two different ways. The first and most detailed method, the Fourier meter, plots the results on a 2D graph (as seen in the stereo image in image 44), with frequency on the horizontal axis and sound level on the vertical. The results are continuously updated and displayed as an animated solid line. A second, broken line displays recent peaks on the same graph to help you build a picture of how what you are seeing now relates to what you saw a second or so earlier. This is a very detailed

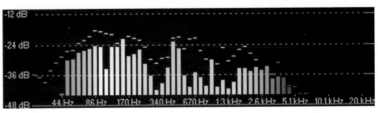

image **45**

method of display, and this method also lets you generate 'snapshots' where you can look at a single frozen moment in time.

The plotted line method can be difficult to get useful information from in realtime, so a more simplified version of the same thing has been developed in the shape of the spectrum meter, as seen in image 45. This presents realtime information as a peak-hold bar graph, giving an easy-to-read display of current and recent peak info.

Another use for sound analysis is to gauge the left and right levels in the stereo image,

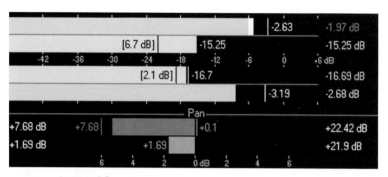

image **46**

either of an individual sound or a final mix. Relative levels can change continuously over time, and it's fine for one channel or other to dominate for brief periods, but it's important that your overall mix is fairly evenly balanced, with similar amounts of energy devoted to both sides – you don't want all the action happening over in one speaker. (This might happen because of the way sounds were originally recorded, or how they've been panned at the mixing desk.)

In image 46 you can see two sets of level meters at the top, one showing peak values (the outer set), the other showing RMS, or average values (the inner set). At the bottom, the pan meter displays when one side of the signal is louder than the other.

Frequency control

As mentioned in Chapter 1, most sounds are a combination of several frequencies (or notes), the loudest or most dominant of which determines whether a listener would call it a bassy, mid or treble sound. There are lots ways in which manipulating frequencies can be crucial to sampling musicians. Here are just a few of them:

- Cleaning up and bringing increased definition to sounds you've just sampled.
- Suppressing a particular aspect of a sound – removing high frequencies from a guitar to make it more mellow and bass-like, for example.
- Enhancing a particular aspect of a sound – adding more bass to a bass sound, for instance, to increase power and depth.
- Suppressing and/or enhancing frequencies so extremely that the dominant frequencies are no longer present, and secondary sounds become dominant, forming a completely new sound.
- Adding a sense of constant change to a sample through realtime manipulation.

There are two main tools for manipulating frequency – namely filters and equalisation (EQ). They both do a similar same thing, but in different ways, and with a different emphasis. Both are crucial to the entire recording/production process, and as such are also an intrinsic part of almost all uses of the sampler. Choosing whether to use a filter or an EQ, and which type to use, is totally dependant on the job in hand.

FILTERS

You'll find filters built into all studio samplers – most provide at least one filter per sampler instrument. This usually means that the filter affects all the samples within the instrument. In these circumstances the filter is often simply 'hard-wired' – it's always there whether you use it or not. Within a modular sampler, like NI Kontakt, you need to select and 'patch-in' the filter. A small number of samplers (like Native Instruments' Intakt) allow you to apply filters to individual samples within an instrument.

There are five main types of audio filter: low-pass, high-pass, band-pass, band-eliminate, and multimode. The most commonly used of the bunch is probably the low-pass, so I'll start with that and use it to explore the basic concepts. A low-pass filter (LPF) reduces the frequencies above a user-defined frequency, allowing all the frequencies below that 'cutoff' point to flow through unaltered. The cutoff frequency can be set anywhere in the frequency spectrum. (A high-pass filter (HPF) is, as you might guess, simply the inverse of a LPF. It reduces the frequencies *below* the cutoff point and allows the frequencies above it to pass through unhampered.)

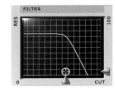

image **47**

image **48**

Listen to CD1 Track 23 and you'll hear a one-bar drum loop. After one cycle of the drum pattern, you'll notice the effect of moving the cutoff frequency slowly and steadily down through the frequency spectrum. This is commonly known as a filter sweep. The first instruments to disappear are the cymbals and hi-hats, and then you can hear what happens to each of the other instruments as the cutoff is moved downwards. Notice how their tonal characters are fundamentally altered as higher frequencies are stripped away – the sounds don't just disappear, their entire character changes and they mutate away to nothing.

It's worth experimenting with passing a range of sounds through a filter, because it can teach you a lot about the way sounds you thought were familiar are actually made up.

Most filters have three editable controls: one is cutoff (which we've just been talking about), and the others are amount and resonance.

Filter amount & resonance

The reason we say a LPF *reduces* the frequencies above the cutoff (rather than completely removing them) is that the amount by which the frequencies are cut can usually be adjusted.

Resonance concerns a very narrow band of frequencies around the cutoff frequency (it's sometimes referred to as 'emphasis', and can be compared to the use of the term 'Q' in parametric EQ, which we'll come to shortly). When you tweak a resonance control you are adjusting the amount by which that band of frequencies is boosted, or cut.

Image 47 and 48 show the filter element of the TC Electronic Filtrator. The arrow at the bottom represents the cutoff, and the arrow on the right edge represents the resonance amount. In the first image there is a zero resonance setting, but in the second the resonance is boosted dramatically.

In image 48 you can see the way in which the removal of frequencies above the cutoff produces a gradual sloping line beyond the cutoff, as the effect of removing 18dB per octave gradually removes the frequencies rather than cutting them absolutely dead. Leaving remnants of reduced sounds in place can have a pleasing effect, particularly with drums.

Just a small amount of resonance boost adds a little bit of edge to the filtered sound, which can help to define and bring extra punch to a sound. A large amount of resonance creates a powerful, piercing sound that will dominate and obscure the filtered sound.

Listen to CD1 Track 24 and you'll hear a filter sweep with just a small amount of resonance applied; Track 25 has a medium amount of resonance; Track 26 has a large amount. Note that by the time you reach full resonance, with Track 26, the results destroy the original

TWO-POLE/FOUR-POLE FILTERS

Filters originate from the days of old analog synthesisers, when the effect was created using resistors made by wrapping wire around a pole. A filter with two of these poles would usually reduce the sound by 12dB over the frequency spectrum of an octave. In practice this produces a less severe effect, with some of the sound in the first octave above the cutoff (in the case of a LPF) still seeping through. A filter with four poles would reduce the signal by 24dB over the width of each octave, which should be a more or less total cut. A simple electrical switch would be used to switch many early filters between employing just two or four poles.

Many modern digital filters still follow this traditional format, referring to a switchable filter amount as being between 'two-pole 18dB per octave' cut and 'four-pole 24dB per octave' cut. Other digital filters employ a variable filter amount, not based on the traditional pole model but simply offering a continuously variable amount of cut.

OFFSET

In the context of music production, offset is used to describe a *relative* value change – where you perform an action that increases or decreases a value, regardless of what the initial value is. For example, you have a sampler instrument with a filter cutoff frequency set to a value of 80, resonance set to 30, and an effect send level set to 20, and you assign a single MIDI hardware control to all three of these parameters. When you turn the knob clockwise, you apply a positive 'offset' value to all three; if you turn the knob enough to increase a value by 10, you will change the three settings to 90, 40 and 30. The knob sent out a positive offset of 10, and anything that was set up to respond had its value increased by 10. If you turn the knob anti-clockwise you apply a negative offset.

A 'literal' value, by contrast, refers only to the setting of each particular control.

sound so much as to make it almost unusable, because of different volume levels for different sounds. (If you wanted to make use of such intense new sounds, you might wish to resample the bits you like and create new sampler instruments and MIDI sequences using them. Resampling is covered later in this chapter.)

With many filters, applying a large amount of resonance causes the cutoff frequency to resonate so much that it begins to produce a constant tone – an effect called self-oscillation.

In image 48 you can see how the extreme setting of the resonating filter produces a curved frequency response rather than straight lines. Both immediately above and below the cutoff there are nice gentle curves to the build-up and trail-away.

The width of the band of frequencies boosted by the resonance control is clearly crucial to the tonal character of the sound. Each filter manufacturer chooses the particular width of frequency band affected by the resonance control, thus producing a slightly different curve – which is largely why not all filters sound identical. Boosting a wider band of frequencies will produce a shallower curve, and this is liable to cause a slightly fatter, rounder filter sound; whereas boosting a narrower band will produce a much steeper curve, giving a sharper, more piercing sound. A concave curve also will produce a slightly different sound to a convex curve. These are not things you can usually edit with filters, just an explanation of what it is you're hearing and identifying as different.

If you experiment with adjusting cutoff frequency and resonance as your sound plays, you can create some unique sounds. It adds a sense of movement and much-needed dynamics to repetitive sound. Sampling musicians are blessed with a number of tools that automate, enhance and expand the possibilities on offer. Envelopes, envelope followers, LFOs and of course MIDI automation are all tools that can be used in this way, and are covered in other areas of this book.

Band-pass filters

A band-pass filter (BPF) is perhaps best viewed as a LPF and a HPF combined. A BPF has two cutoff points: one reduces the frequencies above it, the other reduces the frequencies below, leaving the band of frequencies between the two points unaltered.

Rather than having control of the two cutoff points independently, a BPF gives the user control of the frequency at the centre of the unaltered band of frequencies. The two cutoff points are often then set a fixed width apart from each other (and of course from the centre frequency). Adjusting the centre frequency moves the settings of the two cutoff frequencies in relation to it.

The resonance control on a BPF adds emphasis to the frequencies around both cutoff points. A number of samplers offer an additional 'width' control, which allows you to adjust the distance between the centre frequency and the two cutoff points, and therefore the width of the band of frequencies passed through the filter.

The effect of a band-pass filter can be created by applying a HPF and a LPF to a sample. This arrangement, of course, offers control of the width of the band of frequencies passed through the filters, which has its advantages, but it is inevitably a little trickier to edit (and particularly to adjust in realtime).

If you do want to replicate a BPF with two filters, and be able to manipulate the cutoff settings smoothly while maintaining their relationship, try this: assign the cutoff points of both the HP and LP filters to the same MIDI controller (using an 'offset' rather than a 'literal' controller mode – see box), then use a single hardware control on a MIDI control surface or keyboard to adjust both filter cutoffs at once.

Band-eliminate filters

A band-eliminate filter (BEF), sometimes known as a band-reject filter, is often also called a notch filter. It achieves the inverse effect of the BPF. It still works around a band of frequencies between two cutoff points, but this time removes the frequencies between the cutoff points and lets those above and below them flow through. The BEF uses the same centre frequency and resonance control types as a BPF.

Multimode filters

There are in fact several different concepts of the multimode filter, employed on several different machines (for instance the Sherman Filter Bank and Mutronics Mutator mentioned in the 'Advanced Filtering' box), but I'm going to focus here on the most commonly used features on multimode filters.

image **49**

Image 49 shows the multimode filter in NI Kontakt, which I'll use for illustration purposes, as it's a good example of the breed. It uses three separate filters combined to form one monster filter.

The controls for the three filters are arranged in three horizontal strips, with filter number one at the top. The first control of filter one is labelled Cutoff, and to the right of this the controls run in the following order: Resonance, Type, and Amount. (Within Kontakt the 'type' is continuously variable, which means that with the knob positioned anti-clockwise the filter is a LPF, with the knob fully clockwise it's a HPF, and with the knob vertical it's a BPF.)

These controls are repeated horizontally underneath for filters two and three, but with one important exception. The first control in the row for filters two and three is labelled Shift 2 and Shift 3 respectively. These shift controls set the cutoff points for filters two and three – the cutoff points of the three filters are linked to each other.

The cutoff of filter one is always the lowest of the three (in terms of frequency setting), and its control sets the cutoff point in the usual manner. The Shift 2 control then sets an 'offset' amount for the cutoff of filter two in relation to that of filter one.

The shift control is calibrated in semitones: if you set the shift for filter two to an octave above filter one, it will always stay exactly an octave above the frequency of Cutoff 1. So if you then adjust the cutoff of filter one, the cutoff of filter two will change by the same amount and remain an octave above it. Similarly, Shift 2 then sets the offset between the cutoff of filter two and that of filter three. Adjusting filter one would then alter all three cutoff points but retain the relationships between the three.

In image 49 I've set filter one to be a LPF, filter two to be a BPF, and filter three to be a HPF. You can see the result of the combination of the three filters in the response graph to the right of the window. It's a little like a complex BEF with a central peak of retained frequencies.

You could achieve the same result by applying three separate filters: a LPF, a HPF and a BPF. The advantage with the multimode filter is that, although complex, once it's been set up, all three cutoff points, and therefore all three filters, can be adjusted in realtime simply by adjusting the cutoff of filter one – creating an effect that you'd need three hands to achieve with three separate filters.

I've applied this filter to our now familiar drum loop, and you can hear the result on CD1 Track 27 – the main cutoff is set to pick out the snare with the central peak and the hi-hat with the second higher peak. I then applied a filter sweep to the same collection of settings, as you'll hear on Track 28.

EQ – FREQUENCY-SPECIFIC VOLUME CONTROL

Technically speaking, filters and EQ are pretty much the same thing – in fact you'll find some manufacturers of mixing consoles and other studio equipment who rather confusingly refer to EQ circuits as filters. They're both devices that reduce or increase the flow of specific frequencies. Beneath the surface they work in very similar ways, with one big difference: whereas a filter is primarily designed for reducing/cutting frequencies (boosted resonance is the only way to increase frequencies with a filter), an EQ is quite capable of increasing or 'boosting' frequencies as well.

A lot of the jobs we do with EQ can also be tackled with filters, but EQ tends to offer more control – control over the amount of cut and boost, control over the curves involved in how the frequencies are sculpted – and generally has a different tonal character. Filters can be said to be more brutal and simplistic. Neither is necessarily better, they are just different – and the difference is hard to define. You have to try both and compare the effects for yourself in any given circumstance.

The other difference is historical. EQ evolved as an audio recording and broadcast tool, designed as a way of correcting the vagaries of microphones, with their uneven frequency response curves. As microphone technology improved, the need for EQ lessened, but by that time it was a firm fixture in the studio and concert hall, and remained useful as a means of compensating for poor room acoustics, and general sound experimentation. Although EQ is an important tool for the sonic sculptor on a quest to make new sounds, it can help to keep in mind that, strictly speaking, it didn't evolve as part of a musical instrument in the way filters did with synthesisers. Indeed a lot of EQ is specifically designed to be 'invisible', to alter sounds as naturally as possible, so the listener would never guess it had been used.

There are four broad categories of EQ found in audio equipment, including sampling systems: basic two-band (treble & bass) EQ, parametric, graphic, and paragraphic.

I'm going to run through the four types as though I'm talking about analog hardware – so I'll talk about knobs and sliders as though they're things you can physically reach out and touch. In fact, software developers used these hardware controls as a conceptual starting point in their designs, so most software-based EQ will employ similar principles, even though you may use a mouse or a set of cursor keys and buttons to actually move the controls.

Simple/shelving EQ

The most basic form of EQ you'll encounter is the two-band EQ, as found on a small number of entry-level mixing consoles, DJ mixers, and of course hi-fi. This consists of two knobs, one for bass and another for treble (sometimes labelled Lo and Hi or something similar); so, for example, turning the treble knob clockwise gives a high-frequency boost to your sound.

But how do you know exactly which frequencies are being boosted? The answer is, you often don't. Technically the process is done in one of two ways. The commonest is to use 'shelving' EQ, which is very much like a high or low-pass filter. With shelving EQ, all the frequencies above or below a (pre-fixed) cutoff frequency are cut or boosted.

In some rare instances it's implemented much more like a band-eliminate filter, where a specific range of frequencies is cut or boosted. This is rare with treble EQ, but it can actually be useful with bass EQ, where it's desirable to remove higher bass frequencies and leave lower ones intact. (I'm only mentioning this unusual type of EQ for the sake of completeness, and because you may have encountered it on DJ mixers or hi-fi, although shelving EQ is the norm there too.)

Most budget products do now stretch to three-band EQ, which adds a third knob that's used to control mid frequencies. A mid frequency control will follow the band-pass basic model, cutting or boosting a fixed range of frequencies.

Parametric EQ

This is the type of EQ found on most professional mixing consoles, and the type most commonly copied digitally in samplers. Parametric EQ operates on a band of frequencies too, but it allows you to specify how wide that band will be, and which frequency it's centred around. A fully featured parametric EQ will provide three controls per frequency band: one control sets the central frequency; another sets the bandwidth (and so the sharpness of the band) – this is what's known as the 'Q' factor; and the third control sets the amount of cut or boost. With many systems, the narrower the Q factor, the sharper the perceived effect, though functionality can differ from one manufacturer's products to another.

A very well specified mixing console will provide two sets of adjustable parametric equalisers, accompanied by one high and one low shelving equaliser per channel. This combination is extremely versatile and provides a very good degree of control over any sound.

There are several ways of presenting parametric EQ. Where there's plenty of physical space, separate knobs for each control might be provided. A common solution employed when space is at a premium can be found on the channel EQ found in Cubase SX, and seen in image 50. This particular set-up uses what's called a dual-concentric knob. (On the Cubase channel strip this is the larger of the two knob types.) It comprises an inner knob and an outer, separately adjustable ring. In this version the inner knob is used to set cut and boost,

image **50**

and the outer ring for setting the centre frequency. The smaller knob (to the right and a little below) is the Q control. The little square is an on/off switch.

The numeric displays show precise details of selected frequency, cut/boost amount and Q (rather cleverly the number to the left is multi-function, so actually changes colour and shows the Q or cut/boost amount depending on which of these controls you're using).

Although overall EQ on/off buttons are common on analog consoles, individual frequency band on/off switches are very rare – as are numeric displays, except on top-end 'hybrid' consoles. Such highly desirable features are the province of software systems, digital consoles and of course samplers.

Computers and software often give us incredibly improved functionality and display options, and this has resulted in a great many different types of EQ. A good illustration is the parametric EQ plug-in from TC Powercore (as seen in image 51).

This is a five-band parametric EQ that has low-shelving, high-shelving and three stereo parametric EQ sections. It can be edited either using the controls (moving sliders and knobs and entering values in the number fields) or by using the mouse to grab and move handles within the display.

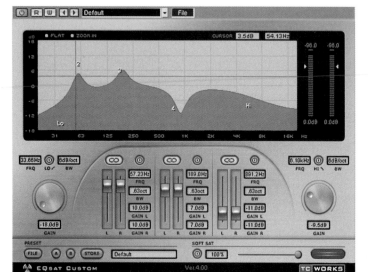

image **51**

The handles are the three numbers and the words Hi and Lo. When you move them, the rest of the EQ curve and all of the EQ settings change, and are shown on the display.

This system offers the best of both worlds: moving the handles and working with visual information is fun, intuitive and fast to use and really requires little theoretical understanding of what you're doing – you simply need to know that the left of the screen represents bass, the right treble, and that pulling handles up or down cuts and boosts frequencies.

Using the controls is precise and fairly technical, but if you know you want to adjust a very specific frequency, it's the most efficient way to do it. When you move a handle, the numbers give you a technically accurate readout of what you're doing.

This type of interface is the perfect way to learn about EQ – you can enjoy experimenting and hearing what specific frequency and EQ adjustments sound like.

Graphic EQ

A graphic equaliser takes quite a different approach to the same subject. The controls of a graphic EQ consist of a row of faders, or sliders, which can vary in number from just three up to 32 (or 64 on a stereo unit). Each fader cuts or boosts a narrow band of frequencies – a 32-band graphic will assign a much narrower band of frequencies to each fader than an eight-band graphic would.

Most graphic EQs are stereo, so will provide a separate bank of faders for each stereo channel. They usually also provide a master level fader and bypass button for each of the two channels.

Dividing the frequency spectrum into dozens of bands provides control over very narrow slices of the frequency spectrum, so larger graphic EQs are well suited to almost surgical removal of very narrow, troublesome frequencies.

Graphic equalisers are not common within dedicated sampling systems, but they are widely available as software plug-ins, and therefore accessible for sample processing within most sample editing packages.

Paragraphic EQ

This is a relatively recent innovation, developed for software-based systems. It's essentially a hybrid between the parametric and graphic EQ approaches: the user interface is almost identical to the graphic EQ, offering a row of faders, but when you're adjusting a particular fader you have the option to spread the effect of your adjustments to neighbouring faders.

What this means is that, for example, when you boost using a specific fader, the faders on either side will also increase, though to a lesser degree. So when the active fader reaches maximum, the adjacent faders might reach 50 per cent. You usually have the option of adjusting the spread of the influence, from only the two faders on either side, or over the entire frequency spectrum.

This can be a very good way of working with EQ, because it combines the sharp, 'surgical' benefits of the graphic EQ with the smooth and rounded feel of the parametric, all in one convenient interface.

Identifying frequencies with a parametric EQ

One of the jobs EQ can do is to enhance what you like in a sound and eliminate what you don't want, all at the same time. EQ is essentially a frequency-specific volume control. First you have to identify the frequency band you want to work on, then you have to decide how wide that frequency band is, then you can increase (boost) or decrease (cut) it as required.

You can use a little trick to help locate the frequency you want to adjust. This involves sweeping through the sound with the EQ set to high boost. First you need to get the EQ set up: set the Q control to something near its lowest setting, so it's only going to adjust a narrow range of frequencies at any given moment. Now turn the frequency control fully anti-clockwise, or so it's set to the lowest frequency your particular EQ can adjust – this will often be around 20Hz. Next, set the gain control to +6dB; this is a substantial increase in level, so turn down the overall volume of your sound at the mixer. (You'll have to judge for yourself whether the volume of the sound is too loud after you've applied this EQ to it, but it's important not to overload your equipment.) Now play the sound.

Because 20Hz is essentially a sub-bass frequency, it's quite likely that at this moment your EQ will be producing few or no noticeable changes to your sound. Now slowly turn the frequency control clockwise, so you gradually work your way up through the frequency spectrum. As you progress through the sound, listen carefully to the results: when you reach around 60Hz you should begin to hear any bass elements of the sound increase considerably; as you work on up to around 100Hz, the deep, punchy elements like kick drums should be picked out; then as you reach about 500Hz, low-mid elements like toms should be boosted.

Remember that, because the Q is set very low, you're only boosting a very narrow band of frequencies at a time as you pass up through the sound spectrum. You'll notice that at some points things sound much more pleasing than at others – at some frequencies things may well sound quite nasty.

Repeat the process, making a mental note of which frequencies sound great and which sound bad. This is a subjective operation, which will be different with each sample, but at this stage it's all about ear-training. The most important tip is to trust your own judgment. Only you know if you think something sounds good or bad, and which aspects of the sound you might want to change.

Repeating this procedure with a broad range of source material is an invaluable learning experience. You'll soon know which instruments tend to inhabit which frequency ranges – with practice you may eventually simply be able to listen to a sound and say what its dominant and even harmonic frequencies are.

The next step is to identify the width of any particular band. Most musical sounds occupy more than just one simple narrow frequency, so when you've identified an 'active' area, try slowly moving the frequency control back and forth slightly, trying to get a feel for the width of the frequency range involved in that particular sound. You might need to repeat this at various points of the frequency spectrum, depending on the element of a sound you want to concentrate on.

A good example might be a percussive sound like a conga. The conga occupies a relatively narrow band of frequencies, but still wider than you'd hear with a parametric Q control set to a low value. It's fairly easy to find out the basic conga frequency using narrow-Q EQ, so try settling on the middle of the conga's range. Now slowly increase the Q setting to widen the affected band of frequencies. The aim is to widen it just enough to take in the whole conga sound, but not the frequencies to either side of it. It takes a little practice, and you may need to re-adjust both the frequency and Q controls several times to get it right.

Like so many things to do with audio production, plenty of small gradual movements and adjustments are needed. This is a precision game, so I'm afraid impatient, violent sweeps and thrashing-about will not produce results.

Once you've pinpointed all the frequencies that make up the full sound, you can choose to cut or boost them as desired.

Identifying frequencies with a graphic EQ

First make sure that all the faders on the graphic are set at their zero position, so they form a flat line (this is where the term 'flat EQ' comes from). Play your sample and, starting at one end of the frequency spectrum, take each fader in turn and follow a simple routine: pull it right down to maximum cut (usually –12dB), slowly slide it back up to the zero setting, then keep going until you've boosted by 6dB, then return it to zero. Do this with each fader in turn, listening to the results and making a note of what sounds good and bad.

Each fader on a good-quality graphic EQ controls quite a narrow band of frequencies, so it's a precise tool. Moving each fader in turn is certainly more time-consuming than turning a frequency knob on a parametric, but it can yield very accurate results.

A graphic EQ is also able to do something a parametric is not. A standard parametric rarely offers more than four sets of different frequency band controls, whereas a 32-band graphic EQ obviously allows for precise independent control of up to 32 different frequency bands at once. So you could slice out, say, 17 different narrow frequency bands from a sound, should you so wish.

In the process of identifying frequencies using a graphic, it's easy enough to gauge the width of the whole frequency band that the sound occupies. Just cut/boost adjacent faders until you come to one that has no effect on the sound – then you know you've reached the frequency band limit.

Most of the time you'll want to use a graphic EQ to surgically remove individual narrow bands from a sound, but it can sometimes sound good if, once you've found the central frequency of the sound you want to EQ, you stagger the effect of your cut or boost over the faders on either side. For example, if you decide to cut a particular frequency by 12dB, it might help to cut the fader immediately on either side of it by 3 or 6dB. The result is a subtly reducing slope around the central frequency.

Identifying frequencies with a paragraphic EQ

The process of locating target frequencies with a paragraphic EQ is identical to that with a graphic EQ. The whole point of a paragraphic is that it automatically creates a slope of cut/boosted frequencies on either side of a central frequency. It becomes a matter of using the width control on the paragraphic to determine how many frequency bands on either side of the central frequency will be affected. A narrow width will only affect the fader immediately on each side, creating a steep slope. A larger width will spread the effect to more faders and create a gentler slope.

The secret to great EQ

For most audio professionals, the main secret of great EQ is to use it very sparingly – if at all. You might think, logically enough, that the reason an EQ system offers a boost control is because using EQ to boost frequencies must be a good thing. Well, in occasional circumstances that might be the case, but mostly it's not. Here's why...

Say you have a sound with three main elements – a bass part, a mid-range part, and a treble part, and you want to make the mid-range element more prominent than the other two. The most obvious solution would seem to be to boost the mid range using EQ – this will obviously make the mid element more prominent in relation to the other two. But it may also sound cluttered or stodgy in the middle frequencies, and unbalance the overall sound. Instead, what you could do is use EQ to cut the bass and treble elements, then boost the overall master volume to compensate for the drop in levels. This will achieve the desired outcome – a relative mid boost – without muddling up the mid tones.

It's almost always possible to achieve better results by cutting EQ rather than boosting... and it often has clear advantages. EQ is all about definition, and you may well find that by reducing the unwanted frequencies you can bring the desired clarity and definition to the target frequency without needing to make it physically louder.

This EQ cutting method has many other benefits in the mixing process as a whole. In a piece of music that's quite complex and dense you'll find that some instruments (and voices) are competing with each other for the listener's attention, both in terms of volume level and frequency range.

To take a prime example, the kick drum and the bass guitar are both bass frequency sounds, and both are fairly high priority. You can't just turn them both up. Part of the answer is to decide which frequencies each will dominate and which they will relinquish.

The kick drum is usually a punchy sound, whose job is to provide thump to the low end. The bass guitar is a more musical and rounded sound, which also carries melody. A good solution is to divide up the entire bass register between the two sounds: say the kick drum will be dominant at around 100Hz, but can afford to be a little less present in the frequencies below this; and the bass guitar can probably get away with being less present at 100Hz. You just reduce a slice of frequencies at around 100Hz in the bass guitar sound, and reduce some of the frequencies below 100Hz in the kick drum. They will lock together to form the single driving force they should be, politely giving each other room to move.

This principle can be applied throughout the entire frequency spectrum, and with all instruments. Try mixing an entire song without allowing yourself to boost frequencies at all. You may well end up with a much greater sense of space between the instruments, and generally within the track. You will almost certainly end up with less background noise (boosting treble sounds, especially, will also boost unwanted hiss), and a superior sense of overall clarity and sonic fidelity.

Cleaning up samples

There are essentially four main kinds of unwanted noise you might find yourself wishing to remove from a sample – especially if you have a habit of sampling from old recordings. These are scratches, crackle, hiss and hum.

The simplest and most convenient method is to use a dedicated audio restoration system. This can take the form of combined audio restoration and CD-burning software packages, like Steinberg's Clean! or Magix Audio Cleaning Lab. But you'll find most dedicated sample-editing packages also contain specialist sample-cleaning effect plug-ins. These systems tend to consist of a basic set of controls that let you strike a balance between the amount of audio that's removed and how badly this affects the material you're trying to preserve.

By all means try this approach first, because it often works just fine. But there are also a few basic manual techniques you can use – which are essentially the same as what's going on beneath the surface with the restoration programs and plug-ins.

The art of the 'manual' clean-up process is to identify which frequencies the desired aspects of your recording might occupy, and which frequencies the various types of unwanted noise might occupy. From there you use filters and EQ to remove or boost frequencies accordingly.

In a manual restoration you'd re-process the sample several times to employ several techniques in conjunction. You'd use a stereo sample editor, like Wavelab, because it enables you to use a broad range of plug-ins, in any order you choose; the plug-ins can be bypassed for pre/post process comparison, and then the sample can be resampled with the entire selection of effects in place (as we'll see later in this chapter).

The effectiveness of the whole procedure will depend on the source material. The simple truth is that not everything can be cleaned. If the unwanted noise is in precisely the same frequency band as the material you're trying to preserve, you are fighting a losing battle. If your sample occupies all parts of the frequency spectrum, the job becomes practically impossible. Cleaning works best with source material that only occupies a relatively narrow band of frequencies – such as speech, for instance.

SCRATCHES & CRACKLE ON VINYL

Vinyl captures and reproduces sound using grooves that are filled with peaks and troughs. As the stylus travels along the grooves it moves up and down in the peaks and troughs and translates the amount of vertical distance travelled into frequency information. (Horizontal distance obviously relates to time, as the stylus journeys around the record). Small troughs translate into high frequencies, and larger troughs into lower frequencies. So when you get scratches on a record they are adding peaks and troughs. Minor scratches create extra small troughs, so produce high-frequency sounds; more serious scratches create additional deep troughs, which become unwanted low-frequency sounds.

Manual cleaning is generally done in one of two ways: either using filters and EQ or, if you have a software-based screen editor, redrawing the actual waveforms to smooth out any blips.

Cleaning with filters & EQ

The technically minded among you may choose to use a Fourier frequency analysis tool to examine your sample and get a graphic illustration of the frequencies that it's made up of. This will show you sharp peaks where anomalies occur, both in terms of time and frequency, and pinpoint areas to be worked on. Personally I've never found the frequency analysis route to be an intuitive or enjoyable approach to the problem, so I'm going to suggest a different option. Use your ears…

The techniques described earlier in this chapter, for locating specific frequencies, can also help identify scratches, crackle, hiss and hum. For the cleaning process itself, you can start with a low-pass filter. This removes much of the crackle of the scratches and gets rid of the hiss that's often present on vintage recordings. Setting the cutoff point for the LPF is a bit of a compromise; by pulling it down through the frequency spectrum you'll hear the unwanted stuff vanish, but eventually you also begin to lose the higher frequencies that you do want to keep from the sample. Losing too much of the high-frequency spectrum can start to make the sample sound muffled and lacking in definition. It can work well to pull the cutoff point down a little too far, so you can hear the definition start to disappear, and then back off slightly until it sounds OK. It's important to give yourself plenty of room for manoeuvre here, as you'll be doing more work on this slice of frequencies in a moment.

Next comes a high-pass filter, to remove the low-frequency thuds and clunks. Choosing the setting for the HPF is essentially the same as the LPF: raising the cutoff from zero gradually cuts away the unwanted thumps, until it starts to make your sample sound a bit thin, so you lower it again a little so it's not really effecting the main body of the sound.

If using these filters is too much of a broad brush approach, and you want to be more surgical about the frequencies you remove, you can use EQ. With a heavily scratched record (assuming you can't find a better version), start by concentrating on the minor, high-pitched scratches. Sweep through the high frequencies looking for a narrow band that contains those high scratches… it is there, you can't miss it. Identify the width of the frequency band, and apply a heavy cut to the whole band. Removing one slice of frequencies should remove a good proportion of scratch noise. Try a –24dB cut to a one-third-octave-wide slice of frequencies around 3kHz.

Next go looking for those major, low-frequency scratches. Repeat the search and destroy process in the low frequency spectrum. Try a –24dB cut to a one-third-octave-wide slice of frequencies centred around 90Hz.

Next you're faced with tackling the mid range – which by now should be sounding much clearer anyway. Use either a graphic EQ or a parametric to identify the frequencies within your source material that sound good and you really want to preserve. But don't actually boost those – the idea is simply to remove everything else. Literally cut away any frequency that's not absolutely necessary to the tonal character of your source material.

HISS & HUM

Hiss is usually related to magnetic tape noise, and is by definition a purely high-frequency phenomenon. As long as your sample doesn't have too much going on in the treble area, hiss can be removed by using a simple low-pass filter. Hum is usually caused by electrical interference in an audio signal, and tends to be a low-mid sound (normally 50-60Hz, the cycle of AC electricity, or a multiple of this). Provided your source material is not primarily a low-mid sound, the hum can be fairly easily located and removed.

By now you should be left with a much cleaner sound. If none of this has helped, your sound is probably beyond redemption – either abandon it, or resign yourself to working with the scratches in place. (Sometimes scratches have been deliberately left in as a feature, adding a touch of retro 'authenticity'. You can even exaggerate them through processing, or add them where there were none before, to dirty-up some over-clean samples.)

Re-drawing waveforms

Re-drawing is ideal for removing single scratches. If you have a relatively unscathed record with only isolated scratches, you can use the pencil tool in a software sample editor to smooth them out. Here's how…

When you zoom in on a sound in a screen editor, you can see the way the patterns and flow of the waveforms combine to make the sound what it is. You can see from image 52 that, if you zoom in far enough, any scratches, clunks, thuds or other brief but loud anomalies appear as spikes that stand out from the rest of the flow.

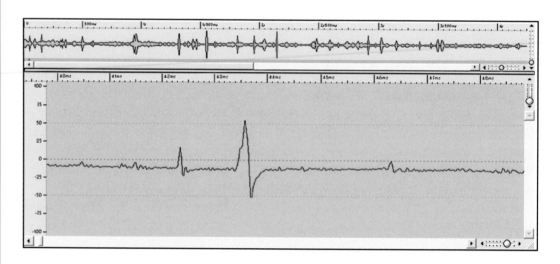

image **52**

In this illustration there is one large scratch and several smaller crackles. The aim here would be to literally redraw the line at those points, smoothing out those peaks and troughs, to match the surrounding 'normal' wave patterns.

Select the Pencil tool (usually found on a button at the top of the screen), and just re-draw the waveform, as if you were using a graphics application. Play back the result and see if it flows OK – you may need to experiment a few times to get something you're happy with. As usual, once you save the edited sample, the changes become permanent, so be sure it's right.

Obviously the zoom factor makes a difference here – if you're not zoomed-in close enough, your changes may not have the accuracy or subtlety required, and the effect can sound too dramatic or unnatural. (You might notice, in our illustration, that the scratch here is actually less than a single millisecond in length.)

In a similar way, an automated scratch removal plug-in goes through the sample looking for peaks like this that don't appear to fit with the surrounding waveforms. Most of the time it guesses right (the more sophisticated the analysis tool, the better its guesses tend to be), but of course it's not human, and can't make aesthetic decisions about the final results. That's down to you.

Re-drawing is possibly the only failsafe method of anomaly removal – it's just a little impractical when it comes to processing large amounts of material. The decision about whether a piece of material is too scratched to restore in this way is also down to personal choices, like time available to you, and your patience for the task.

Suppressing or enhancing certain frequencies

You'll realise by now that simply slicing away frequencies can alter a sound dramatically.

CD1 Track 29 is a big fat synthesiser sound. It contains plenty of bass, mid and treble-frequency components. It could be described as a 'lead' type sound because within a piece of music it would compete with all the other instruments for attention, and demand to be a high-priority sound. This also makes it great raw material from which we can create a wide range of further sounds, simply through frequency removal.

Track 30 is the same sound passed through a HPF. All of the bass and mid tones are gone, and we're left with a nice high-frequency sound. I've added a little resonance boost to give it some extra presence around the cutoff.

Track 31 is the same sample passed through a LPF, and it has now become a workable bass sound. I've applied a little more resonance boost to enhance the low-frequency punch.

Track 32 is the same sound again, this time passed through a BPF, and again I applied a small amount of resonance to add definition. As a mid sound, this is good for rhythmic support-type melodic lines.

Just for fun, I've also layered all three variations of the original sample back together (on Track 33) to show that simply by removing a few frequencies, and boosting a few others through increased resonance, we alter the tonal character of the original sample.

If you want to enhance a particular aspect of a sound (adding more bass to a bass sound for example), this is where using the boost facilities of EQ becomes useful.

CD1 Track 34 is a fairly soft bass sound – it would suit a pleasant, gentle dub-style bassline. But I wanted to tighten it up and give it more punch.

First I used a HPF and LPF filter together (with zero resonance setting) to narrow down the range of frequencies it occupies, just a little. The LPF has its cutoff set at 95Hz and the HPF has its cutoff at 50Hz. Then I used an EQ, first to boost a single note-width slice of frequency around 80Hz by 6dB. Then I boosted 90Hz by 2dB, 70Hz by 4dB, and 60Hz by 2dB. The result is a more powerful, punchy, but still quite low-frequency bass sound. You can hear this on Track 35 – the difference is subtle, but you will hear it when you're listening at high volume.

I then increased the EQ levels to the following: 80Hz by 10dB, 90Hz by 6dB, 70Hz by 8dB and 60Hz by 6dB – then resampled the finished bass sound, which is now more solid still. Listen closely to Track 36, and compare it to 34.

Using more extreme processing, it is in fact possible to change almost any sound into any other. All sounds are made up of layers of waveforms, and although one waveform may be dominant, or primary, there are always many more, less prominent layers of waveforms involved. Without the underlying layers giving depth of tonal character to the primary waveform, it would sound very different.

This opens a creative window for us. By selecting and enhancing the less dominant waveforms we can create very diverse sets of sounds from a single source.

EQ is clearly a crucial part of this process, but EQ alone is not going to get us where we want to go.

Noise gates

A gate is a pretty straightforward device. It has nothing to do with frequency, but is triggered instead by volume level. Its job is to completely close off the flow of sound when it falls below a user-defined volume level. It's mainly used to get rid of low-level background noise.

A simple gate will have only three controls. The most important is the threshold (marked in dB), which is used to set the desired level at which the gate will open and close. When the gate detects sound levels above the threshold level, it remains open and sound flows through. When sound levels drop below the threshold level, the gate is closed and no sound passes through. If you don't play any sound through a gate, it remains closed.

The next control is the attack, which (like all attack controls) determines how quickly the operation will start when it detects a sound above the threshold. In practice a gate sounds a little smoother in operation with a slow attack setting, where the gate opens more gently. Slow attack is great for things like vocals, because you don't really hear the gate in action. But something like drums, which arrive more suddenly, require the gate to open instantly, so need a fast attack setting.

The third control is release, which determines how long the gate will remain open after a sound is allowed through. The release control is there to accommodate sounds with long ambient trails – for example a vocal may have some reverb on it, and that reverb effect (which adds a sense of space to a vocal) may actually be quieter than the threshold, but we don't want the gate to cut it off. So we use the release setting to hold the gate open, for perhaps a second or so, after the vocal sound falls back below the threshold.

The most obvious use of a gate is to cut down unwanted background noise. In pre-digital recording studios, the inherent background noise generated by audio tape would be a bit of an issue.

Gates would be used, among other reasons, to completely close the sound from tracks when there was no music signal present. So, for example, if you had a backing vocal that only occurred every few bars, that track could be automatically turned on and off to remove the tape noise between bursts of activity.

To set up a gate as a simple noise remover, set the threshold quite low (maybe –48dB), with a fast attack. You can then set the release control appropriately for the source material.

The other popular use for gates is on drum kits. When you have as many as eight or even ten microphones on a drum kit at once, and you want to record each individual drum sound to its own track on a multi-track recorder, gates can help isolate each sound.

For example a mike on a tom would otherwise almost certainly pick up the sound of the snare drum – but with a very slight delay because it's further away than the actual snare mike. This could make a kit sound very messy.

By having a gate on each individual instrument signal, set with a relatively high threshold, each gate will only open when that particular instrument is hit. This prevents that mike from picking up other kit instruments.

This process has a happy by-product that can also be of value to the sampling musician. Because of its attack curve, a gate offers a particular type of control over the actual impact of a sound (and each model from each manufacturer can have a quite specific tonal character). Fast attack settings can add punch to drums; and the release setting can be used to add a kind of envelope to sounds with natural ambience trails, offering control over how long the ambience will linger before being cut.

Compression

Compression is one of those aspects of music production that's widely misunderstood, and often poorly used. It can be an incredibly useful production tool, but getting the desired result can be an elusive art. A compressor is essentially an automatic volume control. It measures the volume level of incoming sounds, and if they're too loud (according to how you've set it up), it turns them down.

A high-class compressor will have two level meters, one to measure the incoming level and another to measure the sound leaving the compressor. Machines with only one level meter usually have a switch that sets the meter to measure either incoming or outgoing levels. A top-quality compressor will also often have a third level meter, which displays the amount of gain reduction that's happening (so if the compressor is turning a sound down by 3dB, this meter will show 3dB). Lower-cost compressors may again use the same meter as the one showing incoming and outgoing levels, with a three-position switch to assign the meter to its different functions.

The most important control is (again) the threshold, which in this case is used to set up a maximum sound level. Any sound that's louder than the specified threshold level is reduced in volume, by an amount set by the next control, ratio. Ratio determines how much the level will be reduced by for each db it is over the threshold. A ratio of 1:1 will turn a sound down by one dB for each dB above the threshold it is – effectively silencing the above-threshold sound, an effect known as 'limiting'. A ratio of 2:1 means if the sound is 2dB above the threshold it will reduce its level by 1dB. And 5:1 will only reduce the level by 1dB if the sound is 5dB louder than the threshold.

Next there's an attack control. This sets how quickly the compressor will respond, and so how quickly the sound will be turned down once it exceeds the threshold. A small attack setting will cause a very rapid gain reduction. A larger attack setting will result in the sound being turned down more slowly, and therefore smoothly.

Next comes the release control. Once a sound level exceeds the threshold, the compressor continues to reduce the level for as long as the incoming sound exceeds that threshold. Once the sound drops back below the threshold, the release control determines how quickly the compressor ceases to reduce levels. A short release time allows the sound to flow freely almost immediately; a longer release time returns signal flow to normality much more gently.

More sophisticated compressors may have a couple more controls. The first is a 'soft-knee' control (sometimes called 'over-easy' in the US, after the version pioneered by the dbx company). This often simply takes the form of a switch, though some machines do feature soft-knee knobs. With standard 'hard-knee' compression, the threshold is a single specified level – the moment a sound level exceeds this point the compressor kicks into action. Soft-knee introduces a curve to the threshold, so the compressor starts to work fairly gently as sound levels approach the threshold and the full force of the compression doesn't kick in until slightly above it. The result is much smoother and less obvious to the listener.

The other control is a side-chain input. This is a clever little trick: it allows you to use a different sound altogether to cause the compressor to start to compress. This may seem an odd idea at first, but it can have its uses.

A perfect illustration is working with vocals in a mix. We usually want the vocal to sit nice and clearly, ever so slightly louder than everything else in a final mix, because the vocal usually carries the catchy bit of the music – the hook. But a composition where the vocal only appears for half a song may also contain a lead-type instrument that serves as the hook when the vocal is not present (a guitar playing a riff, perhaps). When the vocal is silent, this instrument may need to be louder, but when the vocal comes back in, the lead guitar, or whatever instrument it is, may need to be turned down again. If you feed that instrument signal through a compressor, then feed the vocal sound to the side-chain input on the compressor, the compressor can be set to automatically reduce the level of the instrument whenever the vocal happens.

So far so good… compressors are devices for adjusting the volume levels of sounds. But here is where the confusion kicks in, because the fact is that not all compressors sound the same, even using the same basic settings. For instance, with the 'knee' controls, most manufacturers have their own 'pre-set' curve – you don't have control over the shape of the curve, merely over whether you want to use it. Similarly with the attack: the time it takes for the gain reduction to kick in, and how rapidly it actually reduces the gain, are choices made in advance by the hardware/software manufacturer. Some compressors are also designed with a particular sound-controlling job in mind, and won't suit other applications.

The bottom line is that if you don't like the character of a specific compressor, or can't get it to perform perfectly for a specific task, you may well need a different one.

Different kinds of compressor

Getting to grips with compression is easier if you think about what you're trying to achieve. This largely depends on whether you're applying it to an individual sound or a whole mix.

Let's start by looking at an isolated bass sound. The different notes and harmonic elements of a bass sound (real or synthesised) are particularly susceptible to contradictions of perception versus actual volume – in other words some notes just naturally resonate more than others in certain circumstances, whether the player intended them to or not. You might also want bass passages played louder or softer to gel together, not to sound like they're different instruments, or suddenly become inaudible or disturbingly loud. By applying heavy compression to a bass sound, you can get that desired cohesion. All of the different frequencies and levels sound more like they are part of a single sound.

This form of compression often actually sounds better if you can hear the compressor in action. The sounds become squeezed together, but with an added sense of dynamic movement (even though the levels are more even) because you can actually hear the adjustments taking place – the sound of the compressor pushing and pulling the different frequencies, or 'pumping', as it's called.

If you examine a live vocal performance, a singer doesn't sing at the same volume all the way through a song. Really good vocalists will vary the tone and inevitably the volume of their performances during different parts of the song. A breathy, whispered passage will have a very different feel to a belted-out section – and the whispered passage will be much quieter (even if the singer's mike technique is excellent).

When it comes to a final mix you might well want to keep the different tonal character of each section, but have them at more or less even volume throughout. A compressor is ideal for this, as it will do a clinical job of identifying the volume of each phrase and adjusting the level accordingly. You may or may not want the compressor to interfere with the actual tone of the material – that's down to personal preference.

Compressing a whole mix uses the same technology to achieve its ends. An obvious illustration within dancefloor music is the 'breakdown', where you might strip away the drums and bass to leave string parts, percussion, secondary instruments and melodies etc to carry the track. These 'ambient' elements are normally quieter than the drums and bass, but you may well want them to be temporarily louder during the breakdown, to keep the energy of the track going – while still keeping the tone and relative volumes between themselves, as an ensemble of sounds.

Running the entire mix through a compressor, which reduces the general level of the track by a few dB, means that when the rhythm section drops (and the sound levels fall below the compression threshold), the ensemble of sounds for the breakdown rises by a few dB. When the rhythm section kicks back in, so does the compression, and our ambient ensemble instruments are returned to their correct relative levels.

When it comes to compression for mastering, you'll want the level adjustments to be as smooth and invisible as possible. You have after all spent a great deal of time and effort perfecting the tonal and dynamic characteristics of your mix, and don't want any pumping noises or obvious volume tweaks to distract the listener.

It helps avoid confusion if you think of compressors as *either* musical instruments *or* mastering tools. We expect a musical instrument, like a guitar or vintage synth, for example, to have a unique sound, depending on the make and model. But somehow many studio musicians fall into the trap of believing that one compressor is much like another, that because they have the same controls, the same functionality, maybe even similar specifications on paper, they must have the same effect on a sound or a mix. And so they'll use their £100 guitar compressor to master their latest mix, and expect it to sound clean and smooth. *Not* a sensible idea…

As a rule, cheap compressors use cheap components (or simplistic computer code), which don't have the sophistication to be invisible. By their very nature they're likely to have a unique tonal character. If what you're trying to achieve is an artificial, chunky, crunchy sound, that sounds like it's been compressed into oblivion, you're better off buying a selection of cheap and cheerful guitar or bass guitar compressors, and simply experimenting to see which one happens to sound good to your ears. If you want a compressor for smooth, professional mastering, expect to pay handsomely for the required increase in quality.

Limiting

Depending on the attack, ratio settings etc, a standard compressor will allow sound levels to exceed the threshold momentarily. The level usually won't stay above the threshold for long before it's reduced again, and to the human ear the period of time involved is hardly noticeable. But with a limiter, or a compressor that can be set up to act as a limiter, absolutely no sound is allowed to exceed the threshold at any time. This kind of extreme compression

MASTERING

Mastering is what happens to a finished mix to optimise it for commercial release. When done well, it can make your track leap out of the speakers when played on the radio or in a club. For many aspiring producers, hearing the difference between a mix that's been well mastered and one that hasn't can be a bit of a revelatory shock to the system. And much of this effect is down to well-applied compression at the mastering stage. You simply cannot achieve the same result during the recording or mixing process – and it's all too easy to chase your tail trying to replicate the effect. This inevitably leaves you feeling that your own, un-mastered mixes just don't seem to have the same smooth power and impact as a commercial release. Experienced professional producers have always known where the boundaries lie, and that some aspects of the production are best left for the mastering engineer. Although state-of-the-art mastering technology, from people like Masselec and Focusrite, costs many thousands of pounds, you can now at least dabble in the process for yourself. With the aid of a computer and some relatively inexpensive software, home mastering has become a possibility, and is well worth exploring. Don't expect the same results as you'd get from a top mastering suite – you usually get what you pay for – but you can still make an appreciable difference to your mix.

can sound a bit harsh in action, but it can be handy, particularly with a digital recording system – like a sampler.

With an analog circuit, overloading sound levels tend to cause distortion – a little of which can be a beautiful thing, adding some punch and warmth to a sound. This is especially true of magnetic tape, which can sound wonderfully crunchy when over-saturated. With a digital recording system, an excessive sound level causes nasty, clicking distortion. There is nothing gradual or nice about digital distortion – overload the recording level (which is known as 'clipping') and you get an unpleasant, grating sound. Using a limiter ensures that this absolutely cannot happen. Even the sound of overdone compression is sometimes preferable to digital clipping.

You'll find that most compressors are described as being compressor/limiters. This is because almost all semi-pro or pro studio compressors will happily limit signals. Simply set a ratio setting of 1:1 and the compressor will usually limit incoming signals to the threshold level. Standalone limiters are actually quite rare things.

Expanders and enhancers

Just as a compressor can be used to reduce the dynamic range of a sound or sample – smoothing out peaks and troughs in level – an expander can be used to do the opposite. An expander *increases* the dynamic range, by making quiet signals quieter and loud signals louder.

Many people seem to confuse enhancers with expanders and/or compressors. What enhancers do is what it says on the box – they 'enhance' the sound, but the way they do it is often not specified, and even deliberately mysterious. It generally involves adding some 'sparkle' by boosting certain higher frequencies.

But enhancers are now much less popular than they used to be – interestingly it's one of the few hardware studio devices that hasn't been widely replicated as a plug-in for software systems. Perhaps one reason is the general improvement in audio fidelity brought about by low-cost digital recording, so there's less need now for that extra added sparkle. One thing that's certain about enhancers is that you don't want to apply one to the same material twice, because the over-boosted frequencies will become too prominent.

EFFECTS & SOUND PROCESSING

When it comes to transforming sounds and sculpting them into new forms, 'effects' are among the most important aspects of the sampling process.

An effect is just that – a processor that has an effect on the physical properties of a sound. Effects can help you turn one sound into a different sound, and, apart from anything else, they're probably the most fun aspects of music production. Proper use of effects can literally transform a dull and lifeless sound into something with sparkle, energy and bags of character.

Although there are hundreds of different variations on each theme, effects can be divided into a very small number of basic categories: delay, reverb, modulation and distortion.

Delay/echo

In an effects context, delay refers to the delayed repetition of a sound, and as such is closely related to echo, a natural phenomenon we are all aware of. It's the thing you hear when someone shouts in a canyon, or towards a mountain range – the sound of the voice bouncing off a distant surface and coming back again. The vital point is that, in nature, the reflective surface needs to be far enough away from the sound source to create a distinct echo – the closer the surfaces are, the quicker the sound reflections come back (and probably the more often too, as they bounce from one surface to another). These faster, more numerous repeats are too close together to be heard as individual echoes, and are known instead as reverberation, or reverb, which we'll come to in a moment.

The echo we use when processing samples emulates the natural phenomenon, as do some of the terms used to describe the different functions of an artificial delay/echo processor. Delay time (often abbreviated to 'delay') is the amount of time it takes for a sound to leave the sound source, bounce and arrive back, usually expressed in milliseconds (ms). A very short delay time (on a single repeat) can sound like a doubling-up of the signal.

The feedback control determines how many times the sound is heard to repeat. Multiple repeats, especially with a longish delay time, can add an atmospheric sense of space – as if you're in that canyon or on that mountainside. Multiple repeats can also be effectively used like loops, creating an extended rhythmic or melodic pattern.

Early echo units were like mini, multi-headed tape recorders, which would literally use revolving loops of magnetic tape to produce delay and repeat effects. The term 'echo' tends to be reserved now for retro-style 'slapback' echo effects – as used in 1950s rock'n'roll. Most studio and digital uses of the effect tend to adopt the term 'delay'.

Different types of delay unit include: standard mono delay; stereo delay – essentially two mono delays, one for each side of a stereo sound field; cross delay – which adds autopanning, or ping-ponging; and multi-tap delay – which can create a highly complex overlapping series of delays that each differ in delay time, feedback and level.

Using delay

Once of the most popular, if perhaps less obvious uses of delay is with drum sounds – creating rhythmic patterns from a single hit.

Try this for yourself… Set the delay time on a digital delay unit to 500ms and feed in a single kick drum sound. Provided there is a decent amount of feedback set, the kick drum will be repeated – another copy of the original kick drum sound will be played back by the delay every 500ms. If you have a kick drum occurring every 500ms (which is half a second), there will be 120 of them in a minute. That's 120bpm – a classic tempo in popular music, especially dance-oriented material, from soul to funk to disco to house.

If you repeat the trick, but this time play the open hi-hat exactly 250ms after the kick sound, you will hear the kick drum repeated, followed 250ms later by the hat, then a copy of the kick, then another hat… and hey presto, you've created the fundamentals of a standard dance rhythm, using nothing but a delay, a single kick drum and a single hi-hat sound.

Now to add a snare. The time interval between the second and fourth beat of the bar in our example is actually two beats, which is double the length of the interval between kick sounds. This is where you need another digital delay (we'll call it delay 2), with its delay time set to 1000ms, or one second.

So you repeat the first steps again, play a single kick sound into delay 1, then play the open hat sound into delay 1 just 250ms later. Exactly 250ms after that first open hat (incidentally right on top of the first kick drum repeat), you play the snare sound into delay 2. Because the delay time of delay 2 is set to double the interval between the kick drums repeating in delay

image **53**

1, it will be repeated at the right intervals to coincide with every other kick drum repeat, on beats two and four of the bar.

This is a bit of a long-winded way of making the point that all music is about mathematical relationships. By playing around with regular and irregular time intervals between sounds/notes, almost any rhythm can be created. So using multiple delay processors can produce incredibly intricate and complex musical relationships from just a single, very short sound source.

Software tape delay/echo

There are a number of software packages that offer tape delay emulation. Image 53 shows the Steinberg Karlette VST plug-in, which is a software approximation of a vintage tape echo unit (something like the old Watkins/WEM Copicat machine). It attempts to recreate the actual tone of magnetic tape – with all its muddy warmth, rather than sounding pristine and accurate like a digital delay system – but with far greater and more accurate control.

For instance it has delay time controls that synchronise the four different virtual playback heads to MIDI tempo, as well as providing individual level, pan and feedback controls. This makes it far more controllable and versatile than a true tape echo – although to some people the sound is not a match for the real thing.

The incredible Spektral Delay plug-in by Native Instruments takes an innovative and unique approach. It allows you to divide the incoming audio into up to 128 different frequency bands, and lets you process each band separately – each band has its own controls for feedback, delay time etc. It's capable of producing rich, complex and fascinating textures, and is also very useful for applying delay to individual elements within a sample loop.

Reverb

Reverb is another natural phenomenon we are all very familiar with. As mentioned earlier, if reflected sounds bounce back from more than one surface, and/or the surfaces are relatively near you, the reflections you hear will be too numerous and close together to be heard as distinct individual echoes. These fast, multi-directional reverberations blend into an ambient aural environment that can be recreated by analog or digital reverb.

Everywhere we go there is reverb, whether we're aware of it or not. It helps give us a sense of the space we are in – how physically near objects and other people are to us. The only place reverb is totally absent is in a deliberately designed 'anechoic' chamber – a highly padded and acoustically deadened room where you can really appreciate how strange and artificial even voices and handclaps sound when there is genuinely no reverb at all.

Different amounts and types of reverb can create instant, if

VINTAGE REVERBS

There are two types of vintage analog reverb that are worth a brief mention.

Spring reverb literally passes sound through a slightly loose spring within a circuit, and became popular in 1950s and 1960s guitar amplifiers. Because of the length (up to a couple of feet) and wobbly nature of the spring, the sound is altered as it passes through and comes out the other side covered in something that sounds a bit like reverb. Spring reverb tends to be metallic in tone, have a very bright high-frequency response, and no controls other than Amount, which in reality means wet/dry mix. It's an interesting texture, but one you're unlikely to meet in the real world. For studio use, you might come across a retro-style hardware reconstruction, or perhaps a digitally modelled software version.

Plate reverb performs the same trick by passing the sound through a large, thin metal plate. The plate is suspended in a soundproof chamber, where a sound is passed through it and back into the air again from its edges, where it's picked up by one or more microphones. There's often a damping pad that can be physically pressed onto the plate to cut down the amount of reverberation. They actually sound very smooth and warm in action and are still in use in some studios.

almost subliminal, aural environments for a listener – you can make someone think they're outdoors, in the street, in a cave, in the bath, in a claustrophobic cupboard, or wherever you wish.

In your average room there are literally hundreds of different surfaces for sound to bounce off – so any sound we make or hear is not only travelling from the source directly to our ears, but we're also hearing hundreds if not thousands of little reflected 'partial' echoes as the sound bounces off the furniture, walls etc. Sound reflects off different types of surfaces differently, depending on their size, shape and consistency: for example a thick, heavy fabric curtain will absorb more of the high frequency elements of a sound. That's why a large room with a concrete floor, or metal roof, or ceramic tiles, will sound very different from a small, carpeted, curtained bedroom.

Architects have known for centuries about the acoustic properties of certain types of construction. Religious buildings, in particular, as well as being physically imposing edifices, have often been perfect for amplifying the volume and tone of the human voice, to give it added perceived power and depth, largely thanks to all that lovely natural reverb. The voice of a preacher in a well designed building sounds like it's all around you – as if it might even be coming directly to your ears from your chosen deity.

Sadly, it's also true that bad building design and construction can wreak havoc with musical acoustics – as I'm sure we've all experienced in certain music venues…

Artificially created reverb is used for two reasons: either to ensure that things sound natural, or else to give sounds an added sense of depth, space, drama and power. It might well be that the big, cavernous reverberant sound is what you're after – the only problem with getting it from real environmental sources is simply that you have less control over it. That's why it's often preferable to work in an acoustically dampened space, and then add the reverb you want at the processing stage.

Reverb is in fact a very complex sonic area, far more so than most people realise. Many elements combine to create the overall effect that reverb can have on a sound.

Room size, shape and 'colour'

The size of a room (whether real or 'virtual') is one of the most important factors. A very small room will produce very short 'early reflections' and lots of secondary bouncing around of the sound, but only for a relatively short period of time. A much larger space will possibly take longer to produce those early reflections and allow much more space for reflections to bounce around in.

The basic rule of thumb is: large rooms (and hard surfaces) increase the length of time the reverberations last for – ie the 'decay time'; small rooms (and soft surfaces) reduce the reverb decay time.

A sound will also bounce off a flat surface differently from the way it will bounce off a curved or angled surface, so it's logical that

EARLY REFLECTIONS

There's a time delay between a sound leaving its source and hitting various surfaces. It will obviously hit the nearest surfaces first and then each of the others in turn. As it hits the closest large surfaces and bounces back, it produces a fairly clear and defined set of reflections, known as 'early reflections'. After this, the sound bounces back and forth between the surfaces and the reflections become less defined as they overlap and blend with each other.
Only some of the more expensive reverb processors offer an editable 'Early Ref' parameter, which might have two controls: Number, which allows you to select how many distinguishable first reflections you hear; and Time, which determines how long it takes for the first one to arrive.

DIFFUSION

Diffusion is where sound reflections are no longer distinct and clean, but merged together in a complex build-up of reverberations. A diffusion control on a reverb processor lets you set a level for this. For instance, a large, hard-surfaced, square-shaped room would produce clearly defined reverb reflections – this would be called low diffusion. In a small, multi-sided room, or one filled with irregularly-shaped objects and a mixture of textures, diffusion will be higher, as reflections overlap, interfere with each other, and are re-reflected as they decay.

DECAY

In a very large space, especially one with hard surfaces, a sound can spend quite a long time bouncing back and forth, before it finally dies away to silence. With most reverbs you are provided with a decay control that lets you specify the time it takes for the reverb to fade to nothing – the longer the decay time, the bigger the imaginary space you're creating.

PREDELAY

In larger rooms there can be a short but noticeable delay between the sound occurring and the reverb being produced. A pre-delay control on a reverb unit allows you to set this time in ms. This can be useful with vocals, for example, so a vocal line can be delivered cleanly before the reverb kicks in, which helps avoid the lack of clarity that heavy reverb can sometimes bring; or in rhythmic material, for keeping drumbeats sharp and tight.

REVERB TIMING

It's a good idea to adjust all the different time-based aspects of reverb so that each matches the tempo, or at least a subdivision of a single beat of the music – eg to one 16th of a beat. (The formula for calculating tempo is in Chapter 4.) It's a subtle thing, but having predelay, early reflections, decay time etc all occurring in time with your music can make the reverb blend with the rest of the sounds and help to draw them all together into a coherent form. Reverb whose timings are all wrong can cloud a mix.

different shaped rooms will produce different reverb characteristics. Flat surfaces, and particularly right-angled corners, tend to deliver much more clearly defined reflections – which is normally not what you'd want in a professional sound studio, which should be more neutral. Rounded and irregularly-shaped rooms tend to produce softer sonic characteristics with less reverb definition.

It's also acknowledged that large, hard-surfaced rooms can produce a harsh sound in the higher frequencies; on the other hand soft furnishings will soak up high-pitched sounds more than low-frequency ones. What a room is made of can have a big impact on reverb characteristics, and how different frequencies respond. This is often referred to as the 'colour' of a reverb.

So for instance hard, flat surfaces reflect more sound in general than soft curved ones, and different fabric and wallcovering materials reflect different kinds of sound more readily. It's also possible to use combinations of materials within certain construction methods that will selectively damp either low or high frequency reflections. On reverb processors that provide damping facilities, you'll often find separate low and high damping controls.

In general, if you mix and match size, shape, colour and damping, as well as diffusion, predelay and decay, you can create an almost infinite, and sometimes unpredictable, variety of reverb effects. Getting the right reverb sound is down to practice, and knowing that each of the different controls affects a different aspect of the finished result. So for instance if you want a very bright, well defined reverb with strong high-frequency response, no low-frequency response, a clear definition of timing and a relatively short decay time – just what you might want on a snare drum, for example – you need to set your reverb to emulate a small, square/rectangular, hard surfaced (perhaps tiled) room, with zero high-frequency damping, some low-frequency damping, and strong early reflections. And so on...

Modulation effects

In songwriting terms, modulation usually means changing key, but in a music technology context it just refers to performing a change in general. With regards to effects, it specifically means adjusting the pitch and/or volume of a delayed signal.

There are three main studio effects grouped together under the heading of modulation: chorus, flanging, and phase-shifting. Others include vibrato (where the pitch fluctuates slightly back and forth), tremolo (where the volume fluctuates rapidly), and wah-wah, but those are perhaps most relevant to electric guitar players.

Chorus

Chorus was in the past referred to as 'ensemble', because it's meant to produce the effect of more than one person playing together – it's often used to create a fuller effect on a vocal or any lead line. Chorus works by introducing a slightly delayed copy of the original signal and detuning it subtly. It does so by applying an LFO to the pitch setting of the extra copy, directing small but rapid rises and falls in pitch. A stereo chorus will usually create two copies of the incoming sound, one for each stereo channel, and provide a complete set of independent controls for each side. The controls for a chorus are as follows:

● Shape – lets you change the shape of the LFO waveform (for instance sawtooth, square, triangle or sine wave), which in turn alters the way the effect is manipulated. A curvy sine wave, for example, would trigger the effect more evenly and smoothly than a sawtooth wave would. The choice would depend on the effect you want to achieve.

● Rate/speed – this sets the speed at which the LFO oscillates, which controls how rapidly the pitch is made to rise and fall.

● Depth – with most choruses this controls the maximum amount by which the pitch can rise and fall.

● Stages – some chorus units provide this setting to create several additional copies of the sound (slightly incrementally delayed). It's usually a case of choosing between one or more extra copies.

● Feedback – the output of the second copy of your sound can be fed back into the input stage of the chorus, making for a more intense and complex effect. This control adjusts the amount that is fed back.

Flanger

Originally developed by allowing two tape machines playing the same piece of music to run back and forth out of synch with each other, but a flanging effect can also be recreated electronically, again by modulating a delayed signal.

This time the delay is not only short, it's constantly fluctuating, going in and out of time with the original signal. This also results in irregular pitch wobbles as the delayed signal tries to compensate for the insistent speeding up and slowing down.

The controls commonly found on a flanger are:

● Depth – can either refer to the amount of the modulated signal mixed into the original dry version, or to the range or 'sweep' of the modulation.

● Speed – adjusts the timing of the modulation.

● Shape – controls the shape of the LFO waveform.

● Feedback – the amount of the modulated signal that's recycled back into the flanger input stage.

Phaser

An electronic phaser artificially replicates phase-shifting and phase-cancellation. Again it creates a delayed copy of an incoming sound, which it shifts back and forth out of phase with the original signal, cancelling out various harmonics as it does so. In many phasers the copied sound is passed through a filter before being added to the

PHASE CANCELLATION

Playing two copies of exactly the same sound at exactly the same time would double the amplitude of its waveform (the height of the peaks and troughs on a graph). But if one copy is delayed by exactly half a cycle (so it still crosses the X axis at the same points), something very different happens. You'd be adding negative versions of the same values to the original wave's values, and they'd cancel each other out.

In a studio, if you take two microphones and point them at the same sound source, but place them slightly apart, you create the possibility of introducing a delay between the sound reaching one mike and the other. If the distance between the two mikes happens to be just right (or rather wrong), you may create a situation where the two halves of the wave cycle are exact opposites. The result would be silence – total phase cancellation.

In fact it's very rare to get complete silence, but it's reasonably common to get one copy of the sound delayed by *almost* half a cycle. When this happens, *some* parts of the sound may be cancelled out. Some frequencies will vanish, and the combined sound of the two will be less full than even one on its own. This is called 'out of phase'. One way around this in a recording situation is to artificially 'reverse' the phase of one mike by delaying it slightly using a phase-reverse switch on a mixing console or preamplifier.

What a phaser effect unit does is exploit this same phenomenon to create an interesting, phase-shifting sound effect.

original, so that only part of the frequency spectrum is subject to phasing. With a stereo phaser, each side of the stereo image can be manipulated independently. The controls commonly found on a phaser are:

- Depth – used for adjusting either the amount, range or sweep of the modulation.
- Speed/rate – adjusts how quickly the phase effect moves through the frequency range.
- Feedback – feeds the output of the phased copy back to the input stage.

Guitar effects

Guitarists have been using effects processors of all kinds to transform the sound of their instruments for nearly 50 years. So it should come as no surprise to find that there are truly huge numbers of dedicated guitar effects units out there. How is this of relevance to the sampling musician? Well, the fact is that guitar processors include all the types of effect I've mentioned so far, and more besides, but they do it in their own sweet way – which just might add a new twist or edge to a particular sample.

One crucial difference between a guitar effects unit and a studio processor is that guitar effects tend to be designed from the ground up to completely transform the incoming sound beyond recognition, and make it more exciting. This trait makes them an intriguing proposition for sampling musicians faced with an ordinary-sounding sample, or a limited budget and equipment set-up.

DISTORTION & OVERDRIVE

Although the dictionary definition of distortion as 'deviation from natural shape' might essentially cover more or less all effects, it's specifically used to describe the kind of gritty, hard-edged 'roughing up' of sounds associated with electric guitar technology.
Most distortion-type processors model the characteristics of loud tube amplifiers fed through speaker cabinets. When you overload a valve amplifier, the first thing that happens is a little gentle compression; as you increase the proportion of overload the sound begins to break up, until the original signal becomes lost amid the grit and debris. The difference between the various subdivisions of distortion – from mild, warm, bluesy, slightly gritty 'overdrive' to full-on, screaming, metallic, headbanging 'fuzz' – will vary from one manufacturer to another. The more sophisticated units offer a greater degree of control over tone, as well as sheer dirt; some even allow individual adjustments of three or four different frequency ranges within the sound for extra versatility.

At the low-cost end of the market there are dozens of little 'stompboxes' – small hardware units designed to sit on the floor for easy foot activation. These usually have a few knobs for adjusting settings and tend to restrict themselves to one or maybe two effects per unit. There are dozens of different models available, most of which offer distinctive versions of the kind of effect types covered already.

Further up the price chain you can now choose to buy a high-quality 'boutique' pedal, usually handmade with superior components, often in a retro style, and sometimes with considerable accompanying hype.

Or you might prefer the convenience and versatility of a multi-effects system, offering several individual effects within a single unit, which you can mix and match at will. (It must be said, though, that such 'multi-FX' units have somewhat fallen out of favour among guitarists since their heyday in the early-1990s, as the trend for specialised one-off 'standalone' effects pedals has gradually returned.)

The drawbacks, especially with cheaper guitar effects, is simply that they're often rather rough-and-ready, not built to exacting studio specifications, and usually designed for live use – which means, crucially, they might be noisy, and probably won't slot neatly into a rack unit.

Bearing in mind that studio musicians already have access to very similar, and probably better quality, effect types through their own specialised hardware and software systems, the one development that might be of most interest from the guitar world is the digital modelling systems. Many sought-after guitar sounds are emulated this way, combining specific guitar amplifiers with specific speaker cabinets, with perhaps a modest dusting of classic effects.

As with analog synth models, the presentation (and effectiveness) of such systems is diverse. There are quite a number of mid-priced, mostly hardware-based systems available offering very impressive collections of preset classic sounds. You turn a knob to choose a basic sound and then use a small collection of controls to tweak it to taste. At the high end of the market are some very sophisticated packages that can be hardware or software based. Some of these offer large selections of impressive-sounding gear emulations for you to mix and match.

SAMPLING & SYNTHESIS

As we've seen, when it comes to processing samples you can employ a mixture of traditional studio-based or instrument effects, and also make use of tools drawn from the world of synthesisers, such as LFOs, filters and envelopes. But there are lots of other synthesis tools that can add new dimensions to your samples, and the best place to find them is in a computer-based set-up using a modular sampling & synthesis system.

The twin paths of sampling and synthesis have run side-by-side for many years. In fact, even though the tape-loop-using experimental musicians of the 1950s and 1960s would rightly point to their creative influence, the technological development of sampling as we know it today actually came about as part of the evolution of synthesisers.

Synthesis is all about processing raw materials, and synthesiser designers initially developed sampling as a means of delivering more versatile and convincing raw materials than oscillators could provide – at least as soon as processing power and storage capacity made samples of more than half-a-second possible.

When using sampled sounds as the basic building blocks (instead of oscillators), the application of synthesis tools, EQ and effects tends to produce uniquely dense and charismatic sonic textures. It also involves a certain amount of retained rhythmic inspiration, which can lead to exciting new artificial rhythmic forms.

Ironically, although the original intent may have been to create more 'naturalistic' results by using samples as raw materials for synthesisers, it soon became obvious that sampling could do that by itself, and all synthesisers tended to do was turn perfectly convincing samples into weird noises. Hence a parting of the ways…

The fact is, not everybody wants realistic emulations of traditional instruments. An alternative, experimental musical school of thought has always sought interesting new sound forms to work with, where the more abstract, weird and wonderful they are the better. That's where sampling & synthesis (S&S) comes into its own.

Modular S&S

In some ways modular sampling & synthesis systems are the state-of-the-art. They exist only as software applications, but that doesn't mean all software samplers are modular. Most are not. Most software samplers are essentially emulations, or clones, of hardware sampling systems: they improve on the functionality and ease-of-use of hardware systems but still operate within similar confines to hardware. This is because they're pre-configured into a single more-or-less fixed structure. Modular systems, on the other hand, give the end user all of the same components, but in the form of a pile of building blocks (or modules, hence the name) for the user to put together in any structure they please. Modular systems can be re-assembled in a potentially infinite number of different ways.

There a number of modular S&S systems available, of varying size and quality, including some notably excellent ones from manufacturers like Clavia and Creamware. But there is one clearly dominant modular S&S system, and that's Reaktor by Native Instruments – so I'm going to use that to illustrate what modular S&S is all about.

Reaktor offers around 100 different tools covering every type of sound-shaping widget you can think of, and quite a few more you never dreamed were possible. It contains everything you might need to create experimental sample-based music, from the usual basic sample playback modules, to more complex and esoteric modules, synthesis elements, sequencers, effects and more. It's extremely well suited to those whose desire is true sonic pioneering, to explore intriguing soundscapes and to generally tinker a lot with pure abstracted sound. It's possible to make quite incredibly intricate, complex musical compositions and textures just using Reaktor – limited only by the power of your computer. Reaktor is, in short, unique.

But the very fact that Reaktor is ideal for experimental sound design means that for many potential users it would be the wrong platform to choose. Reaktor is best not viewed as a standalone sampler, but more as a synthesiser with some powerful sampling features. It doesn't use graphic sample key-mapping, layering, crossfading, and all the other traditional features that make other soft samplers so great for creating multisamples. In fact, trying to set up a standard multisample instrument is considerably more difficult with Reaktor than with most of the other samplers mentioned in this book – even hardware systems. It's not best suited to those who are deeply into chopping up breakbeats, because it doesn't really integrate any beat-slicing facilities, and has no graphic waveform editing. Most people find it's not ideal as a drum sampler either.

Native Instruments have acknowledged Reaktor's steep learning curve in several ways: with a comprehensive set of ready-made instrument constructions that ship with the application, plus a playback module called Dynamo, and crucially some streamlined, user-friendly sampler systems based on the same technology, including: Battery, a drum machine-style sampler; Intakt, dedicated to beat slicing and breakbeat-style sampling; and Kontakt, which sits firmly between the two worlds of traditional sampling and Reaktor.

Using Reaktor

The thing about working with Reaktor is that it's easy enough as long as you have a clear understanding of how synthesisers work, and exactly what you're trying to achieve.

Reaktor has two different main edit screens: one where you actually build or adapt S&S structures and another that represents those structures with virtual knobs, faders etc.

REAKTOR AND INSTRUMENT MODELLING

All the modular S&S systems on the market use similar basic principles and offer fairly similar facilities, albeit in varying quantity. The synthesis side of the operation uses instrument modelling. Software-based synthesis modelling is based on some very complex mathematics, which needs to be done very fast to make the system 'realtime' enough for musicians. The maths needs so much processing power that, when the technology of instrument modelling first emerged, computers just weren't up to the job. The way around the problem for early developers was to add dedicated hardware rammed full of processors that could be used alongside the computer's own processing power to lighten the load.

Clavia got there first with the Nord, which devoted all the power of the most powerful computers around (at the time) just to building instrument structures. Once constructed, the instruments are downloaded into the hardware for playback and MIDI sequencing. Creamware represents the next generation, because their chosen way is to add PCI cards to computers with the extra processing hardware – as does SampleCell within Digidesign's Pro Tools.

Reaktor was essentially the first really good quality S&S system in the shops that didn't need additional hardware. Reaktor relies entirely on the power of the host computer. This makes it much more affordable, and for musicians that's usually enough to make a product a clear winner. The fact that it's since evolved into a massive monster, with a very impressive and individual sound, obviously helps a lot too. Reaktor is also so well suited to experimental sound creation that an ever-expanding community of producers has grown up around it over the last few years. There's a thriving online forum, hosted within the Native Instruments website, that shares tips and technique and contributes to a vast library of user-constructed instruments.

You start with a blank canvas. Pull-down menus present you with a massive selection of different 'modules' – seven different types of sample playback module, a comprehensive range of oscillators covering more or less every known method of synthesis, amplifiers, filters, frequency dividers, sound shapers, randomisers, envelope generators of various types, MIDI inputs and outputs, LFO generators, effects, sequencers, mixers, output routers, etc etc.

Select a module, drop it into your structure, and it appears as a block onscreen. When you have several modules onscreen you drag virtual patch cables between them to 'connect' them together. Sounds simple enough… but unless you actually know how to create a logical sampling & synthesis structure – with a sound source, an amplifier and an output stage – you'll get no results at all. In the same way, if you don't include a MIDI input module, your structure won't respond to MIDI, and so on…

Luckily Reaktor comes equipped with a large selection of preset structures of varying complexity, and most users seem to start here simply because it saves time and reduces that learning curve. For many users Reaktor is the ultimate learning tool for this reason: by starting with a fully functioning structure and disassembling it, adapting it, finding out which bits are doing what and just messing about, you can learn how the system works.

Reaktor sets out its stall to be a single working environment offering every type of sampling and synthesis tool you can think of. Once you grasp the possibilities and the working methods, the potential really is endless.

There are a number of excellent books on synthesis tools and techniques – including some particularly good ones by Jim Aikin published by Backbeat Books. I obviously can't do the subject justice in the space I have here, but I can mention a few S&S techniques that are particularly relevant to sampling.

Wavesequencing

A standard sampler uses a single sample (or a few samples layered on top of each other) played from start to finish, or perhaps looped, to form a single MIDI-responsive sound. Wavesequencing, pioneered by Korg in around 1990, uses a series of dozens, if not hundreds, of short samples played back in a sequence that's triggered each time you hit a note. Each individual sample within the sequence can have independent level settings, and you can set up crossfades between each one. A subsection of the sequence can also be looped and playback started from different points within the sequence.

Korg's original Wavestation synth employed a second technique that was revolutionary in its day, namely vector synthesis. Vector synthesis takes a single wavesequence and feeds it through a standard filter, amplifier and envelope generator combination, with two associated LFOs, and calls this a 'voice'. You can then combine four voices to form a single

---

REAKTOR VS ANALOG MODULAR SYNTHS

Very early analog synthesisers were made up of several different sound-processing units, or modules, which could be 'patched' together in any permutation using short cables, or patch leads – hence the persistent use of the word 'patch' to describe a sound on a synth. The more modules and patch leads involved, the more elaborate and complex – and often unrepeatable – the results. There was no way of saving or storing the sounds you made, other than recording them on audio tape, so you had to try and remember all the connections if you wanted to recreate them. It was also possible to create some horrific noises by accidentally making ill-advised patches…

One of the ways Reaktor differs from a 'proper' analog modular is that it won't let you make wrong connections. It knows you don't use envelopes as oscillators, for instance, so it won't let you connect the 'virtual' patch cable between two incompatible devices. You maybe miss the sheer insanity of totally miswiring a modular synth, perhaps producing a unique and wonderful sound by chance, but at least you know your creative endeavours on Reaktor will achieve usable results.

'performance'. The Wavestation allowed you to assign each of the four voices within a performance to the left, right, top and bottom positions of its joystick. Anywhere in-between gets a proportional mix of the four voices. You can use the same system to apply modulation sources to the four voices. As well as manipulating the joystick in realtime you can also sequence four different stick positions and set the time it takes to smoothly fade from one point to the next.

The combination of wavesequencing and vector synthesis makes for a dense and musically dynamic instrument with a unique sound. Unfortunately, despite the recent re-working of the system for the Korg Wavestation Legacy, it's not yet possible to use your own samples within wavesequences. (Reaktor could possibly replicate something similar using its modular synthesis system – if your maths is up to the task...)

Granular synthesis

Granular synthesis takes a slightly different approach to sampling. Whereas a standard sampler chops sound up into slices, analyses what's in each slice, stores the information and then plays each slice in turn during playback, granular synthesis breaks sound down into much tinier audio fragments, or 'grains', usually between 10ms and 50ms in length. Granular synths tend to offer independent control of individual grain pitch and length, and even density control (ie how many grains are present in a given length of time) and 'sharpness' of each grain. Randomisers are a common feature, as well as the usual filters etc.

Granular synthesis is very much an experimental process. There are few commercial applications using the system, and most of the software devices that adopt it are the work of independent, experimental synth designers, each with their own approach to the technique.

There is definitely a distinctly recognisable tone to sounds produced by granular systems – some would say a unique weirdness – which is probably to do with that independent control over individual grain pitch and length. But the best way to judge granular synthesis is, as usual, to try it for yourself – assuming you can get access to it.

Just about the only mainstream commercial products to blatantly employ granular synthesis are Reaktor and Kontakt, both from Native Instruments. Reaktor has a granular sample playback module, while Kontakt actually has two – the Time Machine (offering knobs labelled Tune, Smooth, Speed and Grain), and the Tone Machine (offering Tune, Smooth, Speed and Formant). A couple of good illustrations of freeware granular synthesisers are 'Granulator', available at www.nicolasfournel.com/granulator.htm, and Crusher X, available at www.crusher-x.de. Personally I prefer Crusher X, which I find more pleasant and musical – you might disagree. In any case, try them and get a taste of how random and experimental granular synthesis seems to be, so far at least. As time passes and the process evolves, perhaps it will become a little more predictable.

Resampling

In a computer-based system, every effect or plug-in you use consumes processing power. But instead of continuously loading more effects on top of the original sample (known as 'online' processing), you can make a fresh recording of a sample with the sound of the effects permanently in place ('offline'), after which you can switch off the various plug-ins, use the new 'processed' version of the sample in place of the original dry version, and so free up vital computer power for use elsewhere. This process is called resampling.

For example, let's say you have a drum break loaded into your sampler, being triggered via MIDI and playing back through an audio+MIDI sequencer. You've then loaded up a reverb plug-in, employed some EQ, added a compressor and a stereo expander – all as insert effects within the channel mixer of your sequencer. All these things are being used solely for your drum sample, and it sounds great.

This might be repeated on other sounds in a busy composition, until you find when it comes to mixdown that you've run out of computer power – and you still desperately need another reverb for a vocal part. But what you can do is resample that drum break, with all the effects in place. So now that the reverb is no longer being used on the drum sample's channel (the drum sound already incorporates it), it becomes available to use on the vocal.

There are broadly three different ways resampling might be done, depending on your own combination of equipment. The first, using on-board effects within a hardware sampler set-up, is usually very straightforward. Because the effects processors are already within the sampler, you simply set up the effects as you like them and use the Resample command (check the manual for its location).

If you want to use an external effects processor, things are done a little differently, although you'll find that most hardware samplers are able to play back samples and record new ones at the same time, or have a facility that enables you to resample routing the sample via an external processor.

With software samplers, or in an audio+MIDI sequencing environment, it get slightly more complex. Most software samplers are designed as sample playback devices rather than actual samplers – they're designed to load and play back samples that have been recorded or created elsewhere. So when it comes to resampling (just the same as creating fresh samples), you'll need to employ your audio+MIDI sequencer. There are two methods here:

● 1: If you want to resample a sample through an external effects processor (via a hardware mixing console etc), you'll need to actually re-record the sound using the standard audio recording facilities within your audio+MIDI sequencer. You set up sample playback, with the effects as desired, set up an audio channel to record to, ensure that you've routed the newly effected sound to the audio input of your interface, test playback to set proper input levels, follow all proper recording procedures… and hit Record.

● 2: To resample using onboard effects within your software sampler or in your audio+MIDI sequencer, it's a little easier. Set up playback and effects as desired; consult your manual to find the Export Audio Mixdown (Cubase) or Bounce (Logic) or equivalent within your system, and use it. This creates an audio file that's saved to disk. You can then either import this new file into your sampler, if you wish to manipulate it further, or simply use it as an audio file playing back on a track in the usual manner.

With most audio+MIDI sequencers (as with a hardware mixer) it's important you remember to mute all other audio tracks, software instruments or incoming audio signals before you proceed, because the operation is designed to capture anything that's set to play back when the function is employed. You only want to capture the intended sound, not any extraneous sounds or noise.

ONLINE/OFFLINE

Using an effect running in realtime is known as 'online' processing; using a pre-applied effect is known as 'offline' processing. A comparison might be made with a factory production line putting together cars. All the bits are made elsewhere (the engine, bodywork, wheels etc) and brought to the production line in manageable units ready to fit together. If every single component of a car was actually constructed on just the one production line, the line would be very long and the car would take ten times as long to make. Building each self-contained chunk offline means that the main online construction process is quicker and simpler – and in a computer sequencing context, less draining on the CPU.

It's also important to note the position of the playback locators/markers, because only events occurring between the left and right locators will be included in the final mixdown. This is handy when resampling, as it's the way to limit the new file to the desired length (eg a single bar). If you want to resample an entire song-length piece of audio, you'll need to place the locators at the very beginning and end of the song.

Problems when resampling with effects

There are two troublesome issues concerning resampling when using effects like delay or reverb, and they relate to the beginning and the end of the finished result.

When sound is passed through an effects unit, the processor takes a short period of time to calculate the effects and produce the result… so the first few tiny moments at the beginning of the sound remain dry (without effects in place). This is usually not too much of a problem when using effects in realtime, because those first few moments will pass very quickly, will sound fairly natural and probably go un-noticed. If you are resampling very long sections of music (like whole passages of vocal) with the intention of simply using your resampled material as though it's playing back from a multi-track recording, the same rule applies. But if you want to loop the resampled material, it can cause problems.

And unless you're using a hardware sampler set to Sample In Place (see box), you'll probably find that when you resample through effects like delay or reverb, these effects create echoes or reverberations that continue beyond the original sample for a period of time. Having these effect 'tails' in place is a desirable thing in many circumstances, but it can cause trouble if you want to loop your resampled version.

The best way to explain the solutions to these two problems is to demonstrate with an audio illustration that addresses them both.

● **Step 1:** CD1 Track 54 is a sample of a turntablist scratching (it's from CD2, the Zero-G sample CD, and called Okay_Scratch_107bpm). I used this to create the four-bar sample you can hear on Track 55. Although the original sample is long enough to use as a two-bar loop, I've intentionally used only the first two beats or so of it and left the short gap you can hear. This was done by using a four-bar long MIDI sequence containing notes that are only about two beats long to trigger it.

The original sample (which is dry) has an inherent tempo of 107bpm, and the sequencer I used to create Track 55 was also running at this tempo. Extract the audio from Track 55, load it into your sampler and place it into a sampler instrument ready for MIDI sequencing. Set your sequencer to 107bpm and create a simple four-bar MIDI sequence (containing a single note that's four bars long) which triggers the sample to play back at the correct speed etc. If you now 'cycle' playback on your sequencer around the four-bar sequence you've just created, you should hear the sample loop playing with regularly spaced short silences.

● **Step 2:** Now set up a simple stereo delay in a way that means the sample will be passed through the delay and is available for resampling (eg using an effects insert or effects send).

SAMPLE IN PLACE

Some samplers offer an option to either 'Sample In Place', which usually erases the original sample and replaces it with the new resampled version, or 'Create New Sample', where you give the new version a different name. With almost all onboard resample functions, the default setting is Create New Sample.

If you're resampling through an effect like delay or reverb, these effects create echoes or reverberations that continue beyond the original sample. The Create New Sample setting usually includes these additional echoes etc in the resampled version, so produces a fresh sample that is longer than the original; Resample In Place limits the length of the new sample to that of the original sample, and so can't include additional echoes or reverb tails.

This means Resample In Place is sometimes a useful alternative to Create New Sample in circumstances where you want to use the resulting fresh sample as a loop.

I've tempo-synchronised the delay and set the left channel to 1/4 and the right channel to 1/8. If your delay effect doesn't have a tempo synchronisation feature, then setting the left channel delay time to 561ms and the right delay time to 280ms should deliver similar results. These delay times are worked out based on the tempo of the sample (60 divided by the tempo of your music will give you the duration of a single beat, so 60/107 = 0.5607s). Stop playback of the sequencer and you should hear the sound of the echoes continue after the sample has stopped playing. What happens next is different for software and hardware systems.

● **Step 3 (hardware users):** If you're using a hardware sampler with an onboard effects unit, use your MIDI sequencer to trigger the sample while you try out your delay settings, and then use the onboard resample function.

If your hardware sampler doesn't have onboard effects or a resample function, you can still achieve similar results by using an external effects processor and either sampling the results in realtime (if your sampler can play back and record samples simultaneously), or by recording the results to an external recorder and sampling the resulting recording.

● **Step 3 (software users):** Ensure your locators/markers are placed at the beginning and end of your four-bar MIDI sequence – to ensure you do actually capture the right section, and to limit the length of your resampled version to four bars – and perform an export or audio mixdown (the name and process varies depending on your system).

● **Step 4 (all users):** The result should sound like CD1 Track 56... or at least the beginning of it should anyway – I'll come back to dealing with the end in a minute. Try loading your resampled version into a fresh sampler instrument and listening to the first four bars of it looped. You should clearly hear that there's a little drop at the beginning of the sample, every four bars, where there's a bit of silence and no echoes and it doesn't sound right. It sounds like Track 57.

● **Step 5:** The solution to the problem is to create a longer version and loop a portion of the sample that *does* have effects in place throughout. In the example that follows, this will actually be a second four-bar section.

If you're using a hardware sampler with onboard effects and a resample function, you'll need to double the length of the original sample by using the copy and paste functions: copy the entire sample, place the cursor at the end of the sample, and paste. This should attach a second four-bar copy to the original dry sample, creating a (dry) eight-bar version. Now when you resample with the effects in place you should get something that sounds like Track 58.

If you're using software or a hardware sampler without onboard effects, you'll need to create a longer MIDI sequence before proceeding. Copy your original four-bar MIDI sequence and place the copy immediately after the original on the same MIDI track, so you now have eight bars of continuous MIDI sequence.

Those using hardware samplers and external effects can now use this longer MIDI sequence to create a longer resampled version containing eight bars of sequenced sound, plus the tail of echoes. This sounds like CD1 Track 58.

Software users need to move the right locator after elongating the MIDI sequence. In this example, moving the right locator from 5.1.0 to 13.1.0 should be sufficient, extending the interval between locators to 12 bars rather than four. This should sound like Track 58.

Remember that it's the position of the locators that determines the length of the resampled version, not the MIDI sequence. If I had the feedback setting on the delay set to a much higher value, so the repeats of the echo continued for longer than four bars, I would have needed to set a greater time period between the locators to capture the extra repeats.

● **Step 6:** Once you have a fresh version of the sample containing eight bars of sequenced sound and then a tail of fading echoes (sounding like Track 58), you need to loop a section of the sample with effects in place throughout. In this example this will entail creating a loop with its start point at the beginning of bar 5 and its end point at the end of bar 8.

Instead of using an actual loop, you could simply have created a copy of the resampled version, and moved its start point to the beginning of bar 5 and its end point at the end of bar 8. This would give you a four-bar sample with effects in place throughout, and would sound like Track 59.

Listen closely to the way Track 59 starts. You can hear echoes that are actually repeats of the very end of the sample, and they occur at the same time as the very first moment of the source material. This is like managing to put the cart before the horse, and cannot be achieved without resampling sounds with effects in place.

In some contexts, having the sample start this way may be perfectly acceptable to you, but in others it may not. Using the eight-bar version and looping the second four bars gets around this, because it means when you play the sample it starts naturally without the echoes in place right at the beginning, and then loops the echoed section.

I can now tell you that you could also have gotten away with looping just a one-bar section, perhaps even just the second bar of the resampled version you hear in Track 56, and you would hear what you hear in Track 59. But this is only true because, for this illustration, I'm using a very simplistic, repetitive MIDI sequence. With a less repetitive sequence – where you have a longer musical passage with, for example, 64 bars of material that changes constantly – you may find the technique of extending the original version useful, as it can be used with passages of as many bars as you need.

● **Step 7:** We've looked at how to ensure you do actually capture the fading trail of echoes or reverberations generated by delay and reverb effects (or any other type of effect), regardless of the type of system you use. But if you want to use it in the context of making a piece of music, there may be a little more to be done. Track 58 is a sample that starts naturally, has eight bars of effected sound, then a trail of echoes – but what do you do if you want the sequenced and effected material to continue for much longer, like 12 bars or 32 bars or 128 bars, before ending with the echo tail?

You could cut Track 58 into three individual samples, place them into a sampler instrument and re-sequence the three samples to get the desired results. Or you can employ a couple of loops.

Using the techniques described in detail in 'Creating Sustained Sounds Using Loops' in Chapter 5, I set up two loops: the first is a 'sustain loop', with its start point at the beginning of bar 5 of Track 58 and its end point at the end of bar 8. This means that when the sample receives an appropriate MIDI note it will repeat the four-bar interval between bars 5 and 8 for as long as the MIDI note is held down. When the MIDI note transmits its note-off message, the sample plays on past the end of bar 8 and plays the tail of echoes.

In general, being able to resample a sound is obviously unbelievably useful when working with a limited or under-powered system (which most of us do). The disadvantage is of course that the changes are permanent – you can no longer 'undo' or switch off any of the effects you may have applied earlier. You have to be very sure that you are ready to resample, especially when the array of effects in use is quite large.

Many systems let you save effects presets, but it can still be tricky to get the combination of effects exactly right – not least because most musicians are too lazy and/or impatient to take adequate steps. Things like taking notes or keeping backups are alien concepts to many musicians, and sometimes not conducive to the kind of speed of creativity that often goes hand-in-hand with making good work. The key would be a good balance between trying to back up what you do, so that you can roll back to previous versions of samples, but not being scared to move forward.

It's certainly always worth saving a copy of the original clean sample before you resample, so you always have that at hand to re-use if necessary.

Resampling has spawned some interesting creative spin-offs. If you listen to drum & bass and some other breaks-based music you might be able to spot the sound of resampled samples with effects in place, which will often have been cut up and re-arranged. In this context all pretence at natural-sounding effects is often abandoned, and the apparent impossibility of the resulting sounds is part of the whole point.

AUDIO ILLUSTRATIONS – USING FILTERS, EQ, ENVELOPES AND EFFECTS ON SAMPLES

To end this mammoth chapter on customising sounds, a few examples of some of the sample-manipulating techniques and tools we've looked at throughout the book so far.

Just like in the real world, where the various sound manipulations are rarely performed in isolation, they've been grouped here in likely scenarios, to give a feel for the way they might work together – and to show just how effective they can be. You can also follow these processes in audio form by listening to the relevant tracks on CD1.

Creating a string part using sustain loop, envelope, and effects

The end result of combining these three processes is the simple but atmospheric string 'pad' on CD1 Track 15. The melody is intentionally simple, because it's just for illustration, but I've made sure the part incorporates notes across a four-octave range so you can hear how different note ranges are affected by various aspects of the process.

The underlying point here is: how do you create the sound in Track 15 from the brief sample in Track 16. And yes, Track 16 really is that short... You'd be forgiven for missing it – it's a tiny little blip of sound – but that's all the raw material I was using.

If you open Track 16 in a waveform editor you will see (as illustrated in image 53), that it is indeed a very short sample, a mere 8ms long, to be exact. It's taken from the Roland Juno 6 again, and contains just two cycles of a fairly pure analog waveform.

In fact what I'm doing in this example only works with samples where the sound is of a relatively pure, repetitive nature – it could be a sustained vocal part (often used to create 'choir' sampler instruments in

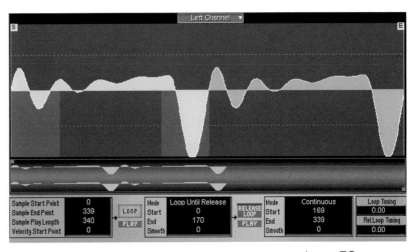

image **53**

commercial sample libraries), or orchestral stringed instruments where the sound is generated by the constant movement of a bow against a string, and so on. The technique works best with sounds that naturally produce long, sustained notes – not everything will sound good repeated in this way. Only trial and error will tell you what does and doesn't work.

At each stage of these examples you can hear, through various CD tracks, what the finished result might sound like before all the pieces of the puzzle are in place.

First I have to admit I did cheat a little here. After I'd created the actual sampler instrument, I wrote a MIDI sequence that produces the string part in Track 15. As a result, the chronological order of events is not as it might be. The reality of the working process is that each element evolves in relation to all the others – so, for example, once I started writing the sequence I found it was necessary to go back and tweak the attack and release stages of the envelope to improve the sense of musical timing.

In image 53 you can see that the first half of the sample is highlighted (it's a lighter shade). This selected area is in fact a single cycle of the original oscillator. The second half of the sample is identical.

The first step was to select this single cycle for looping, which I did by drag-selecting in Halion. If you're using a hardware sampler, you may need to do this by adjusting the start and end points of your loop numerically (within the relevant loop editing page). Note that I've selected between two zero-crossing points, to avoid any clicks or edit noise.

With Halion it was necessary to actually 'activate' the loop via the pull-down menu, located where it now says 'Loop Until Release'. Now the looped section of the sample will continue to play for as long as a note is sustained.

As you can hear from CD1 Track 17, this immediately makes the instrument respond to the MIDI sequence by producing recognisable notes that can be played and held. It's a good start, because it means there's something to work with… but it still doesn't sound too good. The stark way it sounds at this stage does highlight two interesting factors:

Firstly, if you listen carefully you can hear the way the sample really is looping; you can hear the texture of the way the short section repeats, and this happens at different speeds for different notes – illustrating that different MIDI notes play the loop back at different speeds and different musical pitches.

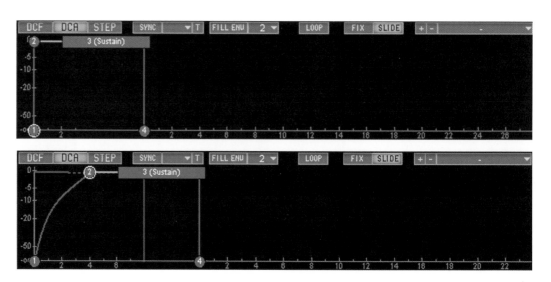

image **54**

image **55**

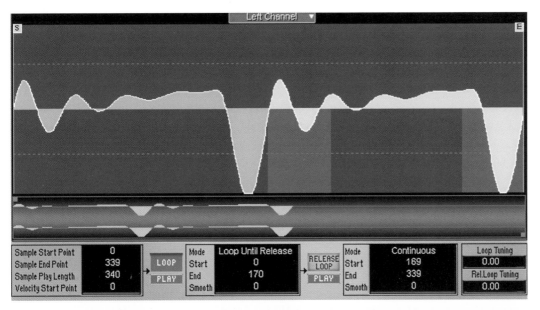

image **56**

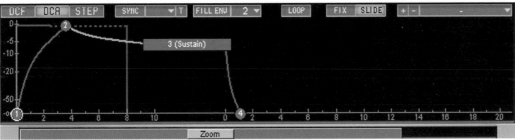

image **57**

You can also hear that the actual MIDI sequence is deliberately messy. I did record this part several times, experimenting with different amounts of accuracy and timing. The fact that the notes are not metronomic adds greatly to the eventual feel of the string part and the way different notes interact tonally. (But this is not a book about sequencing, so I'll leave that subject there.)

The next step was to add an amplitude envelope. When you first navigate your way to the envelope edit view, the envelope looks like image 54.

I first increased the value of the attack stage of the envelope by pulling handle number two across to the right (as in image 55). This causes the notes to fade up gently, as you can hear on Track 18. The notes are still stopping abruptly at their end, though, so the next thing to consider is what happens when note-off information arrives at the instrument.

You need to do several things. The first thing is to reduce the sustain level by pulling down the sustain handle. Then you move the sustain handle a little to the right to increase the decay value. I confess I did this based on experience – I know that the decay and sustain settings will both have a knock-on effect on any release adjustments I make, so I essentially altered all three together. You then move handle four across to increase the release value, in the hope that this will cause the sample to fade away rather than stopping suddenly.

But because I was using such a short sample, before I could get the result I was after from adjusting the decay, sustain and release settings, I needed to add another loop. The problem was that the first loop stopped playing the moment note-off messages arrived from the MIDI sequence. I had to employ a release loop.

You can see from image 56 that I've set the release loop to be continuous, and drag-selected the second half of the sample (that's why I sampled two cycles of the oscillation in the first place). This caused the release loop to repeat for as long as is necessary to fulfil the demands of the envelope release settings… even after the note-off message has arrived. The finished envelope looks like image 57, and produces the results heard on Track 19.

Time to add some effects. Although the string part's starting to sound OK, it could do with being bigger and stronger. To achieve this I added a chorus effect – specifically the standard chorus from Cubase SX2. You can use whichever chorus effect you have, be it within a hardware sampler or a plug-in from another maker. The settings for this chorus were found by trial and error by simply twiddling the controls until it sounded nice: it ended up as a triangle waveform, frequency 2.0Hz, delay 2.0ms, wet/dry mix 50 per cent. The chorused result is on Track 20.

Now I wanted to give the string part a little more presence and an additional sense of structured form, so I employed a little stereo expansion. This pulls the left and right channels of the stereo signal out and places them a little further apart in the stereo soundfield. I used the standard Cubase stereo expander, and like most it only has the one setting for amount – it's at 100 per cent. The part now sounds like Track 21.

Next up I wanted to give the string part more of a sense of space and depth, and this can only mean adding a reverb. Again, in the interest of proving that you don't necessarily need high-end additional plug-ins, I used the standard Cubase 'NaturalVerb'. Its settings were: predelay 20ms; HPF and LPF filters are bypassed; size 12; decay 2.3s; damping 50 per cent; stereo mix is bypassed; wet/dry mix is 50 per cent; sensitivity 50ms; threshold –26dB; and fade-out 20ms. And yes, that little lot is very close to the standard default setting for the plug-in. Have another listen to Track 15 to hear the finished product. (And check Track 16 to remind yourself what it came from.)

To illustrate how using a different effect can make a big difference to the end result, and show what using a relatively high-end plug-in might sound like, I did another, alternative take. CD Track 22 contains a version made with the TC Electronic Native Reverb Plus V3 plug-in, used in place of the Steinberg NaturalVerb. The settings for the Native Reverb (should you manage to get hold of one) are: shape, round; size about 60 per cent; diffuse, very sharp; and colour, a nice pinkish hue… The more sensible settings include an 8ms predelay and 2.5s decay. It does sound different – you can decide which version you prefer.

Rhythmic textures from vocals, using filters, LFO, reverb & modulation

CD1 Track 37 contains a vocal sample, which I chose because it's a series of simple, sustained notes, and again they're fairly pure tones. This is, as you'll realise when you start to experiment for yourselves, taking an easy option. The more complex the waveform you start off with, the less cleanly it can be transformed. So a nice simple one like this can be changed into many things. The vocal tones are quite soft, rounded, gentle and generally mellow in character… but it's deceptive – there's a lot going on beneath the surface.

This time, Track 37 has been altered to sound like Track 42. Here's how it was done… (Again I'm not sticking strictly to the order of activity here because I created a MIDI sequence to play back the edited sound after I'd experimented with some effects. But Track 38 illustrates the extremely simple sequence I did use in the end, without the effects, so you can clearly hear what the sequence is doing. It's just C3 played with varying note lengths at 130bpm.)

The first process I passed the sample through was a 24dB low-pass filter (LPF). It was the Waldorf one from Halion, with cutoff set to 42 (somewhere in the low mid) and resonance set to 31 (which gives a little distortion to the sound). This produced CD Track 39.

Next I passed it through another filter, this time the TC Electronic Filtrator, set like this: LPF 24dB; drive 40 per cent; damp 0; attack 75 per cent. As well as these basic filter settings, the LFO on the cutoff frequency is quite heavy; shape square; env depth 100 per cent; LFO depth 90; and external sync on. It's the LFO that creates the wah effect, and really transforms the sound. Listen to Track 40.

I then added some reverb. The Cubase SX Reverb B was set: room size 27 per cent; time 0.46s; predelay 10.5ms; damp –1.1dB; mix 6 per cent. This softens the sound a bit, and adds a little fluffy depth. Check Track 41.

For the finishing touch I added a phaser – the standard Cubase SX Phaser, set: feedback 72 per cent; stereo basis 95 per cent; rate set to external sync 1x; output 57 per cent; mix 39 per cent. The phaser adds another layer of depth and gives a touch of the 'underwater' feel.

By double-filtering the sound and then bathing it in two washy effects you remove most of the source material, add several layers of distortion, bring in a rhythmic element with the LFO, and then cause these new sonic textures to be sustained and softened.

Changing vocals into hi-hats

I turned the original vocal sample on CD1 Track 37 into a percussion track – the evolving open hi-hat sound on Track 43. Track 44 is the same thing with a kick drum added for a sense of rhythmic perspective.

The first step of the process was to transpose the pitch of the sample by simply playing it further up the keyboard. It was placed into an instrument with its root note at C3, the offbeat is the sample played from C7. I've also entered notes on the second and fourth downbeat of the bar to illustrate where a standard $\frac{4}{4}$ square snare would occur. This note is played at C5. You can hear what this sounds like without any filter or effects in place on Track 45.

Next step was to apply a filter. It was a 24dB high-pass filter with its cutoff and resonance both set at 74. This gives you Track 46.

Then I laid on a flanger – again the standard Cubase flanger, with settings: feedback 60 per cent; delay 54.9ms; depth 100 per cent; stereo basis 66 per cent; shape set to 13 (which gives a kind of inverse sawtooth pattern); output 100 per cent; mix 50 per cent. This is a fairly strong flange, which is set up to change fairly slowly over time, and it's this that gives the sound a sense of constant change. It produces Track 47.

Finally I added some reverb. This time it was the Cubase SX NaturalVerb set like this: predelay 20ms; HPF & LPF inactive; size 20; Decay 350ms; 100 per cent wet; sensitivity 50ms; threshold –26dB; fade-out 20ms.

Turning drums parts into riffs –
using filters, distortion, reverb, modulation & compression

Track 48 on CD1 is a crunchy, atmospheric yet driving riff in an industrial-rock kind of style. It could pass for a heavily distorted guitar or even synth bass, but is in fact made entirely by reprocessing Track 49, which was the clean, simple drum pattern we used earlier in the book. (Again, some adjustments needed to be made as each layer of effects was added.)

First I used a filter – a simple 24dB LPF with cutoff set towards the low mid (in this instance 26 in Halion). This removed the hi-hats and allowed the lower frequency elements of the original drum sound to be expanded upon by the effects. It sounds pretty bad like this, as you'll hear on CD1 Track 50.

Next came the main element of this process: some fairly heavy distortion. I used the Cubase SX Overdrive, a three-band overdrive with separate controls for applying distortion to bass mid and high frequencies. I had it set: bass +15dB; mid −15dB; high −15dB; drive at a hefty 86 per cent; input 0dB; output −7.2dB. And it made it sound like Track 51. I should point out that, unless you're stone deaf, it's wise to reduce the channel playback volume beforehand, because the bass is being boosted by 15dB…

Then the reverb – Reverb A from Cubase SX in fact. I added this to provide a very different kind of atmospheric vibe to the sound. Predelay was 43ms; room size 83; high-cut 7.5dB; low-cut 7.5dB; reverb time 1.4s. You might notice I used mathematical subdivisions of the tempo to set room size and time: $60\text{secs} \div 86 = 697.6\text{ms}$ (a single beat at 86bpm); $697.6 \times 2 = 1.395$ (two beats and our reverb time); $697.6 \div 16 = 43\text{ms}$ ($\frac{1}{16}$th of a beat). This helps make the reverb more cohesive with the rhythmic timing of the final loop. This produced CD Track 52. As you can hear the reverb is a bit wild… but I'm not done with it yet.

To finish I added compression, to squash the whole thing in together, to bring that reverb under control, and give the end result more solidity. I used the TC Native Compressor set like this: attack 0.1; release 500ms; thresh −29.2dB; ratio 2.6:1; all other functions, like the de-esser (for removing sibilance), Soft Sat, etc are off. This gives the final result, Track 48.

Again there's an alternative version. Track 53 used the same set-up but with the reverb bypassed, so there was a signal flow running filter-overdrive-compression. The result is a matched amount of solidity and volume, but a really dry version.

Altering drum patterns using pitch, beat slicing & effects

CD1 Track 65 features a very simple drum & bass-style drum beat. It was made by reprocessing Track 83. This was a raw drum beat that's been 'time-corrected' (see Chapter 7) and then layered with additional sounds to make it a little more sonically dense. Here's what I did to to turn Track 83 into Track 65…

The original tempo of the breakbeat is 86bpm, and most drum & bass runs at tempos in excess of 170bpm, so the first step was to speed the sample up. I tried loading the sample into a fresh sampler instrument and simply playing it back at double speed – by hitting the key on the keyboard exactly one octave above the root note (in this instance the root note was C3 and I played the sample back at C4). Not surprisingly, this wasn't ideal, because the drastic pitch increase meant the sounds of the drums changed dramatically.

The next option was to try beat slicing the sample. I loaded it into Steinberg Recycle and adjusted the sensitivity control until the screen showed that the sample would be divided into 10 individual slices, each containing a single drum hit. The screen from Recycle is shown in image 58, and you'll find each of the slices on CD1, Tracks 66-75.

I then used the Export MIDI File function in the Recycle 'File' menu to generate a MIDI file containing a sequence of notes. Recycle automatically assumes you would want to arrange each of the slices of your sample on consecutive notes on a keyboard map in a sampler instrument, and for convenience it assumes you'll always start at C3 and then map the slices up the keyboard. It then generates a MIDI sequence that places a note for each slice on the correct key at precisely the right time interval for each slice.

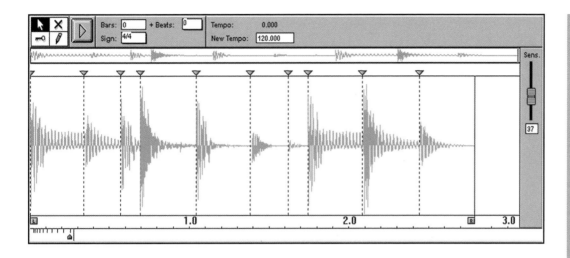

image **58**

The result is that, if you import this MIDI file into your MIDI sequencer, the sequence will play back each slice of the sample in turn at precisely the right moments, so it sounds precisely like the original (providing you have the tempo of your sequencer set to match the tempo of the original sample). You can see from image 59 that the notes of the sequence follow the timing of each drum hit very accurately.

Next I imported all ten of the slices into a fresh sampler instrument. As I was using Halion, I employed a handy function where you can specify a root note by clicking on C3 before using the Import Samples command, then in the sample selection dialogue I selected all ten slices by holding down the shift key and clicking on each sample in the dialogue window. When I hit Open, all ten slices were automatically mapped incrementally up the keyboard from C3.

Then I used the Import MIDI File command from the file menu in Cubase SX. This automatically created a MIDI track for the imported MIDI file, which I then set to send MIDI data to Halion (on the correct MIDI channel, of course). Having set the sequencer tempo to 86bpm, when I hit Play the sample played back perfectly, sounding just like the original, without any sign that it was now a series of individual slices being played back consecutively. The entire process – from loading into Recycle, to setting up a sampler instrument and importing the slices, to importing the MIDI file and setting up the sequencer – took less than two minutes.

The next thing I did was simply double up the playback tempo of my sequencer to 172bpm. Unfortunately the result sounds like CD Track 76 – and that isn't right either. The actual sound is kind of OK, but the beat is cluttered and wrong. Luckily I know from experience that removing one or two elements from the MIDI part will improve things quite a bit.

The original sample is a very common traditional funk-style beat, and I know that the fundamental rhythmic foundations for drum & bass come from the kick drum and snare relationship of this traditional beat, but played at double tempo. So I cut out the notes of the sequence that trigger everything except the kick drum and snare drum. The result looks like image 60 and sounds like Track 77.

I did a bit of sequencing next. I decided that the beat could do with some more hi-hats, so I used the mouse to place a few simple beats into the sequence on the right note to trigger

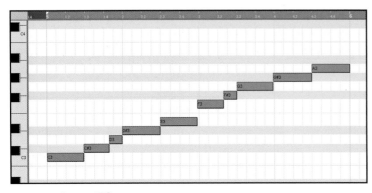

image **59**

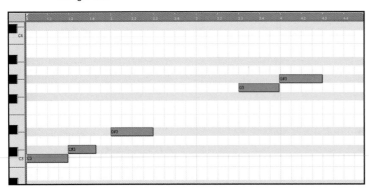

image **60**

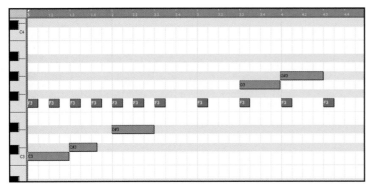

image **61**

one of the hi-hat slices. The result can be seen in image 61, and heard on Track 78.

The next bit was trickier. I wanted to add some effects, but felt it needed different effects on the kick, snare and hi-hats. To make this possible I had to separate the slices into three groups – I ended up using two of the kick drum slices (the ones with the extra sine wave boom added during the layering process in the time correction section), two different snare slices, and just one hi-hat. Yes, that means I did abandon three of the slices.

To achieve this separation I moved the snares and hi-hats to their own separate 'programs' (instruments) within Halion. Halion is multi-timbral, so each of these programs behaves like a separate sampler instrument that can respond to a unique MIDI channel and be routed to a specific set of audio outputs from Halion to different channels in the Cubase mixer.

Most hardware samplers are also multi-timbral, so will allow you to do the same thing, but many software samplers are not. If you're using a non-multi-timbral software sampler, you'll need to move your slices into entirely separate sampler instruments to achieve similar results.

Although more or less all traditional multi-timbral hardware samplers will let you assign each program to a different MIDI channel and audio output, some multi-timbral software samplers (notably Halion) won't. The MIDI channels in Halion's first 16 programs are fixed to channels 1-16; programs 17-32 are all pre-fixed to MIDI channel 1. Unfortunately, with Halion the routing of samples to outputs is also done according to MIDI channel rather than program, so although you can get up to 17 programs to respond to a single MIDI channel, they are all routed to the same audio output. This means I also had to separate the different elements of my MIDI sequence out onto different tracks in the sequencer.

I ended up with three different MIDI parts (one for kick drum, one for snare and the other for hats), each sending MIDI note information on a different MIDI channel to a corresponding program in Halion. Many software samplers allow you to freely assign different MIDI channels and audio output routing to programs as you please.

I then routed the kick drums to Halion audio outputs 1&2, the snares to outputs 3&4 and the hi-hats to outputs 5&6. This meant I then had three stereo channels in the Cubase mixer, with one of my sample groups on each. I could then use the effects send system on the Cubase mixer to set up several different effects, as follows…

First I set up a reverb on aux send 1. I used the very simple Reverb B from Cubase, with the following settings: room size 30 per cent; reverb time 0.7s (this is two beats at 172bpm); predelay 50ms; damp –7.5dB. I used the aux send at about 30 per cent on the appropriate mixer channel to route only the snare samples to this reverb. It sounds like CD1 Track 79.

I then moved onto a modulation effect – a flanger on aux send 2. I wanted a relatively high feedback (68 per cent) to give a metallic feel; high depth (81 per cent) for quite a strong sound; and relatively slow rate (1Hz) so the sound would rise and fall gradually during the course of a couple of bars. Because I had it set up on an aux send I was able to apply quite a lot of this flanger to the hi-hat (about 70 per cent on the channel send) and a relatively small amount to the snare (20 per cent on the channel send). For Track 80, I've switched off the reverb temporarily so you can hear the flanger more clearly.

Finally I wanted to add some power to the kick drum, so I set up quite a heavy distortion on aux send 3. I used the Cubase Quadrafuzz, with the low and low-mid at 100 per cent; the high mid at 0 per cent; and the high at 40 per cent.

I also combined this with a little EQ: +6dB boost at 150Hz (narrow Q) on the kick drum mixer channel. On its own, without the other effects, it sounds like Track 81.

Put the whole thing together, and you get CD1 Track 65.

CHAPTER 7

hands-on
sampling

There's a surprisingly broad range of ways you can play and control your sampler, which in itself can make a difference to the sound it produces. This chapter is mostly about the various types of physical interface available for playing samples, and about how to use MIDI to control different aspects of sample playback. There's even a section on audio time correction, for those who choose not to go down the MIDI route at all.

- MIDI controller data – what it is and how to use it.

- Hardware controls – such as knobs, sliders, buttons, wheels, touch pads etc.

- Alternative controllers – including drums, wind instruments, guitars, light beams, ultrasound.

- Time correction – completely manual adjustment/editing of samples.

Get physical

Computers have undoubtedly opened up new realms of power and sophistication for sample users, both in terms of the sounds and the general functions available. But when it comes down to it, the feel and fun of using a good old hardware instrument is still much more conducive to music-making than pushing and clicking a mouse. Hardware controls offer a much more tactile and intuitive option – as more and more people are realising.

In some circumstances the way to get the rhythmic/melodic feel or dramatic effect you're after may not involve manipulating samples at all. A great deal of the feel of music comes from subtle nuances of timing that can be very difficult to create artificially simply by number-crunching or moving dots and blocks around in a sequencer edit page. With some practice, and trust in your musical instincts, it can be quicker and easier to make like a traditional musician and actually play your musical ideas into your sequencer.

Much of the art of playing (rather than sequencing) rhythms and melodies is about creating a sense of constant change in the sounds you use. When musicians play real instruments they are not mechanically repetitive (no matter how hard they may try to be). There will be slight variations in how hard they pluck strings, strike skins, or expel air. Instruments themselves sound different at certain times, depending on atmospheric conditions, age, construction etc. Even vintage analog synthesisers produce sounds that naturally evolve and change all the time.

Constant, subtle variation is a major factor in the feel of music. And there are plenty of parameters within a sampler that can be used to add such a sense of constant change to your music – you just need to get your hands on them.

Once you know how to access the technology, the rest is all about learning to trust your own physical ability to reach in and literally tap, twist and wiggle the right feel into your sound. Shake your hips, nod your head, feel the groove… you might amaze yourself.

MIDI keyboards

The most common interface used to generate and input MIDI information within a MIDI studio is the keyboard. We've already seen how a MIDI keyboard works by sending note-on, note value, velocity, and note-off messages – I covered this in Chapter 5 in the context of creating an effective sampler instrument to respond to such information. That was about making the right connections and hitting the right keys.

The next skill to start practising is how to tap out rhythms using those keys, and then (having perhaps taken a quick refresher course on musical scales) to start experimenting with melodies. If you can get your fingers to tap out the melody and rhythm combinations you can hear in your head, you really have won half the battle of creating your own music.

The more skilled you get, the more subtlety you'll find you can put into your compositions. After a while the music will seem to make its way directly from your subconscious creative imagination to your fingers, without the process of actually thinking about what you're doing, which can sometimes otherwise get in the way and slow you down.

The section on velocity mapping in Chapter 5 introduced the idea that whether you strike a key hard or softly affects the volume of the note produced. With some modern keyboards, pushing down harder on the key *after* you've struck it sends another type of MIDI data, in this case called aftertouch.

Aftertouch is an example of what's known as MIDI controller data.

So what is MIDI controller data?

Each sampler instrument may have dozens of different parameters that you might want to control remotely via MIDI. For example, a fairly standard sampler instrument will have filter cutoff, filter resonance, four different envelope parameters (attack, decay, sustain and release), and so on. Rather than try to second-guess what each instrument from every different manufacturer might consist of, the creators of the MIDI language realised that something a little more versatile was called for.

The chosen solution was to provide 128 different 'continuous controller' (CC) data numbers. A few of them would be given names (like volume and pan), but the rest would just be left as numbers, from 0-127. Continuous controller messages use a type of sliding scale of settings across the 128 increment range, so a CC message can have a setting of any number between 0 and 127. Switch messages are either on or off.

So if you want to control a specific parameter (let's say your filter cutoff) via MIDI, you need to set it up to respond to a particular CC number. If you then set up your external MIDI device (using a knob or slider on a hardware control surface) to send out CC data on that same number, the parameter – in this case the filter cutoff setting – is changed.

Because the information is just MIDI data, it can then also be recorded to and played back from a MIDI sequencer. So the controller system not only opens up enormous potential for realtime, hands-on control of your MIDI instruments, it means you can automate changes in instrument settings from a sequencer.

HARDWARE CONTROL SURFACE

Any piece of hardware that transmits MIDI control data can be called a hardware control surface, or HCS. They come in a great many shapes, sizes and levels of sophistication, as we'll see throughout this chapter.

As it happens, there aren't strictly just 128 CC numbers at all, as this proved too limited in some cases. It was decided that, although most parameters can be manipulated quite sufficiently by a value range of 0-127, some require a finer level of detail. The solution was to combine various CC numbers into pairs – known as MSB, which technically stands for 'most significant bit', and LSB, or 'least significant bit'.

The first controller in the pair (the MSB) divides the range of possible settings into 128 steps; the second CC number (the LSB) is then used to divide each of those 128 steps into a further 128 steps – giving a possible range of 16,384 different values (128 x 128).

This is great, but it does mean you can have quite large quantities of data flowing to and from your sequencer and around your MIDI network. MIDI is not in general a 'high-bandwidth' system, so this can cause the equivalent of traffic jams and, consequently, sporadic loss of bits of data (commonly called drop-out). You might think that if all you lose is a single step out of many thousands of incremental messages, who would ever notice? But if that one digit you lose in the melee happens to be a note-on or note-off message, you will definitely know all about it.

If you start having such drop-out issues, there are two solutions: either cut down on the number of controllers you're using at any one time, or make use of the MIDI filter systems you'll find in most good software sequencers, which are specifically intended to combat the problem – you should find instructions on how these work in your sequencer manual.

If you send out a volume-type CC message on a particular MIDI channel, any instrument set up to respond to that particular MIDI channel, and also set up to respond to volume-type CC data (which not all will be), will have its volume adjusted accordingly.

The plain truth is that not all MIDI instruments respond to MIDI CC data at all. Of those that do, not all of them are entirely user-friendly. As a broad rule of thumb, the older your instrument the less easy it will be to set up, but unfortunately the level of complexity of MIDI implementation, and how well it has been configured by the manufacturer, can be random.

With several products, only a small number of individual parameters are assigned to controllers, and those are preset, so the only way to assign them to different external devices is to alter which CCs the external device transmits.

Assigning controllers to instrument parameters

The best equipment uses a system often called MIDI Learn. Engage the MIDI Learn function, select the instrument parameter you want to assign a CC number to, and then send an appropriate CC message to it via MIDI. The MIDI Learn recognises the incoming data and automatically assigns your parameter to respond to this data from that moment on. With most systems like this, the moment the learn facility does receive some CC data, it then disengages – so you effectively use it to set up one parameter at a time.

With systems that don't have MIDI Learn, you need to select your instrument parameter, manually assign a CC to it, then manually set up your external MIDI device to transmit the right data. The extent of the MIDI implementation, the approach to assignment, and instructions on how to set your system up, are hopefully to be found in your sampler manual, and in the 'MIDI implementation chart' – a list of the parameters automatically assigned to which controllers, usually found at the back of your manual. If there are no instructions or implementation chart, then your sampler probably doesn't respond to CCs. But almost all of the leading hardware and software samplers do.

There are several other common approaches to controller assignment. NI Kontakt and a number of other products use a 'right-click' approach. You point at the onscreen control for the instrument parameter you wish to control, and right-click (control-click for Mac). A little menu box appears where you specify the CC number you want to use for that parameter.

Most hardware control surfaces also use this approach. They usually provide you with a piece of computer-based editing software that displays a graphic representation of the control surface. Point and right-click on the knob, slider, button etc you wish to use for a particular parameter, and a similar CC number assignment box appears. Tap in the CC number you want the control to transmit, hit return, and away you go.

Tascam's Gigastudio uses a fairly similar approach, but rather than the right-click method, it includes little arrows beside various onscreen controls. Clicking an arrow opens a similar assignment window, where you can choose from a list of CC numbers.

Some samplers provide a separate controller assignment page or area (this is almost always the case with hardware samplers), which takes the form of a list. In one column you either have a preset list of instrument parameters that can be controlled via controller data, or a pull-down menu that lets you choose the parameter to be controlled. Another column lets you specify which incoming controller number you'd like the chosen parameter to respond to.

Sometimes this approach will feature a third column that lets you select a range for your chosen controller. Not all systems have this, but it can be very useful. Range settings specify the extent to which the hardware control affects the setting. A simple example might be pitch: without a range setting, a pitch wheel (which I'll come back to later) usually adjusts sample pitch over a range of 12 semitones (one octave). In a musical sense this is rather a lot, so it's often more desirable to have the pitch wheel only alter the sample pitch by perhaps two semitones.

By specifying a reduced range setting for the pitch controller within your sampler instrument, you can use the total length of travel of the pitch wheel for your two-semitone adjustment. This makes life a lot easier than trying to make a two-semitone adjustment using a smaller portion of the available travel on the wheel. It's equally useful where you wish to make a relatively small but precise adjustment.

Once you have (sometimes literally) grasped the process of assigning controls on various hardware controllers to different sampler parameters, the principles can be applied in many ways. In a modern computer-based studio, more or less all the functions of your sampler, synthesiser, DAW, effects etc can be controlled in this way.

'Conditional' playback using Megatrig

It's worth mentioning one particular, unusual product feature at this point. The Megatrig page within Steinberg Halion is a particularly cool example of complex controller usage in action. Megatrig (short for Megatrigger) is perhaps a misleading name, because it doesn't actually start sample playback in the way a straightforward trigger might; Megatrig is all about causing something to happen when a particular combination of events, or a certain 'condition', occurs.

The idea of Megatrig is to allow you to choose which samples are playing by using controller data from a sequencer or HCS. Imagine you have three percussion loops that are all samples of the same instrument, playing the same basic riff, but the player has played the riff with variations in emphasis each time. Megatrig enables you to set things up so you can swap between each of the variations during playback by turning a knob, or using the modulation wheel etc.

You can see the Megatrig edit window in image 62. Here's how Megatrig works...

Halion is a multi-timbral sampler, which can play back 16 different programs (Steinberg's term for a sampler instrument, remember) at the same time, and each program can consist of a whole multi-layered keyboard map containing dozens of samples. Each program has a Megatrig page. You're given three controller sections, and within each you can choose a controller from a pull-down menu. You can also use two onscreen sliders to specify a CC value range within which each controller will actually have an effect.

Below the three controller selectors is what they call the 'Play If' section. This contains two columns of little pull-down menus. The left column lets you choose between note-on, note-off, pedal-on, pedal-off, and the three controllers from the controller selection section. The

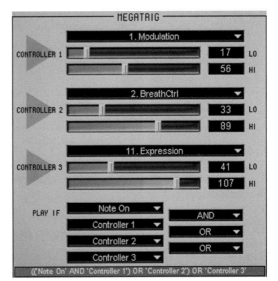

image **62**

right column then lets you set up the relationships between the things you've chosen – it does this by offering you three conditional options: 'And', 'Or' and 'And Not'. So you might decide that the samples in the program should only play if certain conditions are met – if the program receives, for example, note-on *AND* controller 1 *OR* controller 2 data *BUT NOT* controller 3 data.

For your three percussion loops, you might want a situation where all the samples are triggered by the same note-on information (probably from a sequencer), but that by turning a knob you choose which of them plays – this can be great in a live performance. To achieve this you assign each of the samples to a different program, set each program to respond to the same MIDI channel, and ensure that all the samples are set to respond to the same note and across the entire velocity map.

For the first sample, you go to Megatrig and set controller 1 to a controller number (let's pick one at random, say CC22), and then set its value range to min 0 and max 42. Then you head to the 'play if' section and specify that the sample will play if it receives note-on *and* controller 1 data.

Next you select the program containing sample 2, and again set controller 1 to CC22 – but this time specify a CC range of min 43 and max 85. You then use the same 'play if' settings as sample 1. Next set the program containing sample 3 to respond to controller 1, again assigned to CC22 but this time with a range of min 86 and max 127… and again you use the same 'play if' setting.

Now all you have to do is assign a hardware control or sequencer to transmit CC22 using the MIDI channel you've chosen for the three programs. By turning the control, playback will be switched between the samples.

Another obvious practical use for this is with something like a tambourine. It's an instrument with two different sounds to it – one sound when it hits the player's hand and another when it's flicked away. Armed with two samples and Megatrig, you can set up a situation where one of the samples is played when it receives note-on information and the other plays when it receives note-off. That way, pressing down the key on a keyboard will play one sample, and when you release the key again the other sample plays.

Neither of these examples even scratches the surface of the relationships you can set up between different samples and hardware controls by the time you employ all three possible controllers. A fine example might be to make a wide range of things happen at once from a single knob turn. With multiple copies of samples, various effect and filter settings etc, you can create a situation where a single knob turn could progressively swap between different samples with various effects and filters applied; and then, as you turn it further, yet more variations are heard as more samples are selected and different processors applied.

You might only have one pair of hands, but this is a way of programming yourself a whole load of extra ones.

No movement means no transmission

Sounds like a 1960s political slogan, doesn't it? The important message here is simply that all MIDI controller data-transmitting devices remain inactive until you touch them. So although a knob, slider, wheel or whatever may be in a particular position, if it's not in operation it doesn't send data. The moment you actually move it, the data starts to flow.

This is very logical, as the entire process of using controllers exists to allow you to incorporate a little free-flowing, tactile movement into your musical performance. It also makes sense because if they did constantly send data they would make a right old mess of your settings all the time, because they would continually reset values to match their current position, regardless of any alterations you made elsewhere.

But there's still a potential problem. Imagine you have a situation where there's a controller assigned to, say, an effect send level parameter for a delay within a sampler instrument, and a slider on a control surface. The idea is that you can move the slider to adjust the delay send level as a song plays.

Let's say the delay starts the song with a send level controller value of 20, and you want to gradually increase it over a section of the song. You're in a live gig situation, and you've just used the same slider, transmitting on a different MIDI channel, to control a different parameter within a different instrument. So the slider is currently sitting up at the top of its range, at a value setting of 128. But of course, the moment you touch the slider it will start sending controller data – and this will cause the effect send level to jump straight to a value of 127. Obviously not what you want.

There are only two ways around the problem. The first is a little tricky and impractical, but needs must… You have to try and get the slider physically positioned at a value setting of 20 *before* changing over the MIDI channel and assigning the slider to the effect send level. That way, when you move the slider it will have the desired result.

The second solution is a relatively recent innovation that's becoming more common in many samplers as the popularity of hardware control surfaces grows. It's what is sometimes called a 'soft' controller system. In this case, when you switch over the slider to the correct MIDI channel (etc) and move it, it immediately starts transmitting controller data, but the effect send level control will not respond straight away. Instead it will only respond once the slider passes through the value setting of 20, and then moves the value setting away from that initial value. The send level only latches on to the incoming controller data when it reaches the initial value setting. This is an infinitely superior control method, and if your sampler uses it you're lucky – check your manual to find out.

Modulation and pitch wheels

At the front left of most MIDI keyboards you'll find two wheels. One will be labelled Pitch, and will have a little raised or indented bit of some sort that serves as somewhere to put your finger, and as a position indicator. This 'handle' will usually be pointing straight up, so that you can push it away from you or pull it towards you. Pitch wheels are usually sprung, so if you move the handle away from the upright position and let go it will spring back to upright, its default position.

Pitch wheels are intended for applying 'bend' to notes. If you hit a note and then move the wheel, the note's pitch will slide gradually up or down. Most real instruments are well suited to sliding gradually from one note to another in this way, and many musicians and musical styles make good use of the fact. So, for instance, if you want to make an acoustic guitar multisample perform more like the real thing, you'll need to master the physical art of the pitch wheel.

The pitch wheel works by sending controller data. When the wheel is in its upright position it's set at a value of 63. Push it as far as it will go and it will be transmitting the controller value 128; pull it fully towards you and it's transmitting controller value 0.

By default, most sampler instruments obviously have the pitch wheel assigned to control note pitch, but you will probably find you can re-assign it to any other parameter that responds to incoming controller data. Conversely you may also find you can assign other types of control device to note pitch if you wish to.

PORTAMENTO OR GLIDE

Portamento and glide are different names for the same thing – they're basically automated versions of the pitch wheel. If you hit consecutive keys on a keyboard you hear distinctly separate notes, but if you want the pitch to slide smoothly from the first note to the second, you need to use a portamento or glide function. It simulates the effect you get with many 'real' instruments where such sliding between notes is common. There's usually an on/off switch for this function within most sampler instruments.

The other wheel on your MIDI keyboard will be labelled Modulation. Mod wheels are physically quite similar to pitch wheels, except they don't have a sprung action, and the handle's default position is pointing towards the player. In this starting position it transmits a 0 controller value; push it all the way away from you and it will transmit a value of 128. Positions in-between obviously transmit proportionate values.

The idea of the mod wheel is that you can assign any controller you like to it, and so use it to adjust any parameter that responds to controller data. Using a mod wheel to adjust instrument parameters in realtime as your song plays, or as part of the initial musical performance when you're playing your note sequences, is infinitely more responsive and musically inspiring than using a mouse.

Korg and one or two other manufacturers use a combination-type of pitch/modulation lever. This is a bit like a standard wheel but is turned from vertical to horizontal, and the handle enlarged to make it a kind of joystick. The handle sits upright and the lever is sprung so as you move it either left or right it acts like a standard pitch wheel. But you can also push it away from you – this second direction of movement acts just like a standard modulation wheel. The result combines the action of two separate wheels into a single tool that only requires a one-handed movement to operate them.

Hardware control options

As I've said, there's a tactile immediacy to using hardware that injects energy into your music and produces results that are not easily achieved in other ways. Actually changing parameter settings as your sounds play produces a sense of constant change that adds interest and dynamics to your music. But one of the side benefits to hardware control is that your control movements can be recorded to your sequencer, so you can be as wild and experimental as you like and then simply go back and use the best bits.

The practicalities of recording and editing controller data within your sequencer are relatively straightforward. All of the major sequencing software packages provide separate MIDI controller tracks: all you do is create or select one of these tracks, assign it to the correct MIDI channel/instrument and begin recording. On some sequencers, the controller data is recorded within the same individual 'part' or block as the rest of your sequence note information.

Once recorded, the controller data can be cut, pasted and edited with a set of onscreen tools. In fact, the pencil tool can be used to generate fresh controller data, and then the rest of the toolkit used to edit it – which means that almost all your sampler parameters can be automated and sequenced without the use of any hardware controls at all. This approach clearly lacks the tactile hands-on aspect of the process, but it does achieve the sense of dynamic realtime change.

DUB BE GOOD

If you need any convincing about the benefits of constant change through realtime manipulation, have a listen to some good dub reggae – an entire musical genre that grew out of this idea, and became one of the foundations of electronic music, not to mention modern remixing.

During the 1970s, 'riding' the controls of a mixing console became an artform in itself, and is still among the most fun things you can do in a studio. You take a 16 or 24-track master and get each channel up-and-running on a mixer; set up a load of effects, mute out most of the tracks (often stripping back to just the drums and the bassline), and off you go – bringing in and taking out elements as you choose, while whacking effects like reverb and delay up to maximum, creating a huge, atmospheric, ever-changing soundscape.

These days you can select a section, or all, of your song within your DAW and cycle its playback, so you can jam for as long as you please. By adding splashes of echo and reverb, muting and un-muting tracks, applying filters, adjusting envelope settings, and of course tweaking the EQ as the track runs, a whole new arrangement and a whole new set of sounds emerges. It's all about feeling the music, letting it grow from your experiments, listening out for happy accidents (and learning how they happened so you can do similar things again), and letting it flow. It's been said that every multi-track master tape has a thousand songs on it... just try it with a collection of samples and sequences and you'll soon see.

As for the hardware controls themselves, the most common types found on an HCS are knobs, sliders and buttons – each best suited to different types of control. There are also a few more radical alternatives, which are worth a mention here.

Knobs

Although the knobs on an HCS look and feel for all the world like the kind of thing you might find on the front of a hi-fi, there is a subtle but important difference. A knob on a hi-fi (or a synthesiser etc) has a finite amount of available travel. Turn it fully anti-clockwise and you will hit a point where it stops moving, and you have reached a setting of 0. Turn it clockwise and eventually it will be able to move no further and you've reached its maximum setting. By contrast, a MIDI HCS knob (or 'rotary encoder', to give its correct name) just spins and spins. You can keep turning it round and round as long as you like.

The reason lurks in what was said earlier about some instrument parameters possibly having a range of settings between 0 and 16,384, rather than the usual 0-127. Logically, a universal knob needs to be pretty versatile.

Sliders/faders & buttons

Sliders or faders are better suited to adjustment of some parameters, particularly anything where you do actually want a clearly defined and restricted amount of available travel. This can be ideal for sliding a parameter from a current setting to a minimum or maximum setting in one smooth action, where you can see the exact length of journey or amount of movement you'll need to reach the desired final setting. With an HCS knob you don't have the same physical indicator of available travel. The most obvious example is for volume setting, but faders can be useful with any parameter, especially where you are able to specify a controller range, as described earlier.

Buttons are used for single increments. They can be very handy with switch-type parameters, where you just want to turn something on or off.

Touch pads

A touch pad in this context (as developed by Korg) is a square plastic surface, usually about 12x12 cm, with a calibrated cross placed in the middle. The cross is essentially the X and Y axes of a basic mathematical graph. Different controllers are assigned to the different axes of the graph. If you place your finger on the pad, it senses the pressure you apply and plots the position on the axes as you move your finger around, adjusting controller values accordingly.

It can get a bit more complex when you divide the X and Y axes in half and assign different CC numbers to the positive and negative halves of each axis... giving you a total of four different CC numbers assigned to the pad at any time.

Airwaves, soundwaves and light beams

Beyond the standard approaches to realtime MIDI control, there are a few more unusual control methods out there, often built by experimental product designers and musicians. Some of these are particularly suited to using samples within the context of multimedia performance, art installations, museum exhibits, or educational and therapeutic situations.

Ever since Leon Theremin invented the instrument that bears his name in 1919, the practice of making music by waving your hands around in the air has been a part of the experimental musical landscape. The original theremin is essentially a synthesiser, but instead of relying on keys and knobs, its oscillators are triggered by the proximity of the player's hands to its two antennae, which control the instrument's pitch and volume. MIDI versions of the theremin, which could theoretically link to samplers and sequencers, have been attempted in recent years – by such revered designers as Bob Moog, himself a confessed theremin-builder turned synth manufacturer – but not with much commercial success. You still occasionally see MIDI interfaces offered for theremins.

A more mainstream spin-off in the last 15 years is perhaps the MIDI light beam controller. Roland were the first major manufacturer to adopt the technology with their D-Beam, which appeared on several products, including their SP-808 sampling workstation (the 'Groove Sampler') and the V-Synth.

The D-Beam emits several D-shaped beams of light, with the Ds on their back, so the effect is of an invisible dome marked out in space, extending about 30cm above the instrument. If you move your hand (or any other solid object) into the path of the light beams, the light bounces off it and back to a number of sensors, which can detect the position of your hand within the dome. A maximum of four simultaneous MIDI controllers can be assigned to the horizontal and vertical axes within the beam. Different hand positions therefore cause different controller settings – any movement is tracked in realtime, translated into MIDI messages, and the result sent out via MIDI.

A more esoteric and potentially versatile application of related technology, especially for those involved with experimental audio-visual installation or theatre work, is the Soundbeam MIDI controller. This uses pulses of ultrasound rather than light, and was originally invented so that dancers could compose music from their physical movement – it consequently has a maximum range of six metres. It uses use up to four separate beam sensors, looking not unlike little table lamps, routed through an eight-way switching unit that allows you to incorporate other types of MIDI control device alongside it. You can find out more from www.soundbeam.co.uk.

The incredible Notron

I know it's very irritating when music technology writers bang on about something great that in fact you're going to find almost impossible to get hold of... but I'm going to do it anyway.

And it's simply because the Notron is the most original and truly remarkable MIDI control surface I've ever used. It was invented by a nice Englishman, Gerard Campbell, who only ever hand-built them and sold them one-by-one to many of the luminaries of Detroit-style techno production.

The Notron is a two-part concept. The first part is a four-track 16-step sequencer in the style of original analog sequencers. But it has a thousand differences, all of them difficult to describe, particularly in the few words available here. Part two of the concept is perhaps best described by the inventor himself, who said: "Most MIDI instrument designers concentrate on how sound is generated after note-on information arrives. It occurred to me that you might be able to do something interesting if you looked at the potential within MIDI to change the way things sound *before* the note-on message arrives." It goes far deeper, but ask yourself what it would sound like if, rather than using simple on/off switch-type MIDI data as note-on messages, you could use little bursts of waveform-shaped MIDI controller data.

The Notron is a remarkably multi-faceted instrument, and a sublime one to use. Most importantly, it's all about realtime music-making – it's a tool for creating music live, and as such is incredibly intuitive, easy, exciting and fun to use, even with no prior skill. It's also the only MIDI controller you'll find (or perhaps not find) that actually makes almost any sound module or sampler you connect to it sound totally different. Adding a Notron to your studio is like reinventing every other instrument in that studio.

The Notron is sadly no longer in production, and so few of them were ever made (and they were bought by fanatics who are unlikely to part with them), that it's doubtful you'll see one available secondhand. Luckily Mr Campbell has been busy: he has a new DJ-oriented control surface available called the MXF8, and is working on a successor to the Notron, the Genotron. You can visit his company online at www.grexultradynamics.co.uk.

No keyboard? No problem...

Although it's the most popular, the MIDI keyboard is obviously not the only way of getting melodic and rhythmic note data into sequencers, or indeed of playing back sounds. Sometimes it's clearly not the best option, especially if you're trying to reproduce complex drum or wind instrument parts. Luckily, other families of instrument have also been translated into MIDI hardware – with varying degrees of success, it must be said.

A word of caution here: it could be argued that the great electronic lazy Susan that is the MIDI sequencer has managed to remove much of the effort and finely-honed manual dexterity from the music-making process for electronic musicians – but if you're thinking of using some of the following alternative control devices, bear in mind that they are real instruments, which real musicians spend years learning, perfecting the nuances of timing and inflection that give some musical styles their subtlety. You'll need to work at these, from a playing point of view, to get the best from them.

Drums and percussion

The most obvious and perhaps most useful alternative note-generating devices are MIDI drum kits and percussion instruments. These are so effective, and the nuances of rhythmic timing they can deliver is so central to a lot of music, that this family of note generators is now a big and popular business.

When it comes to MIDI drum kits, Roland is perhaps considered to be currently ahead of the field – with the Clavia ddrum (pronounced 'D drum'), a pioneer in the field, coming in a very close second. Roland's 'virtual' drum kit, the V-Drum system, consists of a bunch of drum-shaped rubber pads (a bit like traditional silent practice pads) which you put together much like an acoustic kit. You attach pedals to the kick drum and hi-hat and hit the rest of the pads (and rubber cymbals – no, really) with sticks.

Sitting down at a V-Drum set-up can initially be a bit of a shock to old die-hard 'analog' drummers (especially those rubber cymbals), but the technology has evolved to such a point that the kit responds remarkably like a real drum kit. The feel of the resistance of the pads, the way the stick bounces back up, is very cool. Even those rubber cymbals can be stopped from ringing by grabbing them with your hand the way you would with a real cymbal – a neat touch from the programmers there. The drum sounds assigned to the pads are incredibly intricate, multi-layered multisamples (helped along by a dose of digital modelling), which not only respond impressively to different hit velocities but to a rather detailed positional map on each surface too – something much like a keyboard zoning map spread around the surfaces.

The main alternative to the V-Drum/ddrum approach is the drum trigger. This is a little thing that clamps to the rim of an acoustic kit drum, with a pin-type cylinder that sticks out of the bottom and rests very lightly on the drum skin. The vibration from the impact of stick on skin is picked up by the trigger and turned into MIDI messages.

This is relatively primitive technology compared to the MIDI drum pad concept, and by comparison the essentially note-on/note-off information generated is far less responsive. But the drum trigger approach is still pretty good for drummers who want to play their usual kit, with the added benefit of being able to trigger simple samples. This can be particularly effective when breakbeats (or slices of breakbeats) are assigned to each drum trigger – a good drummer can achieve a fantastic hybrid between the feel of real drumming and breaks programming. (The same technique is even more versatile on a pad kit, but you don't have the advantage of using a real drum and its sound.)

An extension of pad technology has been applied to various hand percussion controllers. Much like an individual pad on a pad kit, the hand percussion controller can be divided up into zones with different samples assigned and layered accordingly. The addition of touch pad-style controller strips opens up the ability to assign the kind of 'slide' associated with things like congas and tabla.

Wind/reed controllers

Wind instrument players have had a MIDI option for years. Akai's EWI (Electronic Wind Instrument) was first introduced in the late 1980s, and was later joined by Yamaha's WX series. In the case of the Akai at least, it's a multi-part system consisting of a controller and/or a pair of sound modules, one that's a modelling synthesiser and the other a sample-based module intended to provide realistic wind instrument sounds that really respond like wind instruments should.

The actual controller part of the system has a mouthpiece with a reed and a similar fingering set-up to a saxophone. The EWI is also based internally on 'control voltage', which is considerably smoother than the somewhat stepped characteristics of the type of MIDI controller data generated by some HCSs. The EWI requires a separate CV/MIDI interface in order to be considered a MIDI controller instrument.

What makes these 'wind synths' particularly appealing is that there are very few controllers you can pick up and walk around with, the way you can with these. (Note that some keyboard synthesisers and sound modules, such as Yamaha's VL range, have also offered plug-in breath controller facilities.)

Brass

It's early days for this development… For a long time it was thought that the reedless brass mouthpiece couldn't be recreated as a MIDI controller instrument, but there's at least one at prototype stage as this book goes to press. The Morrison Digital Trumpet (MDT) is a very space-age-looking bit of kit, which boasts eight MIDI continuous controllers – five breath controllers and three separate thumb controllers (for modulation, portamento etc) – as well as being able to play all 128 MIDI notes, which means a tonal range of over ten octaves. You can read more about the MDT at www.patchmanmusic.com/mdt.html.

MIDI guitar

Using guitars to generate MIDI information has also been rather hit and miss over the years. Problems have often occurred with 'tracking', a term that refers to the speed and accuracy with which the MIDI interface interprets and reproduces the nuances of guitar fingering – there's much more scope for individual variations in ways of striking strings and holding chords and notes than there is with keyboards. Systems have advanced greatly over recent years, although still not to the extent where MIDI guitars could be called a mainstream instrument in the way MIDI keyboards have become.

A modern MIDI guitar may look like (and often be) a normal electric or acoustic guitar, or bass, but will simply have an additional, ultra-sensitive, divided pickup at the bridge – for instance the popular Roland GK-2 pickup – which creates individual output signals for each string. These signals are sent to an interface box that turns them into MIDI note information. Currently the two leading brandnames in the MIDI guitar field seem to be Roland and Axon.

TIME CORRECTION – using samples without MIDI

This section deals with a somewhat unusual approach to working with sampled sound. The idea is to create music entirely by repositioning samples on the audio tracks of a digital audio workstation purely by close-up manual alignment – without involving MIDI at all.

I'm not referring to the live recording of entire song-length performances, I mean quite literally cutting out and meticulously placing individual notes and musical events onscreen to create the manual equivalent of sequences, and eventually entire songs. Without the help of MIDI. It's a process sometimes called time correction, and its devotees swear by the fact that it produces more clinically precise and well-defined results, compared to relying on MIDI – for reasons which I'll come to in a minute.

It's quite a cumbersome way of working, though. The technique doesn't utilise live note input (from a keyboard, MIDI drums, guitar etc), or any of the convenient 'drag & drop' MIDI editing tools available within key, score and grid editing pages of sequencers. Instead you'll need a good natural sense of timing, and a reasonable technical grasp of how music is constructed. It demands a vivid imagination too – you need to be more or less able to write songs in your head and then make them happen onscreen. You need to know precisely which sounds you want to occur in which order, and where you need to place them on the timeline of a DAW to make them sound right.

So why bother with all this extra work...? Well, the main reason is to do with the fact that MIDI is incapable of producing two events at precisely the same time. This may seem daft but it really is true. It's a phenomenon known as latency, and it's the bane of many electronic musicians' lives.

MIDI can produce a *stream* of events, one after another, in such rapid succession that your ear can't really tell that they didn't happen at once. But the bottom line is that if you play a five-note chord on a MIDI keyboard, even if you're skilled enough to hit all five keys at exactly the same moment, MIDI will actually relay your five notes to your sampler one after another, a few milliseconds apart.

MIDI often gets away with it because the latency is generally less than ten milliseconds (although this can vary, depending on the equipment you're using). According to the theory developed by Helmut Haas in the 1940s, your ear/brain can't really discern individual sounds if they're less than about 30ms apart – you hear them as essentially merged into one. So a small number of MIDI notes together might just fool your ear into thinking they're in unison. The trouble is, the larger the number of 'simultaneous' MIDI events you layer on top of each other, the more the timing disparity will become obvious, and you can start to get a rather unpleasant phasing or clouding effect.

Depending on who you speak to, MIDI latency is either a huge problem, or an over-exaggerated one. All I can say is, in my experience, there's definitely a noticeable muddying effect when combining certain MIDI sounds and/or a lot of MIDI layers – perhaps because all those sub-10ms delays add up to more than Mr Haas' requisite 30ms maximum...

Using a process of manual time correction, you can layer sounds more accurately, placing them exactly where you want them. You can have sounds rigidly on top of each other, or shift them slightly to change an emphasis, or throw in a bit of irregular human groove, as and when you wish. It puts you in complete control.

Imagine you want a snare drum, for instance, and can't decide between four different snare sounds that each have a bit of what you want about them: one is deep and powerful, one has a lot of very high-frequency harmonic ring to it, another has a lower mid-range ring, and the other is from a drum machine so it has a pleasantly artificial nature. But each of them on its own is not quite right, and no amount of EQ or effects will really get it either. The answer is to use all four of them... After all, according to Mr Haas, as long as they all occur within 30ms of each other, the listener will hear them as a single sound – a much fuller sound – but not as four separate snares.

When it comes to timing, the quantise function in a MIDI sequencer could obviously be used to pull notes back into time on a grid if they've been played slightly off-beat. And if this made everything turn out too regimented, you could even create quantise 'templates', in which you choose what to correct and what to leave loose, so as to preserve some human feel. But manual time correction gives you the ability to retain tiny nuances of timing everywhere, and let it change in a more personalised way throughout a track.

With time correction you also have the ability to play with adding and removing layers for different dramatic effect within separate musical passages, which isn't so easy to do with a keyzone map within a MIDI instrument.

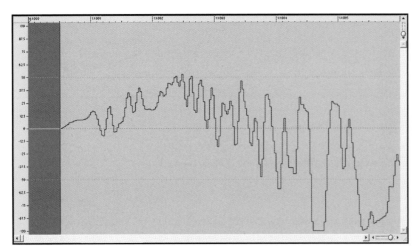

image **63**

Time correcting, step-by-step

The art of time correction basically involves adding or subtracting very small sections of silence before or after audio events, to minutely alter the relationships between them, and control the overall feel and sound of a piece of music.

CD1 Track 82 is a simple breakbeat sample that hasn't been quantised. This is what I've used to try out some time correcting, and you can follow the steps using the same sample if you like. Make sure you keep the original to hand, because it'll be essential for reference later, as you'll see.

(It's always useful to keep a backup of your unaltered samples anyway, in case things don't work out – there can be a lot of trial and error involved in this technique.)

First of all I opened the sample up in a stereo sample editor with its grid set to 'beats and bars' rather than 'time' – I used Steinberg's Wavelab for the job, because it's superior to the onboard sample edit facilities you get in the average DAW.

I then calculated the tempo, using the technique outlined in Chapter 4, and set the sample editor to the correct tempo – so the grid markings related appropriately to the sample.

The very first event in the sample is the kick drum. This was right at the start of the sample, but I moved it – if for no other reason than to illustrate a point and a technique. If you open the original sample and zoom in you'll see a section of flat line before the kick where I've inserted a small section of silence. This is totally imperceptible when played back – which proves the ear cannot distinguish very small silences. What we're going to do now is remove the silence again. Just select the section of flat line before the kick drum, as in image 63, and delete it.

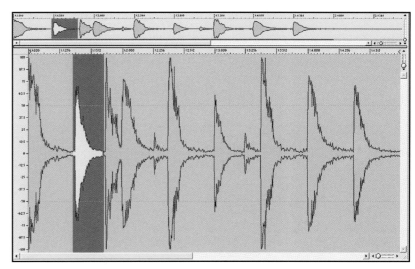

image **64**

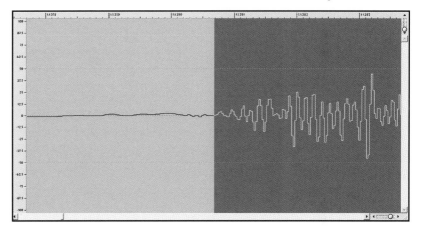

image **65**

Now on to the next significant event in the sample. In this case it's the first hi-hat beat. Onscreen sample editing makes this easy to identify: in image 64 you can see an overview of the entire sample, showing all of the events, and you'll see I've highlighted the first hat hit.

Zoom right in on the very start of the highlighted hi-hat hit, place the beginning of the selected area at precisely the start of the hat, look up the line to the meter calibration, and you should notice that the hit does not fall precisely on a significant grid line. As you might see in image 65, it actually falls just before beat 1.1.381.

Remember the aim here is not to try to quantise this sample, to enforce any mechanically pre-defined rhythm or metronomic timing – the intention is simply to take firm control over exactly where each event is positioned. In this case we're going to move this hat hit so it falls precisely on beat 1.1.381. You might just as easily choose to put it somewhere else – it's a subjective choice, in the end, depending on what sounds good to you. But we'll move it there for the sake of this illustration.

You need to highlight just the area between the current position of the beginning of the hat and point 1.1.381, as shown in image 66. I did this by leaving the start of the selected area exactly where it was and moving the end point to the left. This entailed zooming out, dragging the end of the selection to roughly the right area, zooming in, adjusting the end point, then zooming right in until I could be 100 per cent certain the end point is precisely on 1.1.381.

Once the correct area was selected I used the Insert Silence function from the edit menu. This turns the selected area into silence, and shifts the whole of the rest of the sample accordingly. The result looks like image 67.

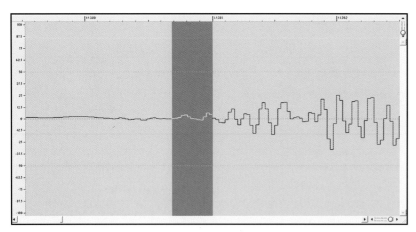

image **66**

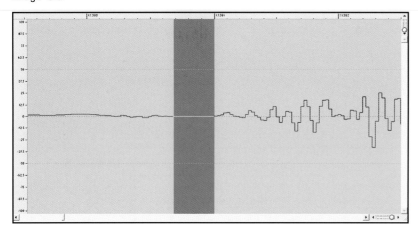

image **67**

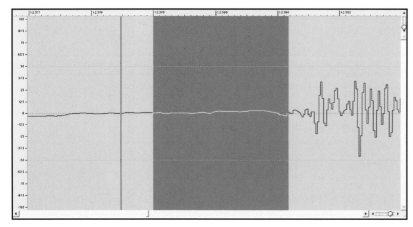

image **68**

Now you need to repeat the process with the next significant event, in this case another kick drum beat. This is where you have to call up the unaltered version of the sample, to determine the correct location for this kick drum – that's because when we moved the hi-hat a moment ago, we also moved the kick drum, so it's now in the wrong place.

In exactly the same way as we did for the hat, zoom in on the very start of the kick drum and you'll see that it should fall onto the grid at around 1.1.632. So you need to insert another section of silence into your 'corrected' sample to push it forward to the new correct location.

Next we come to the first snare beat. This is a perfect illustration of why time correction requires a fair amount of musical knowledge. In the original sample this snare falls quite significantly short of 1.2.000 – which is where the first snare beat would be if you quantised the rhythm, because a traditional 'square snare' falls exactly on the second beat of the bar (or at least it would on a drum machine). But this is a classic funk break, and the snare is a 'hasty' one – the fact that it's early is vital to the swing of the beat. So I decided to move it three ticks short of the metronome, at 1.1.762.

You need to repeat the process again for the little quiet pre-beat kick that also needs pushing ahead by inserting a small mount of silence. But the next event, the next kick, is different.

This kick is the sixth significant event to be dealt with, and we've been inserting little pieces of silence before each of the previous five, which have all added up. In the original sample you'll notice that the kick falls just after 1.2.378 (which still makes it a little early in relation to the metronome), but in the corrected version it's actually late. In fact it's three ticks late, at just past 1.2.381. We now need to pull it back – let's say to 1.2.379 – so select the area between 1.2.379 and the start of the hat, as shown in image 68. Then delete the selected area.

The next event is another hi-hat, which in the original is just before 1.2.763. In the corrected version it's late again, only this time only by half a tick or so. So repeat the process of selecting an appropriate area before the hat, and cut it out.

Now you continue through the rest of the sample, time-correcting each event, until the end.

Once you get a bit practised, this whole process does become a lot easier and quicker as your eyes and ears begin to recognise the imperfections, and more importantly where events should be on the grid. You can hear the finished result on CD1 Track 83.

Does it sound any different? Well, in fact you shouldn't really notice much on this short, simple sample – the idea was to maintain the feel of the original sample. You're not sprinkling fairy dust; it's a subtle and sophisticated technique that needs to be worked at patiently over a whole multi-layered track to achieve satisfactory results.

The benefits of time correction only really become apparent when additional layers of sound are added – and even then only those with sharp ears (and good hi-fi gear) will probably notice the acquired sheen of almost indefinable sonic clarity.

TICKS VS MILLISECONDS

On an editing or sequencing timeline grid like this, the ticks along the top aren't always a standard distance or time apart, but depend on settings within your software. For instance it might be set to show 480 ticks per beat (quarter note) – so at a tempo of 120bpm (two beats per second) there would be 960 ticks per second. Dividing this by 1000 gives us 0.96 ticks per ms – so every tick would be just over a millisecond long (1.04ms).

Creating time-corrected songs

The next step in the time correction composition process entails a move across to a digital audio workstation. You can use any DAW that allows you to place individual audio files onto audio tracks, with one basic proviso – you need to be able to disable the Snap-To-Grid function. The reason will become obvious in a moment…

What's coming up is not intended as an alternative to your DAW manual – depending on your prior skill you may need to use your manual to look up some processes.

As an exercise, I added a number of additional samples, in layers, to the time-corrected breakbeat in Track 83. I did this using Cubase SX2, just because that's what I like to use.

Starting with a breakbeat in this way makes a perfect introduction to how to use individual sample files onscreen to create audio structures. The techniques you'll see here are applicable in a great many ways.

The first step is to assemble the component parts you want to use to start off the song, and to set up one or two aspects of the DAW.

Because of the way DAW systems function, it's necessary to first 'import' these samples into the 'audio pool' (or 'folder', or the equivalent in your DAW) of a fresh song. This process of importing audio is common to all DAWs. It's necessary because it actually ensures that the DAW knows where to find them.

I've used the original un-corrected sample, plus the corrected sample, three additional snare samples, a side-stick (some call it a rim shot) sample, and two additional kick drum samples… so the 'pool' window looks like image 69. You'll find the two kick drum samples, side-stick and three snare samples on CD1, Tracks 84-89.

Media	Used	Status	Info				Type	Date	Origin
📁 Audio		Record							
🔉 DR808 boom			44.100 kHz	16 bits	Mono	1.104 s	Wave	3/4/2004	1(00:(
🔉 DRsnare 2			44.100 kHz	16 bits	Mono	0.596 s	Wave	3/5/2004	4: 00:(
🔉 DRsnare low			44.100 kHz	16 bits	Mono	0.997 s	Wave	3/5/2004	4: 00:(
🔉 Kontakt destinct snare			44.100 kHz	24 bits	Mono	0.266 s	Wave	3/4/2004	1: 00:(
🔉 Kontakt Kick			44.100 kHz	24 bits	Mono	0.545 s	Wave	3/4/2004	1: 00:(
🔉 Kontakt side stick			44.100 kHz	24 bits	Mono	0.200 s	Wave	3/4/2004	1: 00:(
🔉 Kontakt Snare			44.100 kHz	24 bits	Mono	1.600 s	Wave	3/4/2004	1: 00:(
🔉 Shaun Lee half correct	1		44.100 kHz	16 bits	Mono	2.792 s	Wave	3/22/2004	' 00:(
🔉 Shaun Lee Original Mono	1		44.100 kHz	16 bits	Mono	2.792 s	Wave	3/3/2004	3: 00:(
📁 Video									
🗑 Trash									

image **69**

Set the new DAW song to the correct tempo, in this instance 86bpm. Leave 'Snap-To-Grid' engaged for the moment, drag the original sample out onto the screen and place it on audio track 1. It will automatically be dropped onto the nearest bar on the grid, depending on where you release it – it's standard practice to drop it at a left locator position. Drag the time-corrected version out and drop it onto track 2 at the same song position. Set the right locator to the end of the sample and you should end up with something that looks like image 70. The two samples look the same at this zoom factor.

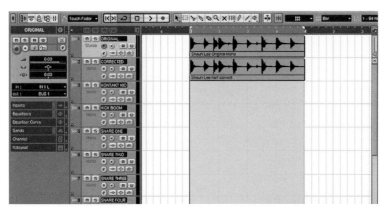

image **70**

Place the DAW into 'cycle' (looped) playback mode and try playing these two samples together. They'll sound phased. Mute audio track 1 so the original sample no longer plays.

Find the sample called Kontakt Kick (CD1 Track 84) and drop it onto track 3. Zoom the DAW arrangement window display in until you see something that looks like image 71.

You should now be able to see the short section of silence at the start of the original sample (which we removed when time-correcting the breakbeat). You'll also see that there's a similar flat line at the start of the Kontakt Kick. Many factory-prepared samples have these imperceptible, short silences at the start to avoid all possibility of unwanted clicks from 'zero crossing' problems (as discussed in Chapter 4). With all the other samples in this illustration, I've systematically removed such silences – I've just left this one in place to illustrate how to work around them onscreen, should you want to.

The solution is simply to move the start of the kick sample to the correct position by dragging the whole block to the left. Before you can do

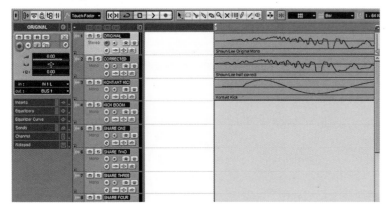

image **71**

this, though, you'll need to turn off Snap-To-Grid. You can see the re-aligned kick drum in image 72, with the area of silence now to the left of the start locator/marker, so the start of the kick itself is exactly aligned with the song start.

Now we're going to align more copies of Kontakt kick with the kick beats within our corrected breakbeat. Zoom the arrangement display most of the way out and place the song position indicator on top of the second kick in the pattern and zoom in.

Cubase has an automatic feature that keeps the song position indicator in the centre of the screen as you zoom in. This is very handy, because as you zoom down further you should find that you weren't bang-on with placing it first time around. You'll need to re-position the indicator right on the start of the breakbeat kick as you zoom down.

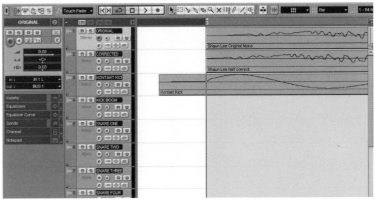

image **72**

Drag another copy from the pool and drop it on track 3, at the right location, and make fine alignment adjustments until the start of Kontakt Kick is spot-on as shown. I've placed the original copy of the break sample onscreen so you can compare the differences between it (at the top of the screen in image 73) and the corrected material below it – this illustrates that you can only see the differences between the two at very high zoom factors.

Play back the results to make sure it sounds right (which it should) and then repeat the process for the remaining breakbeat kicks. It ought to sound like CD1 Track 90.

At this stage I'm not going to place Kontakt Kick beats on top of the little breakbeat half-kick beats, simply because it won't sound right – it would overpower them.

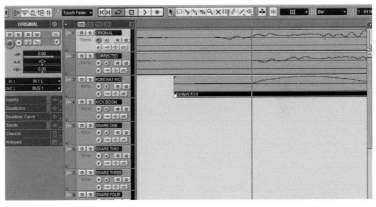

image **73**

image **74**

Time for the side-stick and the snares. Repeat the process of placing the song position indicator on the first snare beat. Zoom in and fine-align the position until it's perfect. Drag out and drop the side-stick and then each snare in turn from the pool onto different tracks, and fine-align their position. This should be easier because I've already trimmed them back so the snares actually begin right at the start of the samples. It should look like image 74.

You could repeat the process with the second snare beat in the breakbeat until you have all four additional snares in place… but there is a quicker way. Get the song position indicator

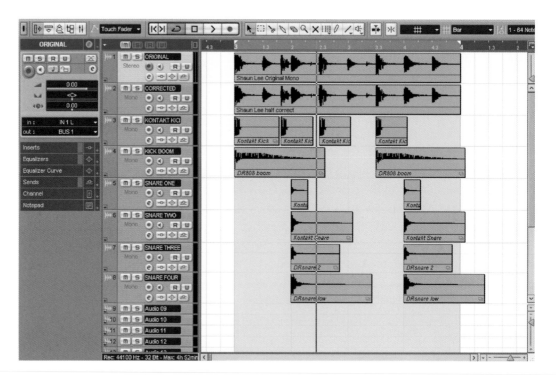

image **75**

aligned precisely with the second snare beat and then zoom right out again. Drag-select all four additional snare sounds, and they will all appear highlighted at once. Hold down the 'alt' key on your computer keyboard and drag them across and drop them so their start is on top of the indicator. This should make new copies of all four samples at once, rather than moving them. As long as you don't click anywhere onscreen except on top of your selected samples, they'll remain selected as a group.

You can then zoom in again and fine-align all four samples as a group. You can copy any audio file by using the method of holding down the 'alt' key.

Now we'll place the Kick Boom sample on top of some of the breakbeat kicks. It wouldn't sound right on all of them, so I've decided we should go for just the first and last kicks in the pattern. By the time it's done it should look like image 75. And it should sound like Track 91.

I made the sample on Track 91 by using the audio mixdown function in Cubase. To use it, you need to ensure that all the individual tracks you'd like included are un-muted. Select the Audio Mixdown command from the sub-menu that appears when you select Export within the File menu. You'll get a prompt to define a location where you would like the new sample to be saved. It includes everything between the two locators.

Most DAWs have a similar mixdown or export function within the File menu – except for Logic, which calls it Bounce and locates the button that activates it within the track mixer, right beside the master level fader.

Now for an experiment… After you've done an audio mixdown, import the new sample into the pool, create a stereo track for it, and drag it out into your song. Using the channel mute buttons, take out everything except the mixdown, then, as it plays, add the other tracks back in one at a time.

You should notice that the original, uncorrected sample causes a distinct phasing sound when played in conjunction with the other layers… and all the other samples and versions don't. That's because everything onscreen has been time-corrected, apart from the original breakbeat. So there must be something in it after all…

It can be very helpful to repeat this exercise with other instrument types, to get a feel for how different instrument sounds look and interact onscreen. By moving samples around on the grid you can create more or less anything you can with MIDI, and you don't need to start with a breakbeat.

If you place bass sounds on top of those kick drums using this process, they will sound different to the result using MIDI – and the same goes for every single instrument or sound you can think of. Any song created entirely within the audio tracks in this way will sound subtly but noticeably different to one created using MIDI.

The few simple techniques we've just covered – how to use the pool, how to align audio events precisely, layering and mixdown – are of immense value when it comes to working with musicians and vocalists. You've just been equipped with more facilities and possibilities than were available to music producers prior to the mid 1990s.

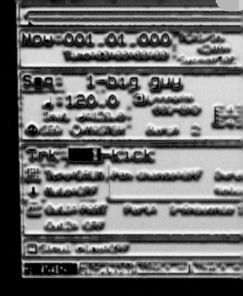

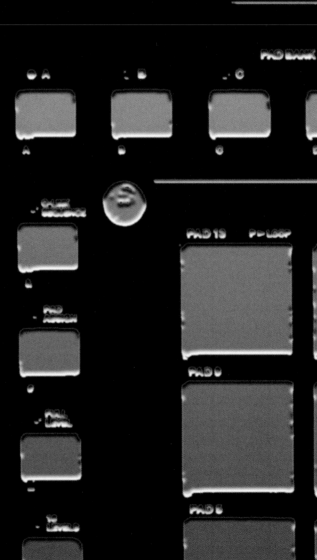

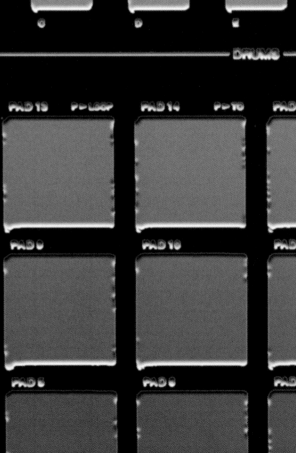

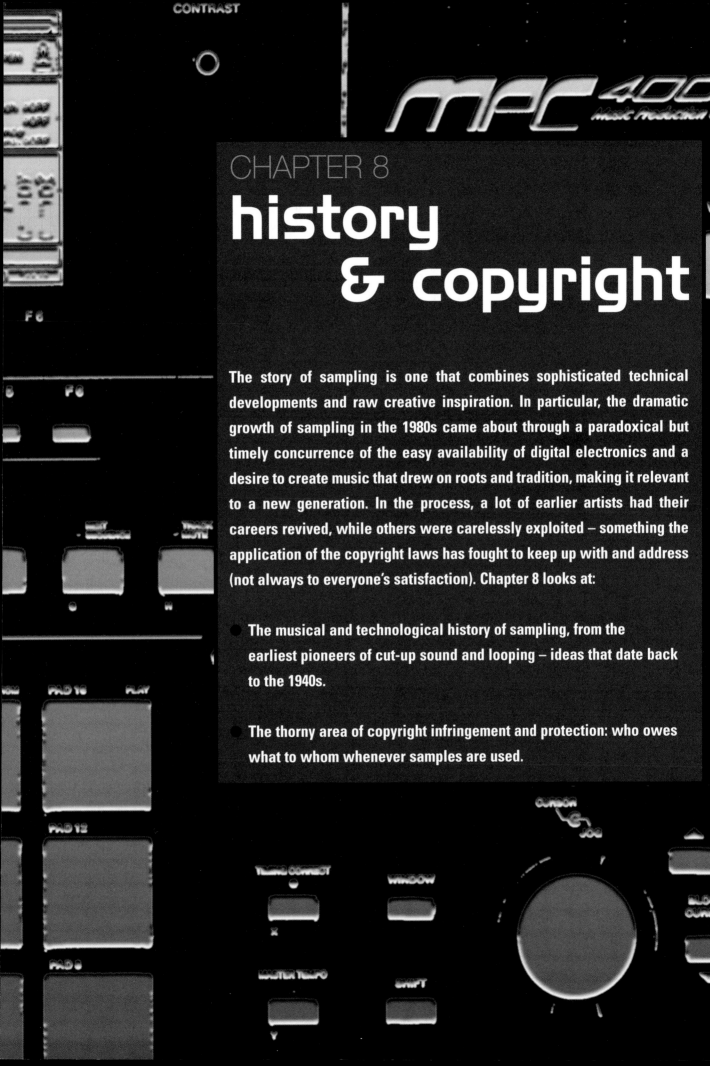

CHAPTER 8

history
& copyright

The story of sampling is one that combines sophisticated technical developments and raw creative inspiration. In particular, the dramatic growth of sampling in the 1980s came about through a paradoxical but timely concurrence of the easy availability of digital electronics and a desire to create music that drew on roots and tradition, making it relevant to a new generation. In the process, a lot of earlier artists had their careers revived, while others were carelessly exploited – something the application of the copyright laws has fought to keep up with and address (not always to everyone's satisfaction). Chapter 8 looks at:

● **The musical and technological history of sampling, from the earliest pioneers of cut-up sound and looping – ideas that date back to the 1940s.**

● **The thorny area of copyright infringement and protection: who owes what to whom whenever samples are used.**

This book is being published at a time of huge change. The computer is taking over, in modern music-making as in many other areas of life. We get the occasional anti-digital backlash, or cycles of back-to-basics nostalgia, but on the whole the trend is towards relentless computerisation.

The current generation of aspiring music producers start their careers looking at a screen and clutching a mouse, with no real understanding of what music-making could be like without their PCs, or indeed was like in the past, before computers.

But there's a lot to be learned from looking at the way things were done back then, and how sampling itself developed.

Early pioneers: on disc and tape

The roots of sampling technology lie firmly bedded in the use of magnetic tape for recording purposes. The introduction of a flexible, metal-oxide-coated plastic tape (invented by German companies AEG and BASF in the 1930s, though not widely adopted elsewhere until after WWII) made sound recording much more versatile – previously it involved gouging grooves into a fragile piece of wax or acetate. Without tape there would have been no advanced sound editing, no multi-track recording, and ultimately perhaps no sampling…

Two of the major boundary-pushers of tape recording development in post-WWII USA were the unlikely figures of crooner Bing Crosby and guitarist Les Paul. Crosby was intrigued when shown the first imported German tape recorder, and saw the possibilities it offered in his own work – for instance he could pre-record and edit his many radio broadcasts, and even piece together the best bits of a performance to produce a perfect 'master'. Bing was soon to be the number one customer of the US-made Ampex tape machines that followed.

Les Paul did more for music than simply lending his name to the famous Gibson guitar. He became renowned for his use of 'sound-on-sound' overdubbing, adding one new track at a time over his own pre-recorded backing track – a process that paved the way for full-blown multi-track layering. Paul also fiddled with the timing and pitch of his recordings, producing what sounded like impossibly fast lead guitar lines and harmonies.

The beauty of tape, of course, was that it could easily be copied, repeated, cut up, played backwards, and generally messed about with. And of course if you take a short length of tape, thread it through the tape play and record heads, back up around the two spools of a tape machine and then join the two ends to each other, you have a tape-loop. Hit Play and the loop will repeat over and over again until you hit stop. Sound familiar?

In fact, some basic sampling-like techniques even predated tape… particularly in the pioneering work of avant-garde musician Pierre Schaeffer. Born in France in 1910, Schaeffer had been through some basic music training and worked as an acoustic engineer before he introduced the music world to the concept of 'musique concrète' in the 1940s. This was defined as music inspired by and constructed from real-world sounds, as opposed to what he saw as more 'abstract' conventional composition, where notes are written on a page and performed on specially-made musical instruments. Schaeffer made a comparison between his method of working with sound and the way photography captured visual images.

And Schaeffer initially did this with discs, which he'd use to record and play back the sounds he wanted to combine. He was clearly a pioneer of turntablism as well as sampling: he even found a way of making a stylus stay within one groove on a disc – a lock-groove technique – effectively playing that section of the disc over and over in a loop.

Schaeffer first came to public attention in 1948 when his *Concert de Bruits* (*Concert Of Noises*) was broadcast on French radio. Moving on to work with tape in the early 1950s broadened his options, allowing him to edit sounds more accurately by physically cutting the tape (removing the attack from sounds was a popular ploy), and splicing it back together in any order he required. He could even add basic filtering, EQ and processors – like echo and reverb – although Schaeffer liked to draw a distinction between his musique concrète and the bourgeoning 'electronic music' movement at the time, where adding filters, envelopes and strange effects was inherently a more crucial part of the whole process.

Naturally Schaeffer had his critics right from the start, who rejected his work as "not real music" and a hodge-podge approach to composition. His argument was that his concept of making-it-up-as-you-go-along was closer to how music originally came about, before it became tied-down, formalised and inhibited by the 12-note octave and strict time signatures. Interestingly, Schaeffer also later said, "I don't consider myself a real musician ... What I am is a good researcher."

In the early 1950s, Schaeffer was joined at his 'Groupe de Recherche de Musique Concrète' studio by engineer Jacques Poullin and composer-percussionist Pierre Henry, and between them they came up with a range of groundbreaking equipment, including multi-headed and multi-track tape machines. Schaeffer's acclaimed collaborations with Henry included *Symphonie Pour Un Homme Seul* (*Symphony For A Man Alone*) in 1951.

Henry's own influence became far-reaching. In the 1960s, as well as making an album with prog rock band Spooky Tooth, Henry joined up with composer Michel Colombier to create music for the modern dance piece *Messe Pour Le Temps Present* – a much-quoted (and sampled) recording, which prompted an album of remixes in 2001 by contemporary stars like Coldcut, William Orbit and Fatboy Slim.

HENRY, ELECTRONIC HERO

Pierre Henry's experiments with tape and sound included dragging pre-recorded strips of tape at different speeds across the playback head of his tape player – a forerunner of the one-shot sample. Henry also experimented with playing back several copies of the same sound on different tape recorders, messing about with tiny delays between them to get phasing… an early example of sound processing work. And what he called 'reintroduction' – the art of layering sound by recording different performances on several machines and blending them back together by playing them 'live' – was another obvious forerunner of multi-track recording. For many years afterwards, people assumed Henry had made most of his sounds using the very early analog synthesisers that were being built at the time. He wasn't – he was working with the first sample-based, experimental multi-tracked sound palette in the world.

Stockhausen & Cage

German-born Karlheinz Stockhausen, who spent some time with the musique concrète group in the early 1950s, is renowned (and in some traditional circles perhaps reviled) as the first 'serious' classical composer to use electronic tone-generators. He also experimented with the changing relationships between rhythm and musical pitch that occur when you alter the speed of recorded material. For example the fact that a low rhythmic sound that's systematically sped up, and getting higher in pitch, will eventually sound more melodic than rhythmic. And, similarly, rhythms can unexpectedly emerge when you slow down a high-pitched melodic sound.

Stockhausen made whole pieces of music out of single short phrases/notes, and also did a load of experiments with repetition and systematic splicing of equal length pieces of tape. Weird as hell, but highly inventive.

Also in the early 1950s, veteran US avant-garde composer John Cage (who'd been exploring the frontiers of musical sounds since his invention of the 'prepared piano' in the

1930s) started experimenting with using pre-recorded sounds on tape. To Cage, a sound was "just a sound" – it made no difference to him whether it was played or recorded, conventionally 'musical' or not. His works famously include an entire piece consisting of silence – or more accurately containing whatever ambient noises happen to occur as it's performed, so it does actually sound different every time.

1960s: experimental noises in pop

Steve Reich, another great American musical experimenter, 25 years younger than Cage, was also intrigued by the unconventional possibilities of sound recording, but (as a drummer himself) he preferred music to have more of a recognisable 'pulse' – and possibly even more of a tune…

Reich is perhaps best known for gathering together teams of musicians to experiment with musical repetition and controlled, drifting rhythm (which means he clearly has a place in the history of sequencing too). But by 1964 he was experimenting with tape loops: using multiple tape machines and loops he created seminal works like 'Come Out' and 'It's Gonna Rain' from a single recorded voice and a few simple effects. The results were considered weirdly radical, even for the 1960s, but will strike a very familiar chord with a modern sample-friendly audience (especially those familiar with the work of Fatboy Slim).

Reich soon realised what fun it was to play live over such repeated patterns, and in the 1970s, 1980s and beyond he went on to record groups of musicians playing different musical phrases on top of various loops, creating pieces like 'NY Counterpoint'.

Reich's work is often compared to the driving, repetitive minimalism of contemporaries like Philip Glass and to some extent Terry Riley, the forefather of ambient music – himself always a keen user of loops. Their kind of quasi-mechanised repetition anticipated what was to come with Kraftwerk and then acid house in the 1980s and 1990s.

One (in)famous adaptation of the tape cut-up technique came from a man who specialised in what might be called electronic easy-listening. Jean Jacques Perrey was also known as the main proponent of the Ondioline (a small, proto-synth-type keyboard, which had appeared on hits like Del Shannon's 'Runaway'), and he later helped popularise the Moog synth – as well as being asked by Walt Disney to provide electronic music for his theme parks…

But in the mid 1960s Perrey decided to try applying Pierre Schaeffer's found-sound and tape-splicing methods with a lighter touch, creating a version of Rimsky-Korsakov's 'Flight Of The Bumble Bee'… using real bees. Having made his own field recordings of bees buzzing, Perrey says he spent 46 hours slicing and pasting hundreds of 1cm-long snippets of tape to create the two-minute track. It's perhaps the earliest example of sampling humour – although Perrey himself said later: "I think I was a little crazy back then."

Another great Sixties father (or mother) of invention, also well known for his own humour, was Frank Zappa. His 1967 album *Lumpy Gravy* is one of the crazed benchmarks of the decade's sonic weirdness – and again, loops, tape reversal, pitch changes are all part of the mix. Zappa was a constant champion of the work of Edgard Varese, a composer born well before his time (1883 to be exact), who himself used and abused every sound-making object he could think of, but ultimately believed his musical visions would only be fully realised with the advancement of electronic instruments. Varese died in 1965, before technology could truly catch up with his ideas.

The sound of revolution

The UK's contribution to the golden era of tape is not inconsiderable. It reached its peak with the experimental sound crew at Abbey Road studios in London in the 1960s: George Martin on production duties, engineer Geoff Emerick, and The Beatles on creative genius. The Beatles' clout in the industry was such that, by the mid 1960s they could decide to retire from live performances and devote their energies entirely to studio work. It also meant that when they asked for some new effect or innovative sound on a record, the technical boffins at Abbey Road got on the case smartish. There's no doubt The Beatles advanced the art of recording in their time.

A good few of the techniques we now consider to be standard practice in sound recording were invented or established on Beatles sessions at Abbey Road, especially during the making of the *Revolver* LP in 1966. For instance they pioneered the use of tape loops on 'Tomorrow Never Knows' – improvising by wrapping the loops around pencils, mike stands, or whatever was handy – along with flanging, tape echo and ADT (artificial double tracking) throughout the album.

As recording technology advanced, tape could be made wider, allowing more tracks to be recorded at once: first two, then three, then four, until The Beatles' sonic landmark in 1967, the first eight-track recording, *Sgt Pepper* – achieved by synching together two bulky four-track machines.

On the even more adventurous *White Album*, the aeroplane sound that sweeps across the stereo image at the start of 'Back In The USSR' is perhaps the first time a 'found sound' was used in this way on a mainstream pop record.

The Beatles also helped popularise the Mellotron, an early and much-loved (if flawed) attempt at a sampler keyboard, which they used on tracks like 'Strawberry Fields Forever' (it's that 'flute' sound you hear the beginning).

A Mellotron looked a bit like a big old Wurlitzer cinema organ; inside, it was something else altogether. Without going into all the nuts and bolts (or springs and levers), each key on the keyboard caused different pieces of tape to start playing, for as long as you held down the key (or until the tape ran out). When you released the key, the tape rewound. It came supplied with factory-prepared tapes of real instruments – or you could prepare your own tapes for it, if you were feeling especially adventurous.

Meantime over in Germany... Holger Czukay, a Stockhausen devotee and founder of the group Can, recorded an album at the end of the Sixties called *Canaxis 5*, which featured tape loops of Vietnamese women singing as a basis for the track 'Boat Woman Song'. This was, perhaps, the first example of loops used in this way by a non-classical composer – and though it wasn't particularly widely heard at the time, could certainly have been an influence on some of the more experimental rock artists that followed.

THE MELLOTRON STORY

The original technology behind the Mellotron came from an American called Harry Chamberlin who, in 1946, built the Model100 Rhythmate, a bulky box that contained about 14 drum pattern loops. Harry continually refined the idea, and by 1960 he'd developed it into the keyboard-operated Music Master 600 (which was at one point rivalled by Canadian Hugh Le Caine and his experimental, keyboard-controlled 'Special Purpose Tape Recorder'). But Harry was apparently having trouble satisfying demand, and keeping on top of technical problems. His salesman, Bill Franson, took a couple of 600s to England to try and find somebody to take the idea a step or two further (with or without Harry's permission). By 1963, the UK's Bradley brothers had launched their own remarkably similar offshoot, the Mellotron – which subsequently featured on the Moody Blues *Love And Beauty* as well as some Beatle tracks. In 1965 the BBC had a custom Mellotron FX built for laying sound effects or 'spot effects' – it held an awesome 1270 recordings of seven seconds each, and was famously used on the soundtrack of the TV sci-fi show *Doctor Who*.

1970s: analog heaven...

Apart from the Mellotron, the early 1970s really belonged to the analog synthesiser – from huge monolithic modular synths with their monstrous walls of knobs, sockets and wires (as exploited by the likes of Keith Emerson in ELP), to more homely, wood-encased string machines (like the ARP/Solina String Ensemble), the Seventies analog equivalent of using an orchestral string sample.

Pink Floyd, who'd already proved themselves masters of challenging 'progressive' rock music with albums like *Ummagumma* and *Atom Heart Mother*, released their era-defining *Dark Side Of The Moon* album in 1973, complete with tape loops and the little EMS VCS3 synth, already brought to prominence by Brian Eno in Roxy Music.

German bands were more often than not at the forefront of the electronic and sonic revolution in the Seventies – not just Czukay's Can, but Faust (who adapted Schaeffer/Henry's musique concrète for a rock audience), Neu! (a looser, rockier Kraftwerk), and head-music synthesists Tangerine Dream.

And of course not forgetting Kraftwerk themselves – whose own uniquely controlled and rhythmic soundscapes were to become the most heavily leaned-on and 'borrowed' in all of electronic music when hip-hop and techno artists started looking for samples.

Unlike some of the big 'prog' bands of the time – like Yes and Genesis, whose music veered towards the classical in its complexity and length – the German bands of this period appealed to later new wave/punk and then dance-music-oriented artists because of their concentration on rhythm and tone rather than melodic elaboration and musical virtuosity.

ONLY ONE ENO

Brian Eno was one of the great sonic pioneers of the 1970s. Inspired by the work of Steve Reich, at the start of the decade Eno had made some sound loops for an experimental film; then after his pivotal role in Roxy Music – where he'd contributed synth sounds previously unheard in pop, as well as electronically 'treating' the band's output onstage – he linked up with King Crimson guitarist Robert Fripp to experiment with heavy tape delay on *No Pussyfooting*. By the end of the decade Eno was producing Talking Heads, and in 1979 started work with Heads' frontman David Byrne on what would be a landmark in the use of samples (even before the word itself was used), the album *My Life In The Bush Of Ghosts*.

Dance, dance, dance

By the mid 1970s, hip-hop was already becoming established in New York, where its driving forces were Afrika Bambaataa and DJs like Kool Herc and Grandmaster Flash. Using a combination of proto-sampling DJing techniques – picking out breakbeats worth repeating, backspinning to replay sections, rapid cross-fading between decks etc – they changed the face of dance and club music for the next 20 years. Many of the turntable techniques involved had been imported from Jamaica, where former DJ King Tubby had already invented studio remixing and dub by stripping tracks back to just drums and bass before adding copious random effects.

What those New York club DJs were doing perhaps marked the start of a modern phenomenon that would have been inconceivable in the music industry of earlier eras. Ever since this period, a great deal of fine, inventive music has been made by people who'd never even thought of themselves as musicians at all. It was DJs, and later dance music producers/engineers, who first saw the opportunities presented by samplers, and who propelled the subsequent rampant expansion of digital sampling technology.

The roots of modern dance music can be traced back to the turntablist's art of 'beat-juggling' – using two copies of the same record, on two turntables, cued up to play the same excerpt, one after the other, over and over. When DJs like Herc and Flash started repeating the instrumental 'breakdowns' of records to make those sections longer, all they were trying to do was keep people dancing – to make the funky, hypnotic, vocal-free grooves last longer. Dancefloors, after all, have always been driven by repetitive rhythms.

What they did, before the invention of the sampler as we know it now, was to take one part of a record – however short in its original form – and repeat it many times; in effect playing it as though it was in a loop. It was all done in realtime with nothing but those two bits of vinyl, a very acute ear, and lightning-quick reactions to flick back and forth between decks without missing a beat. By changing the context of the sounds in this way, they could essentially make these short repeated sections into new pieces of music.

Towards the end of the 1970s, technical innovations were coming thick and fast… The bourgeoning electronic movement in the UK threw up groundbreaking acts like Cabaret Voltaire and Throbbing Gristle, whose music was littered with tape extracts and innovative musical twists. In fact, Throbbing Gristle keyboard player Peter Christopherson even made his own one-off sample-playing keyboard (actually more like a reinvented DIY Mellotron), whose keys triggered individual cassette players.

It wasn't long before 'proper' sampling would make its debut – the only trouble was, hardly anyone could afford to buy the equipment when it appeared.

1980s: birth of digital sampling

The Fairlight CMI (computer musical instrument) was considered the first commercially available digital sampler, but it was unfeasibly large and impossibly expensive – ranging from £20,000 ($35,000) to over £50,000 ($85,000) for later models. Only big stars at the time – forward-thinking ones like Peter Gabriel and Stevie Wonder at least – had both the money and the interest to seek it out and use it.

Launched in 1980, the Fairlight's eclectic samples also opened western ears to the potential of previously obscure ethnic instruments. And of course you could record your own samples, manipulate them with the built-in sound-shaping tools, and play them back, either as a one-off sound or as part of a programmed sequence.

The instrument was also a large part of the impetus behind the formation of the group Art Of Noise by producer Trevor Horn – the group's name was taken from an Italian Futurist text that suggested sounds could be assembled in an audio collage. With the help of the Fairlight, the band introduced this concept into the world of modern pop music.

Horn was an early convert to the Fairlight, and remained faithful to it long after most other musicians had moved on to other samplers. It didn't do him any harm: he had several huge hits with Frankie Goes To Hollywood between 1983-86, produced almost exclusively using the Fairlight. Movie score composer Hans Zimmer was another keen user, as was singer/writer Kate Bush.

The fervour created by aspirational products like the Fairlight (and its even more expensive rival, the Synclavier) certainly set the sampling ball rolling. But because computer processing power and memory was very limited at the time, the

FAIRLIGHT – A NEW DAWN

The Fairlight was also a digital synthesiser and a primitive multi-timbral sequencer, but its sampling ability was the big attraction – even though it was only 8-bit resolution and had a pretty low sampling rate by later standards. At the time it was state-of-the-art, and the sounds it produced astonishingly powerful, albeit just a few seconds long. Being offered such a facility in a world still dominated by magnetic tape was heavenly – being able to digitally record a small length of sound and then play it back simply by hitting a key on a keyboard opened up a momentous world of possibility.

most effective samples were initially short ones – which made drums an ideal source material. Analog drum machines had been used throughout the Seventies – basically synthesised drum emulations, initially in pre-configured patterns – but now a new level of realism, and rhythmic control, was on offer.

With the arrival of two drum-sample players in 1980 – Roger Linn's LM1 drum computer and the Oberheim DMX – the drum machine began to have a profound effect on popular music. The DMX became the rhythm unit of choice for many hip-hop acts, while the Linn Drum (as the LM1's successor was called) was adopted by groundbreaking electronic artists like The Human League and Gary Numan, as well as Vangelis and Prince. Suddenly music became much more rigidly 'in time' than it had ever been, as the electronic metronome took over. The dance-music revolution wasn't far off…

More affordable sample-using drumboxes started appearing in the early 1980s, of which the most famous was probably E-mu's Drumulator. Despite containing only eight 12-bit sounds, its price and quality meant it acquired a devoted following, and E-mu followed it with the SP12 and SP1200 drumboxes.

The next major advance for sampled percussion would come in the shape of 1984's Clavia DP1, the 'digital percussion plate', which by the end of the year was called simply the 'ddrum', short for digital drum. Originally just a flat box with a rubber pad on top, Clavia soon introduced drum-like pads (with real drum skins) that could trigger the sampled sounds – though still only 8-bit, 16kHz samples at first. Gradually this developed into an entire kit of these drum pads linked to a sophisticated sound-editing module – the forerunner of the 'virtual' or digitally modelled kits we see today.

(Strangely, though, drummers didn't take up this kind of kit to anything like the extent that sampling in general began to be adopted – most drummers seemed to prefer to stick to the more traditional acoustic kit.)

ANALOG REVIVAL

There was an unforeseen set-back for sampled-drum products at the end of the 1980s and early 1990s. Ironically, a lot of up-and-coming dance producers and artists at the time began to reject sampled 'real' drum sounds altogether in favour of the thumping 'electro-beats' of the earlier generation of synthesised drumbox units. This meant previously out-of-fashion and often discontinued analog machines like the Roland TR-808 and 909 rapidly became essential items in any dance music production studio. This preference later spread to all areas of electronic music production, as the analog backlash took hold – almost before digital technology could even establish itself. Fifteen years later, digital has improved enormously, but for some people the jury is still out on which sounds best...

As regards sampling *keyboards*, the first of the relatively-affordable mid-1980s alternatives to the 'sell-your-house' Fairlight and Synclavier was E-mu's Emulator, at a mere £5,000 ($9,000). The Emulator II was particularly popular, and was the first instrument to offer a CD-ROM of extra sounds. There was also the much-admired, high-spec'd Kurzweil K250; the remarkably affordable Ensoniq Mirage, forerunner of the more intelligent EPS (Ensoniq Performance Sampler); the Sequential Circuits Prophet 2000; the PPG Wave, co-developed by Tangerine Dream; and the first sampling keyboards from Korg and Roland, the DSS-1 and the S-10 respectively (the latter was followed up by Roland's more professional-standard S-50 keyboard sampler).

After the analog Seventies, the Eighties was undoubtedly the era of the digital synth – Yamaha launched their DX7 in 1983, and Roland's D-50 S&S synth arrived in 1987, closely followed by Korg's M1. But so-called 'home keyboards', often cheap-and-cheerful entry-level mini-synths, were big business too. And in terms of bringing easy, useable sampling to the bourgeoning 'home-recording' market, it could be argued that 1987's Casio FZ-1 made one of the biggest impacts. Before this, most of the easily-affordable sampling keyboards could offer just snippets of sampling time, but the Casio FZ-1 could manage almost two minutes – albeit if you opted for a low sample rate. It was undeniably a major step-up from the company's 1985 effort, the SK-1, a gimmicky 'toy' keyboard-sampler (which nonetheless had its own kitsch appeal for some).

But if you were after a standalone, professional-quality, rackmountable sampler in the mid-to-late 1980s, the choice was really between E-mu's Emax (which also came in keyboard form), or Akai's S range – initially the S900, soon superseded by the superior (and still in-demand 15 years later) S1000. By the end of the 1980s, samplers like this were offering 16-bit sound, 44.1kHz sampling resolution (ie CD quality), up to 32MB of RAM, and hard disk recording facilities.

Good times

Music and technology developed in tandem throughout the 1980s. As samplers gained more memory and improved in audio fidelity, a new phenomenon started to emerge. Instead of just throwing in brief lo-fi sonic references, it became possible to lift whole sections of existing records and incorporate them into new forms. But there is some debate over who was actually first to do this…

It's often claimed that the first substantially sample-based track to cross over to the mainstream was the Sugarhill Gang's 'Rapper's Delight' back in 1979. But no… Although that was certainly one of the first rap tracks to make the pop charts, and is clearly built around the bassline from Chic's disco stomper 'Good Times', it doesn't actually use a sample at all. Sampling technology didn't permit such a lengthy steal at that time (certainly not at high enough quality), so those Chic rhythm and bass tracks were reconstructed in the studio by session musicians. This didn't stop Chic from suing the 'Gang' for ripping off the riff, of course, which they'd done without seeking permission or paying royalties.

Others believe the breakthrough track for sampling was the 1982 single 'Planet Rock'. By that time New York's hip-hop pioneers were finally managing to reach the record-buying public, and Afrika Bambaataa showed the way forward with this mould-breaking electro-rap track, which seemed to blatantly lift the synth riff from Kraftwerk's stark Seventies classic 'Trans-Europe Express'. But in fact, if you listen to 'Planet Rock' closely, you'll hear the riff is played ever so slightly differently, and is again just a re-creation, as is the Kraftwerk-style beat. (Apparently Bambaataa didn't adopt digital sampling until 'Looking For The Perfect Beat' the following year.)

Inevitably, though, 'Planet Rock' itself soon became one of the most sampled records in hip-hop, starting a trend that continues to this day, where records that are themselves based on earlier recordings become new source material for the next generation of samplers.

Another track that's sometimes quoted as influential by sample-users and remixers is Steinski & Double D's 1983 'Payoff Mix'. This was never commercially released. It was voted winner of a remix competition held by Tommy Boy Records (home of Afrika Bambaataa), but was impossible to clear at the time because it sampled from over 20 sources, including old movies and records, obscure and famous – for instance Culture Club and Herbie Hancock tracks, as well as Humphrey Bogart in *Casablanca* saying 'Play it!'. Steinski followed it up with the major underground dancefloor hit 'Lesson 2: The James Brown Mix'.

Two other names leap out from the history books as pioneers of sample use in this era –

there were undoubtedly others who had similar ideas, but never achieved the same level of recognition (but then that's the way history works). The man who co-produced Afrika Bambaataa's 'Planet Rock', former DJ Arthur Baker, went on to have a big impact on 1980s studio production methods in his own right.

As soon as sampling technology would allow, Baker made a pivotal 'cut & paste' track with the Criminal Element Orchestra, 'Put The Needle To The Record', before working with New Order and a host of big-name acts. The other sample-using pioneer from this period is revered New York DJ and producer Todd Terry, often credited as the man who introduced sampling into US house music.

DJs everywhere soon realised they could use the fledgling technology of digital sampling in the recording studio to emulate the turntablists' live beat-juggling effect, and in doing so revolutionised dance music in the late 1980s.

In the UK, the first recognised use of a digital sampler on a commercial recording was Paul Hardcastle's thought-provoking, Vietnam-referencing '19', a huge hit for him in 1985. Apparently he used an Emulator for the repetitive samples, though he went out and bought a Synclavier with the profits from the record's success.

But it was Coldcut – Matt Black and Jonathan More, a duo already known as DJs on the acid house/rave scene – who produced what's believed to be the first British hip-hop-style sample paste-job on their white label EP 'Say Kids, What Time Is It?' around 1986. They soon came to wider attention with their weird-and-wonderful seven-minute remix of Erik B & Rakim's 1987 hit, 'Paid In Full', before having hits of their own with various guest vocalists. Ever-inventive, Coldcut were also behind the launch of an innovative video sampler, the Vjamm, which pointed the way to the future in the audio-visual field.

Even more successful – the first sample-constructed track to really get everyone's attention – was 'Pump Up The Volume' by M/A/R/R/S, which reached Number One in the UK in October 1987, and was a US Top Ten hit. It featured colliding slices of everything from James Brown to alarm clocks and strange voices to recent pop songs, and even cheekily sampled Coldcut.

Perhaps because it sold so many copies, it also opened the door to the world of sampling litigation – though it took a few years for the record industry, and their lawyers, to wake up to what was happening.

Walk this way...

In the States, hip-hop had always been at the leading edge of sampling. Right from their debut album *Yo! Bum Rush The Show* in 1987, Public Enemy amply demonstrated the incessant raw power in the repetition of borrowed funky beats and atmospheric loops, which underpinned Chuck D's relentless social comment. While De La Soul and The Jungle Brothers were proving there was still life in those old disco, soul and jazz records, many hip-hop artists turned to a new source to find harder, cutting sounds they could loop and rap over. They looked to heavy rock music.

Run DMC were probably first – though in truth their 1983 experiment 'Rock Box' was a slightly lame attempt built around a cheesy AOR guitar riff. But by 1986 they'd perfected the formula, and their blending of the Aerosmith rocker 'Walk This Way' with their own streetwise rap style appealed to an unexpectedly huge worldwide audience. Even Aerosmith loved it, and what had begun as a looped guitar and drum sample became a fully-fledged collaboration between the two acts – one that relaunched Aerosmith's languishing career into the bargain. The Beastie Boys were quickly in on the act too, sampling everyone from AC/DC to Zeppelin. (After James Brown, the most popular source for samplers seemed to be Led Zeppelin, especially John Bonham's drum pattern from 'When The Levee Breaks'.)

By the end of the 1980s, the sampling floodgates were well-and-truly open. Suddenly everyone was sampling everything. You couldn't move for 'Funky Drummer' rhythms, and umpteen other James Brown samples, often appropriated by the most unlikely artists – 'indie' guitar bands, for example, with barely a funky bone in their bodies.

Such was the transformative power of sampling. You could even imbue any lacklustre house or techno instrumental with some much needed gravitas by dropping in a few choice words from historical orators – Martin Luther King, Malcolm X, JFK…

In those almost carefree 'pre-legislation' days, anything seemed fair game. Movies and TV shows were frequently trawled for useable sound clips. According to Peter Cigéhn's exhaustive 'Top Sample List' website (in case you're wondering), the most popular source of spoken-word samples is Ridley Scott's 1982 movie *Blade Runner*; and the group that's used the most non-music samples is Canadian 'avant-industrial' band Skinny Puppy. In Britain it was probably the fearlessly opportunistic and appropriately-named Pop Will Eat Itself, who sampled everyone from Robert De Niro and Rod Serling to Lipps Inc and The Who.

HIP-HOP IN A BOX

1988 saw the launch of probably the most significant music production tool of the late 1980s, the Akai MPC60. This all-in-one sequencer-sampler workstation (following in the footsteps of the Sequential Circuits Studio 440) was designed by Roger Linn, and became a huge success with hip-hop and techno artists. In fact, regardless of the rapid technological developments that ensued, the MPC60 retained its status as the music-making tool of choice for all kinds of rhythm-centred music producers, particularly rap and R&B, throughout the next decade – as much for its slightly lo-fi sampling resolution as its overall ease of use as a sequencer.

At the smoother, less noisy end of the sampling neighbourhood, two of the most musically inventive bands around at the end of the 1980s were De La Soul and A Tribe Called Quest, whose eclectic tastes and unpredictable melodic juxtapositions were a refreshing alternative to the growing batch of heavier, more one-dimensional gangsta rappers. With their intelligent lyrics and jazz-inflected grooves, they helped bring rap, and sampling, to another new audience. They didn't please everyone, though – especially the record labels from whom they 'stole' the samples…The carefree times couldn't last – but sampling was here to stay.

1990s: sampling in the mainstream

By 1990, sampling had become a dominant force in music production. Most modern studios offered sampling facilities, and it became an increasingly important part of a home-recording set-up during the decade – certainly crucial for anyone making dance or hip-hop tracks.

Not surprisingly, for an instrument with a limitless sound palette, the sampler helped take electronic music in countless different directions at once. There was an astounding explosion of experimentation and musical creativity. In the first few years of the decade so many innovative things happened, music evolved so fast, that most of us missed most of it… As the decade progressed many of the ideas first aired in those early years were picked up by subsequent generations of young producers and turned into entire movements.

The early 1990s in the UK saw the hardest, fastest forms of techno take a dark twist when they crashed headlong into dub. Thanks to producers like Dillinjah, Rob Playford and Grooverider, the tempo pushed up so far that hip-hop-style funk breaks could be layered over

1990s' GROUNDBREAKING GEAR

So much new musical gear – hardware and software – was launched in the 1990s that it's impossible to offer any kind of comprehensive list here, but some of the technological highlights might include:

AKAI S1100 – the first sampler with a hard-disk

KORG WAVESTATION – with vector synthesis and wave sequencing

DIGIDESIGN SAMPLECELL – the first DSP-based software sampler

ENSONIQ ASR 10 & EPS16 – a couple of advanced, intelligent sampler-keyboard workstations

STEINBERG CUBASE – first audio+MIDI sequencer for Mac & PC, followed in 1996 by VST version

DIGIDESIGN PRO TOOLS – soon became the industry-standard top-end audio+MIDI recording system

ROLAND S-750 – their best sampler to date

KURZWEIL K2000 – a quality sampling workstation;

CLAVIA NORD LEAD – revolutionary 'virtual analog' synth, followed three years later by the Nord Modular

AKAI CD3000 – sampler with built-in CD drive

EMAGIC LOGIC – new software sequencer, evolved from C-Lab's Notator

AKAI MPC3000 – almost limitless upgrade of the MPC60, six minutes of CD-quality sampling at a time

PROPELLERHEAD RECYCLE – audio loop production/editing software

STEINBERG WAVELAB – audio editing software

ENSONIQ ASRX – their answer to the MPC3000

PROPELLERHEAD REBIRTH – software emulations of Roland/Boss drum/bass machines (808, 303)

AKAI REMIX 16 – DJ-oriented phrase sampler

YAMAHA A3000 – powerful 'control sampler'; later 4000/5000 models featured complex filters and effects

SONIC FOUNDRY ACID – audio/loop sequencing software

KORG KAOSS – dynamic realtime controller/effect pad

KORG TRITON – their first proper sampling keyboard since 1987

half-tempo dub-style heavy basslines to bring us jungle, which mutated into drum & bass as some of the more straightforward dub references became less prominent.

The launch of the sample-slicing software Recycle in 1992 made it infinitely easier to chop up the old breakbeats into slices, so the rhythm could be changed while the feel remained intact. The facility to manipulate breakbeats was set to drastically alter almost all forms of electronica. As the second half of the Nineties spun on, not only did 'breakbeat' become an entire musical sub genre of its own, with the likes of Fatboy Slim enjoying massive chart success worldwide, but adding the break to everything from house to techno to ambient sent rhythmic stimulation through each genre.

The Nineties was also the decade where the personal computer began to take hold of music production. As soon as a computer acquired the power to do what a hardware sampler, or synth, or sequencer, or multi-track recorder could do, somebody wrote a program to make it happen.

21st century: what's next for sampling

After the intense activity of the previous decade, almost inevitably the inventive progress of sampling has slowed down somewhat over recent years. Not that this spells a gloomy future for sampling by any means – just perhaps an end of its hyper-active and over-hyped adolescence. It can now settle down, maturely, to its deserved place at the heart of any recording set-up. After all, compare the evolution of the electric guitar: the fundamental design has remained unchanged for over 40 years, and it's currently enjoying yet another renaissance in terms of popularity. If it ain't broke, why fix it?

The sampler is now a well-established, even essential component in a modern music-making environment. The main technical advances of late have been in computer processing power, which has brought incredibly sophisticated sampling options into the hands of everyone with access to a home computer. Computers have made it possible to cram almost every aspect of the music production process into today's audio+MIDI sequencers. They're unimaginably powerful compared to tools even a decade old. If you're meeting one for the first time, you're being handed a hundred instruments at once – and most of us will only use a tenth of what computers can actually do, no matter how long we use them. Computers also allow us to go to ever more unrealistic extremes, creating music that simply wouldn't be possible without the modern crop of power-hungry hardware and software sampling products.

Having said that, some people choose to ignore this 'progress' altogether: Norman Cook (aka Fatboy Slim), who cheerfully admits to being a "computer luddite", still uses his ageing Atari ST to create his multi-million selling records. He says that's the only computer he owns. It's all about what you're comfortable with. The end result, as always, is the important factor.

So where are we now? In 2004 the breakbeat still rules the roost in R&B and hip-hop, though these genres are showing signs of flagging, and really represent dance music's last foothold on the popular music charts. The 'mash-up' (or 'bootleg', or 'bastard pop') can be seen as the art of sampling taken to one extreme. In this influential and ubiquitous stroke-of-genius, two entire records are mixed together and released as a new one – often illegally, at least at first, when it's issued as an anonymous 'white label' 12″.

The ability to merge two existing, sometimes recognisable, pieces of music to form a new composition has always been at the heart of DJing and dance music production. In these bootlegs, one well-known song is layered on top of another well-known song – the more incongruous the better – and the results, when they work, are at worst amusing and at best unexpectedly inspiring. It's one ultimate use of all the sampling and synthesis tools we've looked at in this book, from timestretching and looping to filtering and beat slicing – but because of its cavalier approach to copyright, few examples make it through to the mainstream. Plenty on the net, mind…

As always, this latest musical genre is dismissed by some as a passing fad. It may be. Musical tastes inevitably change. But the sign of a strong technology is if it can adapt to suit new circumstances. Samplers clearly pass this test. You can, after all, make any kind of music with a sampler.

Songs (once derided by the dance generation as 'boring') are back in fashion, and yet the sampler clearly still has a role to play – and can even be said to have helped create this new appetite for riffs and melodies. Songwriting can be looked at and appreciated in a new light now. Sample-based dance music helped sweep away rambling Eighties AOR ballads (in the same way punk did with bloated Seventies rock). Sampling technology allowed music-makers to cut-to-the-chase – you only needed to use the interesting bits, the hooks and breakbeats, because much of the rest was 'filler' anyway. The current generation of songwriters can now call on the technology of the Nineties, as well as the musical inspiration of the Sixties and Seventies…

This awareness of what makes a song work, and the editing skills, attention to detail, and confidence required to leave out what's not working, are among the priceless lessons that sampling has brought us. Live performances and 'real' instruments have an undoubted appeal, and always will – but there's also no doubt that samplers will remain essential composing and recording tools, no matter what style of music is in vogue at any time.

21st CENTURY HARDWARE & SOFTWARE

Again, just a few juicy items from recent years:

EMAGIC EXS24 – software sampler designed for Logic and Pro Tools

NI REAKTOR – superior and versatile modular S&S software, three separate sophisticated sampler modules

SYNTRILLIUM COOL EDIT – audio editing software, later rebranded Adobe Audition

PROPELLERHEAD REASON – all-in-one studio in a software 'rack'

KORG ELECTRIBE ES1 – rhythm production sampler

ROLAND VP-9000 – sampler/vocal processor, realtime manipulation

AKAI Z-SERIES – 24-bit, 96kHz samplers, controlled by AkSys software

STEINBERG NUENDO – new generation software audio sequencer

STEINBERG HALION – their own virtual sampler

ROLAND V-SYNTH – variable oscillator modelling sampler-synth

AKAI VZ8 – software version of Z series

MOTU MACH FIVE – sophisticated plug-in sampler

ABLETON LIVE – comprehensive software production system, for use in realtime

MAKING WAVES – complete music production software

CAKEWALK SONAR 4 – latest version of audio production software

YAMAHA 01X – mLAN music production studio

EMULATOR X – hardware & software hybrid sampler

COPYRIGHT – SAMPLING & THE LAW

Pablo Picasso apparently once said: "Good artists copy – great artists steal." Sadly, he wasn't put in charge of formulating the copyright laws.

Musicians and composers have always borrowed ideas from earlier creations. When we're writing music, we're all influenced by the music we love, even if we don't always realise it. Blatant theft is certainly a major part of the evolution of dance music, but it can be argued that it's impossible to make any kind of music without 'borrowing' ideas from those that inspired you. Digital sampling, of course, has made this a lot easier.

So why do people do it? Why can't everyone create something totally original? Maybe it's because, in popular music, there are few completely new ideas left to discover. Everything is variations on a theme. The fact is, whether we like it or not, if something is too 'new' and different, fewer people will listen. Messing around within familiar boundaries is where we're generally happiest. Copyright law is about judging whether something is just *too* familiar.

It's undeniable that the act of musical recycling, or re-contextualisation, can have enormous power. It can be as devastatingly simple as the repetition of some beats or a section of an existing piece of music, with the intention of making people dance, or it can be a highly political and emotive use of controversial spoken material… or many things in-between.

When a crowd on a dancefloor hears a record they recognise, it can cause a rush of adrenalin. When they subsequently realise that what they thought they knew is in fact now an element of a *new* piece of music, one that's playing with the crowd and their communal recognition, they love it even more, and there's a frenzy of excitement – especially if the new version presents the familiar sounds in an innovative way.

Take the current trend for mash-ups, or 'bastard pop'. The potential source material is obviously vast, but it's also still a largely underground and illegal movement, done for fun rather than profit. Some people would argue that's what music should be about – enjoyment, not cash. Trouble is, it's also a profession and sometimes a crucial source of income for some artists. And of course it's become a huge global industry, with a large amount of money to be made… and often argued over.

WHAT RIGHTS?

What exactly does being a 'copyright owner' involve? Essentially, owning the copyright of a piece of music grants you certain specific rights:

● **The right to reproduce or copy the work.**
● **The right to distribute, sell or lend the work to the public.**
● **The right to perform it in public, either live on-stage or by playing a tape or disc.**
● **The right to broadcast it on TV, radio, internet etc.**
● **The right to adapt the work or make a derivative work based on it (a remix, for instance).**

Anyone else who does any of these things, or authorises someone else to do them, without consent from you, infringes your copyright.

What does copyright mean for you?

Copyright nowadays involves a complex web of rights and collection agencies, which will vary from country to country – but I'll try and go through roughly how the systems work.

First, a brief definition of copyright. The way the law stands at present, in the UK and the US, copyright exists as soon as you (or anyone else) *creates* a work. Not when you first think about it, or just have an idea, but when you actually commit it to paper, or tape, CD, or hard disk. You then immediately own the copyright, automatically – strictly speaking you don't have to do anything to make it happen. The complications arise if you have to *prove* that you created the work on a particular date, say if someone disputes this in the future. So in order that your ownership of the copyright is officially noted, you ought to register the work in some way.

All you need to be able to do is prove that you had a copy of the work on a certain date, so if anyone else says they wrote it, they have to prove it was in their possession at an *earlier* date. That's why it's important to register your creation as soon as possible.

In the UK, this can simply be done by sending a copy of your work to yourself via Special Delivery at the post office, so the date of posting is clearly visible, and the package is well-sealed – and stays that way, permanently, at least until required in a legal challenge. Alternatively you can deposit a copy of the work in a bank vault, getting a detailed, dated receipt – but this is obviously a pricey option (and you don't know how many years you'll have to pay for it to be kept there). You used to be able to register your work(s) officially at Stationers Hall Registry in London, but this facility ceased in 2000.

In the US, the self-addressed envelope option is a non-starter; instead you have to register your music with the US Copyright Office. You can choose to register just the composition, or the composition and performance/production. It costs $30 per registration (which can include more than one piece of music).

Protecting and collecting

That's all very well, you say, but how can you keep track of who's recording what, all around the world? How do you know if someone in Japan is infringing your copyright? Or maybe lots of people want to record your songs legally, but don't know how to find you… You're going to need help.

As the copyright owner, you can transfer your rights, in part or in full, to a third party – for example by signing a publishing deal or record contract. A publisher will do most of the administrative legwork and paperwork for you, and collect your royalties from their particular 'territories' – in return for a percentage of your songwriting royalties. A record label will, similarly, make and sell recordings of your work, for a rather large cut of the profits. You can do either or both of these jobs yourself, if you have the time and the know-how. The main music rights you need to be aware of are: performing rights, mechanical rights, master rights, and moral rights.

Performing rights

If you're doing cover versions of someone's songs at a gig, or you're a DJ playing records, then the club, venue, radio station etc should already have a 'public performance' licence – in the UK from the PRS, and in the US from either the BMI, ASCAP or SESAC. These companies collect money on behalf of songwriters, and their publishers. If you've written a song that's being published or recorded, you ought to be registered with one or more of these bodies, so that if someone else wants to play or perform your song, you can receive a royalty.

MUSICAL WORK VS SOUND RECORDING

The law uses the term 'musical work' to describe the combination of melody, rhythm and lyrics that go together to make up a recognisable piece of music. A musical work can be written down on paper in traditional notation, or as lyrics, or exist as a stream of data from an audio or MIDI sequencer. If you wish to perform or record that musical work, you need to get the writer or publisher's permission first.

The term 'sound recording' is used to mean the actual master recording of a musical performance, regardless of the recording medium, be it analog tape, hard disk, wax…

If an artist performs a musical work and agrees for a sound recordist to record the performance, a situation of joint ownership arises. The artist owns the musical work but needs to compensate the recordist if they wish to sell copies of this specific recording of their work. The recordist in this situation owns the recording, but needs to compensate the artist for use of the musical work if they wish to sell copies of it. Both parties have to get together and agree upon a split of the proceeds from selling copies of the recording.

This is exactly the situation when a record label pays for a composer to record their work. The record label (not the artist) owns the recording, but the record label still needs to compensate the composer (and/or publisher) for use of the work. Which in turn highlights a common trend in recording contracts: many record companies now insist that composers sign 'publishing and recording' contracts where they sign away the rights to both the musical work and the sound recording – it's naughty, often unfair but common practice, and you need to be in a very strong position (ie already famous) as an artist to avoid it. It remains illegal to record an artist (or even someone speaking) without their permission.

Mechanical rights

If you want to make a *recording* of someone else's compositions – whether it's strumming their chords on your guitar or sampling from their record – you are legally obliged to pay a royalty to the songwriter (or their publisher, who would then forward a cut to the writer). Record companies have to obtain a mechanical licence before they can make records, and the fees they pay go to the relevant writers/publishers. If you're just on your own, making a one-off recording of someone else's song, you could try approaching the writer/publisher yourself, rather than going through the mechanical licensing 'middle-men'.

If you're just recording your own songs (with no samples or any 'borrowed' tunes or lyrics), you don't need any permission or mechanical licence – you already have the right to do this. The same is true if the song you are covering is in the 'public domain' (which we'll come back to in a moment). But it might be worth joining one of the relevant agencies anyway – MCPS in the UK, HFA or AMRA in the US – just in case someone wants to record or 'borrow' bits of your material in future... that's assuming you want your music to be a possible source of income.

In fact, efficient royalty collection is only really feasible if you join the various rights collection bodies, listed at the end of this chapter.

Master rights

Whenever a record company pays for a recording to be made, they feel protective of their investment, and don't want anyone stealing their 'baby' – the record they've paid for. Master rights cover everything to do with the physical item they release: the actual performance of the music in the studio (though not the composition itself), the disc and/or tape it's recorded on, the sleeve artwork... none of this can be copied without the say-so of the master right holder. So if you sample from an existing recording, without permission, the label that issued it will very likely get upset. Presuming they still exist... And even if they don't, chances are the master rights will have been acquired by another company that's taken over their back catalogue. Sadly, just because a label is defunct, you're not let off the copyright hook.

Moral rights

As defined by the MCPS, this is: "the right to say, 'I do not like my work being included in these recordings – I do not want to be associated with something like this.' If a vegetarian had their song used to endorse McDonalds, for example... This is a right which should be retained by the writer, but in a lot of publishing deals these days, artists are expected to waive their moral right."

New, young or inexperienced artists are often under pressure to agree to amending, or even signing away, some rights – often before they even know exactly what they are. There's a crucial point here: before signing **any** contract at all, with a publisher, record label, agency – even a seemingly casual pre-contract agreement – get proper legal advice from a specialist music lawyer. There are plenty of books and internet sites out there with lots of useful information and horrific case histories, but every situation is different, and contracts complex and varied, so don't take a chance.

How does all this affect you?

So where does this leave a potential sample-user? Well, if a track you've created has involved using an excerpt, however small, from another recorded work – whether taken from vinyl, CD, or off the radio, TV or internet – you're infringing at least some of those rights we've just looked at. In fact if you rip a sample from someone's copyrighted, commercially released material, drop it into an outrageously obscene new track you're working on, then play the finished disc in your DJ set in an unlicensed venue, you're probably breaching all four of those rights in one attempt. Well done, the full set...

Despite its controversial reputation, sampling per se is not illegal. If you make up all your own samples from scratch, without using any pre-recorded material at all, you basically run little risk of infringing anyone's copyright. But in the real world, if you own a sampler, the chances are at some stage you'll be tempted to sample a quick riff, vocal line or drum break off an existing record... and that's when the can of worms spills open.

Even if it's only for your own amusement, at home in your little bedroom studio, the fact is that as soon as you re-record something for use in a different context – ie other than just listening to it on your hi-fi or iPod – you're breaching copyright. (You did pay for those records, didn't you...? Let's not even go into illegal mp3 downloads.)

Now, you may well be thinking to yourself, "But if it never goes outside of my bedroom, who's going to know?" And you may have a point... but legally, even this can't be condoned, ridiculous as that may seem. And if you want to put that sample on a track you're making, even if it's just to play to friends, let alone making a demo CD to send to record labels, or, perish the thought, release commercially, you're potentially in big trouble.

Whether or not anyone has actually been prosecuted for any of these seemingly minor transgressions is something the official bodies are not keen to talk about – partly because the answer is probably "No, they haven't, though that doesn't mean they won't in future", but also because if legal action were threatened, there would at worst be an out-of-court settlement before court expenses were incurred. And if you never get a chance to make any money from it before the 'cease and desist' order comes through the mail, it might be enough just to agree to stop distribution and destroy any copies you've made.

Even if you don't think you're going to make any money from the track that contains the sample, legally you still need to get permission from the copyright owner, and come to a financial agreement – just in case there is some money generated at a later date.

The public domain minefield

Even if a song is out of copyright (or 'in the public domain', as it's called) – which should happen roughly 70 years after the death of the songwriter, though it varies in different countries – you need to bear in mind that the recording itself might still be in copyright.

The other complication in recent years is that, because there's so much money at stake from the songs and recordings of some older big-name acts, the goalposts for copyright expiry seem to be constantly shifting...

CREATIVE COMMONS

For the more forward-thinking among you, there's a novel alternative to standard copyright on offer, known as Creative Commons – indicated on works by a double C symbol instead of the usual single ©. It's an intriguing new agency whose aim is to make copyright a more flexible concept. They've come up with the idea of there being four different levels of copyright, and as a writer/composer you can choose which one you want to apply to any particular work:

● The CC *attribution* licence, "permits others to copy, distribute, display, and perform the work and derivative works based upon it only if they give you credit."
● The CC *noncommercial* licence permits all of those rights, but "only for noncommercial purposes."
● The CC *no derivative works* licence permits others to, "copy, distribute, display and perform only verbatim copies of the work, not derivative works based upon it."
● The CC *share alike* licence permits others to "distribute derivative works only under a licence identical to the licence that governs your work."

Stanford law professor and copyright-reform campaigner Lawrence Lessig argues that, "Extending copyright is a theft in itself – a theft of our common culture." Increasingly, though, it seems like there's no common culture any more – almost everything is owned by someone, and they damn-well want paid for it.

There's a controversy raging in Europe at the moment because the current EC law states that the copyright in a sound recording expires 50 years after it was first made. The thing that's focused attention on this now is that Elvis Presley's earliest recordings, for the Sun label, will be out of European copyright at the end of 2004. (In the US, the 50-year limit was recently increased to 95 years for pre-1978 recordings, and 70 years after death for post-1978 – for reasons too arcane to go into here...)

But don't get carried away just yet – that 2004 deadline only affects the rights held by Elvis's record label, RCA/BMG. It simply means they'd no longer have automatic, exclusive ownership of those old Sun recordings (which they'd acquired), and then gradually their other Elvis records would follow, assuming the law isn't changed. But the copyright will still exist in many of the songs themselves, till 70 years after the death of the particular writer...

What you could do is find some other, perhaps more obscure records that are past their 50-year expiry date, *and* contain songs that are also out-of-copyright (perhaps cover versions of very old songs), and then you'd think you'd be on pretty safe ground... But with copyright, and especially public domain areas, it seems you can never tell. It's always best to double-check – see the contacts list for more information on public domain music.

Legal dos and don'ts

The financial implications of sampling – for all parties concerned – can't be ignored, and they might just influence your approach to how you work with samples. But because the issues surrounding the legality of sampling and copyright seem to cause a great deal of confusion, I thought we should hear from the people in the know.

The Mechanical Copyright Protection Society (MCPS) is the agency that administers mechanical copyright in the UK. I asked them to clarify just what is legal and what's not, when we might need the MCPS and when we don't, and how musicians and record labels can negotiate the muddy waters (not to mention the James Browns and the Led Zeppelins).

The MCPS didn't put together a specialist sample department until 1993, prompted by the experience of DJ/production team Shut Up And Dance, who had a huge UK hit with 'Raving I'm Raving' but didn't clear the samples and were hit with a crippling lawsuit.

Now, say the MCPS, there's a "clear procedure in place – clearing a sample is now a cut-and-dried, standardised process. Every major label has their own sample manager who negotiates all the samples. They're all very happy to agree for samples to be used, because it's revenue from lost artists."

There had obviously been legal disputes before 1993, but the reason things became more regulated at that point was, the MCPS admit, to do with "how big the songs became, how much airplay they were getting, how many sales – and whether the men in suits in their offices were going to hear them."

The way things currently work is like this: "When a publisher registers a work, if it contains a sample it will generally have been cleared beforehand. When a record company sends us a record for a licence application, it will usually have all of the samples credited on the sleeve notes and we will simply work from that and query our members accordingly. The majority of work these days is all sorted out beforehand. Gone are the days of stuff being sorted out after a release, where a record has already been in the charts for weeks before you find out it's got three samples in it."

But if you want to ask permission to use a sample, how do you know who to ask? And will they say yes...?

"MCPS keeps a database of all the owners of all the songs released in the UK [note: in the US your first port of call would be HFA and/or AMRA], so all you need to do is phone us with either a title or an artist and we then tell you who owns both the master and mechanical rights and can give you names and contact numbers."

The first thing to point out here is that the MCPS is only there, "to protect the people who choose to become members. If the owner of the publishing rights is not an MCPS member, we don't collect the royalty. The vast majority of artists on the dance scene are not members of MCPS and are not officially published." (Of course there's nothing to stop an individual artist making a claim for copyright infringement themselves and seeking recompense through the courts if they wish.)

Your next step, going by the book, would be to approach the copyright owners with a recording of your work containing their sample, to seek permission for its use.

"There are a few artists – like The Beatles, Michael Jackson, Oasis etc – who always refuse all licensing," say the MCPS, "but the vast majority of artists are quite happy to clear stuff. The only way you'll get an absolute no is if another more-established artist has asked to clear the same sample. If the publisher has a multi-platinum-selling artist wanting clearance, they'll get it, because it's going to make more money. For mechanical rights you really have nothing to lose by trying.

"It's a good idea to send them a recording of your entire new song, followed immediately on the same CD by just the sample that you've taken, followed in turn by the song you've sampled from. If you've sampled from some old back catalogue song, it might take them three months to find the original recording, listen to it, work out the differences between your song and the sampled song, work out how big a part the sample plays in your song. You may even have sampled it in such an obscure way that they can't figure out what you've sampled at all. So isolate the sample and provide written notes about where exactly you sampled it from. You'll also need to send them as much release information as you can, in terms of how many copies you're pressing, distribution etc. They'll then have to actually send it to the writer a lot of the time for approval of moral right."

By the way, if you're wondering how some uncleared samples make it onto recordings and into the shops, the answer is very simple. Sometimes musicians lie. They submit a work to MCPS for registration saying that it's "100 per cent written by the artist credited on the cover". Because it's not part of MCPS's job, they don't check content – but it may well be spotted at a later date by whoever owns what's been sampled, and come back to haunt you.

Here's a very practical suggestion at this point. When you're sitting in your studio, making music, and you sample something... make sure you write down where you sampled it from, what exactly you sampled, and where you used the sample. Put this information in a text file and store it with the rest of your song and instrument information.

The reason is simple. You're extremely unlikely to be able to remember what you've sampled a week later, let alone months or years later. If or when your track becomes a big hit, you might just save yourself a lot of work.

Share and share alike

OK, let's check the practicalities of a simple, common scenario: say an artist is making a CD of a track that contains a sample from another record, and they want to release it by themselves, making say 1000 copies. What are the financial implications?

MCPS: "Because mechanical rights are calculated on a percentage, it's easy enough to work out that the total royalties on a thousand copies is going to be a couple of hundred pounds. So if the owner [of the sample copyright] asks for 50 per cent of the mechanical rights in return for the use of a sample, you only have to give them a hundred pounds or so, and you're all legal and above board."

So 'mechanicals' might not be too much of a burden, on limited runs at least, but it seems the *master* rights are more of a financial problem…

MCPS: "Clearing the master rights for a sound recording can be anything from a few hundred to a few thousand pounds, which is quite costly – and it's normally a one-off fee payable *in advance*. How much the record company will charge is based on the extent to which the sample forms a 'substantial part' of your composition."

Ah yes, substantial part… So how big is 'substantial'?

MCPS: "There are huge misconceptions regarding what constitutes a 'substantial part' of a recording. You can use quite a long string sample that isn't particularly distinctive and sit it quite low in the mix and, despite its length, it won't be a 'significant part'. Or you can take a tiny little vocal snippet from the chorus of a well-known record, so that the moment people hear it they recognise it, and lay that over a really minimal drum & bass track and… what's the track without the vocal? That would be a substantial part, so although it might be very short, the owner might demand 75 per cent for it. You can take 30 milliseconds or you can take four bars, and the royalty will be different every time." In other words it's to do with its musical importance within your track.

What's the procedure for an artist who thinks their own copyright has been infringed?

MCPS: "What we advise is that, as well as approaching us, it's good business practice to approach the publisher that owns the record in question. Explain that you think their work is infringing your copyright, you believe it contains a sample of your work, you've approached MCPS and requested that we withhold royalties pending negotiation.

"The way MCPS actually enforces disputes, all our members are treated equally. We've got one member saying, 'This is an unauthorised sample of my work', we've got another member saying it's not. Unfortunately we're not in a position to make decisions, that's not our job, it's down to the individuals concerned to negotiate an agreement from there. Our procedure is to suspend royalties so that nobody gets the publishing share. We look after it until everyone has done all their negotiating, sorted out their splits of who gets what, and then we pay accordingly.

"The next step [before court] in a disputed scenario is that the member who is saying their copyright is infringed has to bring in a musicologist to analyse each musical element and note. [A musicologist's evidence is liable to be particularly convincing in a court, so if you produce

---

COPYRIGHT INFRINGEMENTS

If an infringement occurs, the copyright owner is legally entitled to bring civil proceedings for infringement, and obtain remedies as follows:

● Obtain an injunction to prevent the continuance of the infringement.
● Be awarded damages to compensate for the loss, and/or account of profits.
● Obtain an order for the infringing copy/copies to be returned to the copyright owner, or destroyed.

According to the MCPS, "Some acts of copyright infringement are also a criminal offence and, as such, the offending person may be liable to a fine and/or imprisonment."

a respectable musicologist's report in advance that says you're correct, you may well get an out-of-court settlement.]

"When a work is a total infringement and the writer doesn't want to be associated with it, and doesn't want it released, they can ask us to refuse a licence. We then issue a letter telling the offending label/artist to 'cease and desist manufacture' and perhaps even threaten to seize any remaining product. Damages will often be requested [by the copyright owner] to compensate for the trauma of having their copyright infringed.

"If there's a record out there with an uncleared sample in it, the publishers know they can request 100 per cent of the publishing royalty, and they will get it. Most of the time the publishers will say that, for instance, if there's 1000 copies of a record out there, as long as the record is not licensed any further for compilations, or TV or whatever, and they can have 100 per cent of the royalties, the label can sell the offending 1000 copies."

What if you sample a section of a record that in itself already contains samples from some older recordings?

MCPS: "The copyright is in the recording you have sampled from. Technically the publisher of the record you've sampled should have cleared their own use of the sample with the original copyright owner. So when the royalties from your record are shared out, a proportion would go to the original copyright owner too.

"If you've sampled from some old white label that doesn't have any information about the copyright owner on there, the chances are it's dodgy and hasn't cleared any of its content. Our advice, as MCPS, is don't sample it."

Alternatively, tell the MCPS you couldn't identify the owners, but you want to register your music regardless. That way, if the owner does surface at a later date, your position is strengthened when it comes to negotiating percentages. It proves you weren't deliberately trying to avoid payment.

And that raises another interesting point, which a lot of people either don't realise or refuse to accept: it doesn't matter whether or not your intention was to make any money from your work. As far as the law is concerned, it's enough that you've sampled someone else's work, without permission, and there's at least the potential that you could exploit that in some way in future. It's your word against theirs.

But as our official copyright spokesperson confirms, there are some cases where one or more of the licences mentioned are not required at all…

MCPS: "If you are simply re-playing elements of a song – say for example you've sampled the bassline from 'Walk On The Wild Side', and you then pick up a bass guitar and *play* the 'Walk On The Wild Side' bassline [and scrap the sample], it's classed as an 'adaptation'. In that case you don't need to clear the master rights, you only need to clear the publishing/mechanical rights with the relevant publisher, or via MCPS."

(Be aware though that a note-by-note 'adaptation' of a part of a song can still land you in serious legal trouble – there are plenty of high-profile examples to prove the point, from the Sugarhill Gang's Chic reconstruction to The Verve's 'Bittersweet Symphony', which started off as a short sample loop, was replaced by their own orchestration, but they still had to forfeit 100 per cent of the writing royalties.)

The MCPS say they won't get involved unless they need to. "If someone sits in their bedroom and makes their own music, without any sampling at all, just getting on with it and putting the music out themselves, then it's nothing to do with us. If they want to let a label release their music, without an agreement in place for us to collect their publishing, it's nothing to do with us. But if, at a later point, their song suddenly blows up – like Craig David & The Artful Dodger, who initially put their stuff out with a small label and didn't expect it to do much – then it would be worth their while being registered with us. The moment the song gets licensed to a major, or for broadcast or films or whatever, we will know about it and collect royalties on our members' behalf."

And thanks to new technologies, especially the internet, new kinds of copyright and new licences have appeared over recent years… "A few years ago we only had four different types of audio product licence," say the MCPS, "now we have ten. Things like magazine covermount CDs have their own type of licence. We now have an internet licence – it's a joint licence to cover the performing and mechanical rights. One phone call to us can ensure you're covered for various activities on the web – that's a recent development."

FURTHER COPYRIGHT INFORMATION & ADVICE

Check the views from both sides of the copyright fence...

- ● www.patent.gov.uk/copy – UK Patent & Copyright Office
- ● www.copyright.gov – US Copyright Office
- ● www.riaa.com – Recording Industry Association Of America
- ● www.bpi.co.uk – British Phonographic Industry
- ● www.mcps.co.uk – UK's Mechanical Copyright Protection Society
- ● www.prs.co.uk – UK's Performing Right Society
- ● www.ascap.com – US performing rights license/collection agency
- ● www.bmi.com – US performing rights agency
- ● www.sesac.com – US performing rights agency
- ● www.nmpa.org/hfa.html – HFA (Harry Fox Agency), US mechanical rights licensing & collection agency
- ● www.amermechrights.com – AMRA, US mechanical rights agency
- ● www.creativecommons.org – alternative to conventional copyright
- ● www.pdinfo.com – public domain information
- ● http://fairuse.stanford.edu – copyright information
- ● www.superswell.com/samplelaw – copyright info
- ● www.eff.org – Electronic Frontier Foundation
- ● www.illegal-art.org – lots of interesting stuff
- ● www.negativland.com – heavy sample users offer opinion & advice
- ● www.lessig.org – US law professor & copyright campaigner

The 'Fair Use' excuse

In the multi-layered and pretty-much watertight world of sampling copyright, there is one defence that has occasionally been used to excuse some otherwise blatantly illegal 'borrowings' – and has been desperately clung on to as a potential life-raft by some samplers (who are more often than not deluding themselves).

In the UK, and Commonwealth territories like Canada and Australia, there's a clause in the copyright law about 'Fair Dealing', which allows, for example: journalists to quote short extracts from a song in a review or criticism; or TV news channels to use a snippet of music for free, but only if their story is about that song or artist; or a teacher or student to make a copy of something for educational or research purposes (although the quantity may be restricted); plus a few other less obvious but similar scenarios. Unfortunately, simply sampling someone's work to make a new work of your own is *not* sanctioned under Fair Dealing. End of story.

But in the US, where there's a similar clause known as Fair Use, there's a crucial addition, and that's 'parody'. If your use of a sample is judged (and it will often come to a court judgement) to be parodic, in other words poking fun at the original version of the song or its creator, that might just be OK. But even then, every case is assessed on its own merits, and might come down to a subjective opinion from a judge – who might not share your particular sense of humour.

Other relevant factors come into play within Fair Use – for instance the commercial aspects. Not just the success or otherwise of your 'infringing work' (again, your non-commercial intentions are unlikely to be seen as justification, but may lessen the severity of any penalty), but also how much damage your work might do to the market for the original.

Perhaps the most famous, and hotly contested case of recent times – and certainly the one that brought the issue of Fair Use to public attention – was when rap group 2 Live Crew sampled the classic guitar riff from Roy Orbison's Sixties hit 'Oh, Pretty Woman'. In fact, their track was basically a rap version of the same song, with the same verse structure and even some of the same lyrics, and they did credit Orbison on the sleeve (they could hardly not have). When they were taken to court by Orbison's publishers – who'd been approached initially but refused to clear the sample – the judge concluded that the new track was in fact a parody, allowed by the Fair Use clause of the US act, and so did not infringe copyright.

Many thought this a bizarre and totally unexpected decision at the time – especially considering the scandalous reputation of the 'bad-boy' 2 Live Crew, as against Orbison's wholesome and iconic image. Perhaps the judge was tickled by the humorous re-wording of the song, which added verses about a "bald-headed woman" and "big-hairy woman". Maybe he also concluded from the nature of the track, and the artists involved, that there was unlikely to be much crossover in the audience, so no damage would be done to the sales or reputation of the original.

The judge did make clear, though, that this wasn't to be taken as a precedent, and even seemingly similar disputes would have to be dealt with on a case-by-case basis.

Credit where it's due

Although it's a debate that can (and will) go on forever, the bald fact is this: if you sample from a record, the source material you are 'borrowing' was written, performed, recorded and ultimately owned by somebody else. Think of it this way – if that person was in a band with you, they'd expect a cut of any money made... and you probably wouldn't think twice about giving it to them. There's a simple moral question here.

But in this author's personal opinion (not strictly from a legal standpoint, you understand), there should still be some flexibility within the law. If you sample something and re-process it to such an extent that even the original writer wouldn't recognise it in a million years, I reckon you've been creative enough to at least warrant arguing about how much you owe the original writer. If you straightforwardly sample a piece of somebody else's music and loop it up and simply place it in a different context (just like thousands of filtered disco or hip-hop tracks)... you do deserve *some* of the creative credit for the work you've done, but don't you owe a large chunk to the people who wrote and recorded what you sampled?

It's only fair…

ON THE CDs

There are two CDs with this book: CD1 is largely for tutorial purposes, and needs to be listened to in conjunction with reading the book. CD2 is a bonus sample CD featuring over 500MB of quality samples from Zero-G.

CDI track-by-track (I-96)

These tracks essentially relate to specific audio illustrations that are featured in the book. If you wish, the relevant tracks can be loaded into your own sampler for you to try out the various processes for yourself. Most of the original samples used as raw material here (with the exception of Track 1, the Shaun Lee breakbeat) come from the Zero-G demo disc, CD2.

1	Shaun Lee original mono breakbeat	42	ahhhs, Filtrator, LFO, reverb, phaser
2	triple loop, pitch-up & sequence	43	vocal 'hi-hat'
3	triple loop, original tempo	44	vocal hat with kick
4	triple loop, pitch-up	45	vocal hat, clean sequence
5	beat sliced, re-order, low-sensitivity	46	vocal hat, filtered
6	beat sliced, re-order, medium-sensitivity	47	vocal hat, filtered & flanged
7	beat sliced, re-order, med-sensitivity, tidied	48	drumbreak 'riff', distortion, reverb, compress
8	velocity-mapped drums, not layered	49	original drumbreak, layered mix
9	velo-mapped drums, layered, no crossfade	50	layered mix break – just filtered
10	velo-mapped drums, layered, crossfade	51	layered mix break – distortion
11	Juno single sample, spread	52	layered mix break – distortion, reverb
12	Juno three samples, spread	53	layered mix break – distortion, compressor
13	Juno six samples, spread no crossfade	54	original Okay_Scratch_107bpm
14	Juno six samples, spread, crossfade	55	scratch, shorter, sequenced
15	string part	56	scratch, delay, four bar only
16	two cycles (8ms)	57	scratch, delay, resampled, but wrong
17	string part, no effects, no attack or release	58	scratch, delay, eight bar, tail
18	string part, no FX, no release	59	scratch, delay, four bar, echo, loop, repeat
19	string part, no FX	60	sinewave, one cycle
20	string part, chorus only	61	sinewave, sustained note
21	string part, no reverb	62	cello C1 original
22	string part, Native Reverb version	63	cello C1, looped, 32 bar
23	drum loop, filter cutoff sweep	64	cello C1, looped 32 bar, volume LFO
24	drum loop, sweep, subtle resonance	65	final drum & bass break mixdown
25	drum loop, sweep, medium resonance	66	Recycle drum slice 1
26	drum loop, sweep, full resonance	67	slice 2
27	loop, multimode filter, fixed cutoff	68	slice 3
28	loop, multimode filter cutoff, sweep	69	slice 4
29	LFO, filter, slow	70	slice 5
30	LFO, filter, slow, HPF	71	slice 6
31	LFO, filter, slow, LPF	72	slice 7
32	LFO, filter, slow, BPF	73	slice 8
33	LFO, filter, slow, but different	74	slice 9
34	bass, soft dub-style	75	slice 10
35	bass, EQ'd	76	beat sliced break, double speed/pitch
36	bass, EQ2	77	beat sliced break, kick & snare only
37	ahhhs	78	beat sliced break, added hi-hats
38	ahhhs, clean, sequenced	79	beat sliced break, hats, reverb on snare
39	ahhhs, 24db LPF	80	beat sliced break, hats, flanger, no reverb
40	ahhhs, Filtrator, heavy LFO 'wah'	81	beat sliced break, hats, flange, rev, dist, EQ
41	ahhhs, Filtrator, LFO & reverb	82	Shaun Lee original mono

83	Shaun Lee mono, time-corrected	90	corrected sample with just layered kicks
84	Kontakt Kick	91	corrected, layered, mixdown, four bars
85	DR Boom	92	Scratch, delay, EQ, phaser
86	DR snare 2	93	Scratch, delay, EQ, ring
87	DR snare low	94	Scratch, delay, EQ, phaser, ring
88	Kontakt Snare	95	Scratch delay, EQ, ring, reverb
89	Kontakt Side Stick	96	Scratch delay, EQ, phaser, ring, reverb

CD2 track-by-track (530MB)

The samples on this CD are grouped into folders, the names of which are based on the titles of the Zero-G CDs the samples originally come from. For full details on how these samples can be used, make sure you study the Read Me file on CD2. For full information on the Zero-G sample CD catalogue, visit the Zero-G website at www.zero-g.co.uk. (All samples in 'wav' file format.)

Afrolatin Slam
Afrofunk congas 125bpm – 1.3MB
Afrofunk dondo-shekere-blok – 1.3MB
Afrofunk Drumkit 125bpm – 5.8MB
Afrofunk full mix 125bpm – 5.8MB
Afrofunk Perc NoDrumkit 125 – 1.3MB

Beats Working In CUBA
Bolero Modern Mix 084bpm – 2.9MB
CongaMod Mix 130bpm – 1.2MB
Mambo Modern 112bpm – 1.4MB
Pilon Mix 102bpm – 1.6MB
SonMon Mix 095bpm – 1.7MB

Koncept & Funktion (D&B)
Into The Night-Demo – 5.0MB
Bass-Subbass Catch Me-C – 962kB
Beat-Latin Fever – 481kB
Beat-Scata Rolla – 481kB
FX-Dub Time – 1.0MB
Organ-In Motion-G – 1.9MB
Pad-Ahijah-G – 1.9MB
Synth-Intuitive-C – 1.9MB
Vocal FX-Into The Night-G – 754kB

Nu Jointz
Foolz 145bpm
Foolz Bass – 1.1MB
Foolz Drumz – 1.1MB
Foolz Eko Rhodez – 2.2MB
Foolz Fx – 2.2MB
Foolz Mix – 2.2MB
Foolz Swirl – 1.7MB

The Operating Table
079 05bpm – Slaps.nov – 33kB
079 05bpm – Slaps – 2.1MB
088 28bpm – Jellyroll 02 – 2.0MB
095 06bpm – Swampy 01 – 1.7MB
112 08bpm – Brokenlaughs 01 – 1.4MB
160bpm – Powerpak 03 – 1.0MB

WIRED (Total Trance V1&2)
909 Techno 4 – 591kB
Acid Science F – 2.3MB
Loop It 5 – 591kB
Techno Heaven 2 – 591kB

Ambient Textures Refill
MALSTROM 1 – 11.7MB
MALSTROM 2 – 4.8MB
NNXT 1 – 6.5MB
NNXT 2 – 6.2MB
NNXT 3 – 6.4MB
NNXT 4 – 5.8MB
NNXT 5 – 6.3MB

Analog To Digital
Ambient Chords – 1.3MB
Boom Da Bass – 326kB
Crumar Multiman – 956kB
Jupiter Suite – 1.1MB
Mr Pad Returns – 494kB

Analog To Digital 2 (A2D2)
Alien Pad – 2.2MB
Analog Bass – 278kB
Black Smith – 575kB
Digital Rez Pad – 1.9MB
LFO Filter Slow – 597kB

Beats 'N The Hood
Beijing 101bpm – 819kB
Drum Fill 99bpm – 418kB
Office World 96bpm – 861kB
Sega 97bpm – 853kB
Smart Knob 103bpm – 803kB

Beats Working
Brushes 093bpm – 891kB
Medium Pop 2 108bpm – 768kB
Modern Kit 110bpm – 377kB
Quick Funky 7-8 204bpm – 712kB
Up Pop 1 120bpm – 691kB

Brutal Beats
Big Sticks 108bpm – 766kB
Crumpled Underfoot 110bpm – 752kB
Dancin Daze 117bpm – 707kB
Foggy Hill Jump 133bpm – 622kB
Gamble On 100bpm – 827kB

Celtic
Northern Pipe 120bpm – 1.3MB
Northumbrian Small 120bpm – 1.3MB
Overton B 080bpm – 1.0MB
Uilleann Pipes 120bpm – 1.3MB
Wooden Flute 110bpm – 1.5MB

Cuckooland Ghost In The Machine
Fairground – 3.3MB
Laugh School – 2.4MB
Rolling – 2.0MB
Siren – 3.1MB
Swirl – 1.8MB

Cuckooland Unhinged
Latin-124 – 1.3MB
March Beat-127 – 1.3MB
Reverse-114 – 725kB
Stalker-90 – 919kB
Wood Drum-132 – 627kB

Deep House – dh v2.0
Bungalow 120bpm – 689kB
Coal Train 140bpm – 295kB
Gangsta Boogie 125bpm – 662kB
Shake It Down 130bpm – 318kB
The Chaser 135bpm – 613kB

Deepest India
Ajanata – 1.5MB
Heer – 2.0MB
Saharhar 90bpm – 1.8MB
Shentabs 110bpm – 1.6MB
Sitar Phrase 90bpm – 860kB

Downbeat Dance Grooves
Full 808 – 262kB
junk hip hop 3 110bpm – 754kB
Mad scientist – 3.6MB
pure groove 2 100bpm – 1.6MB
Ricochet – 514kB

Escape From Planet Of Breaks
Booty Luchy 91bpm – 1.8MB
Fry Pan 83bpm – 1.9MB
Iron Mann 84bpm – 1.9MB
Psych 2 93bpm – 1.7MB
Pyschedelic 126bpm – 1.3MB

Ethnic 2
Congas 148bpm – 559kB

Congas Bells Blocks 115bpm – 1.4MB
Sitar – 617kB
Tibetan Flute – 1.4MB
Zither 77bpm – 537kB

eVolution
Loop231-134bpm – 309kB
Loop275-137bpm – 302kB
Metaphysic loop – 1.3MB
Scenary – 2.8MB
Sound FX – 506kB

Flamenco Sounds
Arpeggio – 489kB
Bulerias – 1,004kB
Castanets – 642kB
Male Cantaor Vox – 921kB
Tango – 560kB

Freak Beats
Fresh Meat 100bpm – 827kB
Life Of Crime 100bpm – 827kB
Scratch 105bpm – 394kB
Sharp Spike 75bpm – 1.1MB
Solidstate 95bpm – 871kB

Funk Bass
Deep Throat 99bpm – 835kB
Easy Going 96bpm – 431kB
Hard Days Night 121bpm – 683kB
Head 4 Home 101bpm – 409kB
Jazz It Up 108bpm – 383kB

Funk Guitar
Croakin 90bpm – 459kB
Funk-E 111bpm – 373kB
O-Push 96bpm – 431kB
S-Shot 88bpm – 470kB
Synthfonic 112bpm – 738kB

Guitar Odyssey
Digital Wah 118bpm – 701kB
Distwah 126bpm – 328kB
Flanges 110bpm – 752kB
Heavy Wah 135bpm – 613kB
Twintime 105bpm – 788kB

Harmonica
Diddlydit De Dee – 426kB
Falling Boogie – 1.1MB
Phrased – 761kB
Sonny Pockachee – 521kB
Sonny Train – 667kB
Syncopated Sonny – 466kB

Jungle Warfare 1
Full – 1.5MB
Illegal 160bpm – 517kB

perpetual 162bpm – 511kB
Reverse Bass – 236kB
Sonic 162bpm – 1,021kB

Jungle Warfare 2
808 Standard 166.5bpm – 497kB
Harsh Bk 166.5bpm – 497kB
Mad Filter Bass – 479kB
Metallic Rolla 166.5bpm – 497kB
Ruffige Bk 165.5bpm – 500kB

Jungle Warfare 3
Jazz Ridez 166.5bpm – 497kB
Klanga Bk 165.5bpm – 999kB
Menace Throb Bass 166.5bpm – 497kB
Old Organ LP – 722kB
Programmed Stepz 165.5bpm – 500kB

Junk Percussion
Chain On Metal – 175kB
Log 158bpm – 523kB
Sheet Log 102bpm – 811kB
Sheet Squash 128bpm – 646kB
Spring Twang – 410kB

Malice In Wonderland
Arpeg Soft Bass + Noise 100 – 827kB
Fearsome Bass – 1.1MB
Glissing VCS – 2.0MB
Jungle Hyperflange 160bpm – 1.0MB
Vocoder Beat 160bpm – 1.0MB

Mo' Funky Elements
Disco Beat 115bpm – 360kB
Funky Horns – 518kB
Jaz Rap Beat 90bpm – 459kB
Superbad Stab – 122kB
Swing 100bpm – 414kB

Monster Beats
Attitude 098bpm – 422kB
C19 C 116bpm – 713kB
Manic B 113bpm – 732kB
Rolli A 075bpm – 1.1MB
Top End 120bpm – 689kB

Nu House – Hard House & Nu NRG
Acid 144bpm – 289kB
Breakbeat 147bpm – 283kB
Main Riff 138 – 600kB
Main Stabs 145bpm – 572kB
Percussion Loop 140bpm – 296kB

(Old School Flavours) Houseparty
Boogie 124bpm – 1.3MB
Disco Vinyl 128bpm – 1.3MB
Hustle 124bpm – 1.3MB
Philly Disco 124bpm – 1.3MB

Weekender 122bpm – 1.3MB

(Old School Flavours) Rare Groovin
Blue Funk 110bpm – 1.5MB
Freestyle 114bpm – 1.4MB
Organic 116bpm – 1.4MB
Polyrhythmic 110bpm – 1.5MB
Soul Jazz 122bpm – 1.3MB

(Old School Flavours) Superfunk
Godfather 94bpm – 1.7MB
JBs 73 104bpm – 1.6MB
Kool 106bpm – 1.5MB
Southern 100bpm – 1.6MB
Streetfunker 118bpm – 1.4MB

(Old School Flavours) Vintage Soul
60s Detroit 116bpm – 1.4MB
Marvellous 98bpm – 1.6MB
Mellow 96bpm – 1.7MB
Southern 98bpm – 1.6MB
Supafly 100bpm – 1.6MB

Return To Planet Of Breaks
096 summerbelly – 432kB
108 pekingduck – 384kB
127 noisefunky – 327kB
142 justice – 584kB
194 punky – 428kB

Ross's Rising Funk Guitar
Fever 115bpm – 719kB
Porno Tash 120bpm – 1.3MB
Sandwich Chain 90bpm – 1.8MB
Space Hopper 110bpm – 1.5MB
Voodoo 115bpm – 719kB

Saxophone Legacy
Acid Jazz 120bpm – 644kB
Blues 92bpm – 905kB
Funk 92bpm – 810kB
Jazz 130bpm – 876kB
Latin 100bpm – 1.1MB

Seismic Frequencies
Birdscape – 6.4MB
Blaze 1 – 516kB
Dead Valley 2 – 7.5MB
Mistchoir – 2.0MB
Tap Drums 108bpm – 1.5MB

Skinned (Skinny Puppy)
80s 125bpm – 662kB
Aqua Chainsaw – 2.2MB
Foghorn – 1.8MB
Mad Monks – 1.6MB
Monsters – 337kB

Total Funk
- Banging On 95bpm   –   871kB
- Bass Is Extra 90bpm   –   919kB
- Goin Up Ab   –   192kB
- I Got Ma Own Thing   –   132kB
- Partay 100bpm   –   414kB

Total Hip Hop
- All Black And White 75bpm   –   1.1MB
- Licker 100bpm   –   414kB
- Six-Shooter 95bpm   –   870kB
- Sweet 100BPM   –   829kB
- Workin 85bpm   –   973kB

Upbeat Dance Grooves
- Beyuss   –   976kB
- Nova   –   3.7MB
- Real Phat 140bpm   –   1.2MB
- Statik dreams 148bpm   –   1.1MB
- Subdown 135 bpm   –   1.2MB

Vindaloops
- Choo Tight Variation 100bpm   –   827kB
- Mando Octave 115bpm   –   719kB
- Reck Pot n Lak 91bpm   –   909kB
- Shava Oh Balleh   –   496kB
- Vin Heavy Fall 123bpm   –   336kB

Vocal XTC
- Ahhhs   –   1.6MB
- I Feel The Music   –   641kB
- Listen Up   –   625kB
- Tonights The Night   –   1.2MB
- Vibbin Trippin   –   708kB

(Creative Essentials Vol 03) Brass Elements
- Ascending Line 132bpm   –   627kB
- Attack 132bpm   –   313kB
- Descending Line 110bpm   –   376kB
- Get Ready 76bpm   –   272kB
- Honky 96bpm   –   431kB

(Creative Essentials Vol 04) Dance Vocals
- Deep Space   –   711kB
- Don't Let Go (x3)   –   559kB
- Hear The Music   –   536kB
- Ooo Hey   –   823kB
- These Sounds   –   459kB

(Creative Essentials Vol 05) Electric Dreamz
- Dream Scapes   –   1.0MB
- Electron 32   –   835kB
- Full Rez   –   1.2MB
- Lead Ramp   –   351kB
- Trans Technology   –   2.3MB

(Creative Essentials Vol 06) Trance Formation
- Dark Drone   –   1.7MB

- Deep Sea   –   1.8MB
- Synth Loop-01 120bpm   –   689kB
- Synth Loop-10 120bpm   –   689kB
- Trancy Sequence   –   1.3MB

(Creative Essentials Vol 07) Dream Zone
- Ambient Pad   –   1.8MB
- Bell Drone   –   2.1MB
- Deep Atmos   –   1.2MB
- Hard Fog Horn   –   798kB
- Sci-Fi Atmos   –   819kB

(Creative Essentials Vol 08) Spices Of India
- Balti   –   199kB
- Dolli Lak 124bpm   –   667kB
- Kion Zindagi   –   1.2MB
- Pullit 85bpm   –   243kB
- Rounds 89bpm   –   465kB

(Creative Essentials Vol 09) Guitar Separates
- Cl Strat 5ths   –   674kB
- Cl Wah Repeat Major   –   663kB
- Fender Chorus Single   –   642kB
- Jazz Guitar Major 7th   –   695kB
- Steel Rolled Major   –   669kB

(Creative Essentials Vol 10) Global SFX
- Lawn Mower   –   2.1MB
- River   –   3.1MB
- Siren   –   2.1MB
- Telephone   –   516kB
- Vehicle   –   402kB

(Creative Essentials Vol 13) Jungle Frenzy
- Body   –   663kB
- Dark   –   274kB
- Get With The Music   –   974kB
- Half Step 160bpm   –   517kB
- Very Very Upset 160bpm   –   517kB

(Creative Essentials Vol 14) Live Bass Grooves
- Chase Me 110bpm   –   376kB
- Partay 100bpm   –   414kB
- Ripe Tripe 100bpm   –   414kB
- Take Your Pick 110bpm   –   376kB
- What Goes Up 90bpm   –   460kB

(Creative Essentials Vol 17) Bass Separates
- Dark Bass   –   118kB
- Fill   –   42kB
- Real Bass   –   129kB
- Thumb Bass   –   135kB
- Woody Bass   –   129kB

(Creative Essentials Vol 18) Rock & Pop Vocals
- Badad Hey Hey Ohh Baby   –   1.4MB
- Fall Down On My Knees...   –   359kB
- Got To Have It...   –   236kB

Opera Vox   –   1.4MB
There's A Tear In My Eye...   –   788kB

(*Creative Essentials Vol 19*) *Dance Drums*
Crash   –   159kB
Hat   –   6kB
Kick (909)   –   37kB
Open Hat (808)   –   29kB
Snare   –   32kB

(*Creative Essentials Vol 21*) *Ethnic Flavours*
Bombay Mix 100bpm   –   414kB
Clam Pot Groove 120bpm   –   345kB
Panpipe Hard   –   402kB
Sitar Note   –   355kB
Tabla Groove 100bpm   –   414kB

(*Creative Essentials Vol 22*) *Reggae Connection*
Brass Riff 100bpm   –   414kB
Drum Loop 100bpm   –   414kB
Guitar Chop 100bpm   –   207kB
Piano Chord   –   142kB
Steel Pan Roll   –   142kB

(*Creative Essentials Vol 23*) *Techno Prisoners*
Flush Me   –   952kB
Hat Loop (140-bpm)   –   295kB
Rez Arp (120-bpm)   –   1.3MB
Rez Stab   –   251kB
Zap Bass Loop (140-bpm)   –   295kB

(*Creative Essentials Vol 24*) *Funk Construction*
Funky Soul 92bpm   –   450kB
Guitar Riff 102bpm   –   405kB
Moog Bass   –   279kB
Rhodesy E Piano   –   345kB
Street Funk 107bpm   –   387kB

(*Creative Essentials Vol 25*) *Synth Bass Loops*
303 Groove 120bpm   –   689kB
Fuzz Seq 120bpm   –   1.3MB
No Fuzz Groove 120bpm   –   689kB
Phazed Riff 120bpm   –   689kB
Wood Slap 120bpm   –   689kB

(*Creative Essentials Vol 26*) *Vintage Keyboards*
Hammond Tone   –   115kB
Hohner Clavinet   –   259kB
Mellotron Cello   –   295kB
Mellotron Organ   –   120kB
Vox Continental   –   85kB

(*Creative Essentials Vol 27*) *Voices Of Africa*
Chakoo Bayoo Bangoo   –   460kB
Go Kalama Hi-a-ho   –   546kB
Long Note   –   755kB
Ni Ya Be Saba Hai   –   800kB
Oobaye Oobayo   –   394kB

(*Creative Essentials Vol 28*) *String Textures*
Arco Basses   –   448kB
Arco String   –   902kB
Pizzicato String   –   174kB
Spiccato String   –   173kB
Tremolando String   –   741kB

(*Creative Essentials Vol 29*) *Woodwind & Brass*
Clarinet   –   431kB
French Horn   –   441kB
Trombone Section   –   846kB
Trumpet Section   –   930kB
Woodwind Section   –   875kB

(*Creative Essentials Vol 31*) *Jungle Frenzy 2*
Open Growl Bass   –   147kB
Rhodes Chord   –   230kB
Rhodes Riff 170bpm   –   487kB
Together Beat 166bpm   –   498kB
White Lines 168bpm   –   492kB

Creative Essentials Series
Pentatonic Chord   –   725kB
Piatti   –   552kB
Strings Arpeggio Major   –   830kB
Timpani Roll   –   2.2MB
Tutti Hit Major Glissando   –   723kB

Creative Essentials Series
Keyboard Bass   –   425kB
Rhythm Loop 120bpm   –   345kB
Rhythm Loop 130bpm   –   636kB
Riff 130bpm   –   636kB
Stab   –   39kB

Creative Essentials Series   3.1MB
Congas 85bpm   –   487kB
Conga Groove 68bpm   –   608kB
Djembe 122bpm   –   678kB
Reco-Reco 112bpm   –   738kB
Tambourine 132bpm   –   627kB

Creative Essentials Series
Faith Strum 85bpm   –   487kB
Funkpick 100bpm   –   414kB
Funk 110bpm   –   752kB
Posh Funk Wah 132bpm   –   313kB
Shaft 110bpm   –   752kB

Creative Essentials Series
Bass   –   518kB
Bass Line 90bpm   –   1.8MB
FX   –   555kB
Rhythm Loop 100bpm   –   827kB
Rhythm Loop 110bpm   –   376kB

Creative Essentials Series
Contemp Progression 91bpm   –   909kB

Hard Hat 108bpm – 766kB
Old Skool Funk 108bpm – 383kB
Slide – 539kB
Summer Wah – 868kB

Creative Essentials Series
Bell Tree – 1.6MB
Forest Skin – 238kB
Gong – 2.8MB
Soft Click – 40kB
Timpani – 1.7MB

Creative Essentials Series
Acid Jazz 90bpm – 460kB
Hip Hop 85bpm – 487kB
R&B Soul 95bpm – 435kB
Swing 95bpm – 435kB
Trip Hop 85bpm – 487kB

iFX Games
Battle fx – 665kB
Servomech – 116kB
Sword – 445kB
Teleport – 1.2MB
Whip – 72kB

iFX Matinee
Ambfx – 1.1MB
Button – 298kB
Click – 19kB
Event – 101kB
Rollover – 58kB

iFX Midget Gems
Atari Game – 181kB
Comedy – 36kB
Metal Door – 246kB
Watery – 25kB
Wizz – 52kB

(ProSamples 06) Experimental & FX
Buttons 71bpm – 582kB
Heavy 89bpm – 465kB
I've Got A Worm In My Head – 576kB
Multivoices – 2.9MB
Stew 128bpm – 1.3MB

(ProSamples 07) Future Beats 1
072-BPM – 574kB
104-BPM – 398kB
136-BPM – 608kB
Phazey Bass – 518kB
Trashy Loop – 426kB

(ProSamples 08) World Vocals
Hek – 1.0MB
Ishaq – 461kB
Joom – 1,017kB

Koka 90bpm – 459kB
Pardesi – 366kB

(ProSamples 09) Future Beats 2
Fuzz Piano 90bpm – 459kB
Interzone 142bpm – 582kB
Loop 8 Full Mix 111bpm – 745kB
Percussion 137bpm – 604kB
Splutter Rings 111bpm – 745kB

(ProSamples 10) House
Belle Star 125bpm – 667kB
Filter Me 125bpm – 662kB
Hurry Right Down 140bpm – 593kB
Love Unlimited 130bpm – 636kB
Rebus 125bpm – 664kB

(ProSamples 21) Drum & Bass 2
Drum Loop 160 – 521kB
Drum Loop 165 – 252kB
Drum Loop 170 – 490kB
Guitar 160 – 1.0MB
Piano – 624kB

(ProSamples 22) Hip Hop 1
8th Note Voco Groove 73bpm – 1.1MB
Krush Groove 82bpm – 1,008kB
On The Mello Tip 90bpm – 919kB
Sax Lick 85bpm – 454kB
WahWah Groove 94bpm – 1.7MB

(ProSamples 23) Trip Hop
Deep Breath-92 – 899kB
Electric Bass FX – 244kB
Guitar Loop-109 – 759kB
Medium Wave-114 – 1.4MB
Rework-108 – 766kB

(ProSamples 25) Pop & Funk Brass
Brass Crescendo-A – 981kB
Brass Riff-110 A♯ – 188kB
Brass Riff-132 A♯ – 313kB
Brass Riff-96 A♯ – 215kB
Trumpet Sax Fall-A – 151kB

(ProSamples 36) Chillout
Analog Echo 3 – 530kB
Aquaphone – 886kB
Hot Mud – 854kB
Mystery 2 – 1.4MB
Odd Vox 5 – 333kB

(ProSamples 37) Dance Synths
Acid Bass – 148kB
Cymbalizer – 29kB
Sub Bass – 318kB
Techno Chord – 150kB
Wasp Sweep – 255kB

(ProSamples 38) Trance
- Bass 9 – 374kB
- Brandy 138bpm – 2.3MB
- Buzzer 145bpm – 286kB
- Pad 1 C3 – 2.1MB
- Porta Lead 144bpm – 288kB

(ProSamples 39) Hip Hop 2
- Big Chord Tip 99bpm – 1.6MB
- Clav 94bpm – 331kB
- Old Pop Tip 88bpm – 1.8MB
- Rhodez Riff 68bpm – 457kB
- Sneeky Joint 69bpm – 2.3MB

(ProSamples 40) Breakbeat
- Boom Boom 107bpm – 3.0MB
- Bossa Back 115bpm – 2.8MB
- Mondo Bongo 112bpm – 743kB
- Sizzle 123bpm – 677kB
- Vag 084bpm – 3.9MB

(Pure Series) Pure Brazilian Beats
- Axe Samba Fills 105bpm – 394kB
- Bossa Acid Ride 058bpm – 713kB
- Samba-Funk 093bpm – 445kB
- Samba-Funk Dirty 103bpm – 401kB
- Samba Snare & Hat 105bpm – 394kB

Pure Hip Hop
- Evil Eye 075bpm – 1.1MB
- Fever Fever 089bpm – 465kB
- Furry Beast 089bpm – 465kB
- Okay Scratch 107bpm – 773kB
- Rhodes 075bpm – 551kB

Pure Mayhem
- Auteching 100bpm – 414kB
- Bounce 140bpm – 591kB
- Breaking Intro 130bpm – 636kB
- Hole Head 100bpm – 414kB
- Octave 130bpm – 318kB

Pure RnB
- Coral Sea 98bpm – 211kB
- Dalliance 86bpm – 962kB
- Skanker 85bpm – 243kB
- Smooth Chic 103bpm – 803kB
- Spin Doctor 94bpm – 220kB

Pure Tabla
- Birur 100bpm – 414kB
- Hardoi 115bpm – 719kB
- Jamekunte 140bpm – 591kB
- Jamtara 100bpm – 414kB
- Khetwadi 80bpm – 517kB

Pure Trip Hop
- Drumloop 90bpm – 919kB

- Lazy Days 82bpm – 1,008kB
- Longlife 111bpm – 373kB
- Mingin 96bpm – 431kB
- Sirens 85bpm – 973kB

(Soundisc Series) Darwin Chamber
- Break 2 Scratchin 84bpm – 246kB
- Hollywood Drive 103bpm – 402kB
- Let Go Pad – 494kB
- Object Guitar 129bpm – 321kB
- That Way 136bpm – 304kB

(Soundisc Series) George Clinton
- Kneeler 113bpm – 366kB
- March 107bpm – 386kB
- Thick 95bpm – 435kB
- Twang On 102bpm – 811kB
- Wassup Groove 115bpm – 360kB

(Soundisc Series) Gloss
- Happy Piano 125bpm – 331kB
- Horn Space Delay – 159kB
- Sharper 125bpm – 331kB
- Swish Block 130bpm – 318kB
- Thumpy Loop 131bpm – 158kB

(Soundisc Series) Hardcore
- Accordance 160bpm – 517kB
- Fake ID 160bpm – 517kB
- For The Road 160bpm – 517kB
- Scissors 160bpm – 517kB
- Toothbrush 160bpm – 517kB

(Soundisc Series) Heaven
- Horney Ting 132bpm – 313kB
- MBongo 130bpm – 318kB
- Popadom 100bpm – 414kB
- Roll With It 100bpm – 414kB
- Yahoo 130bpm – 318kB

(Soundisc Series) K-Klass
- Hoppy Break 125bpm – 331kB
- House 125bpm – 331kB
- Pitch Tinker 125bpm – 662kB
- Route Bass 125bpm – 331kB
- Shake The Room 125bpm – 331kB

(Soundisc Series) Lo-Fi Transmission
- Ambisynth 126bpm – 328kB
- Feel Good 126bpm – 328kB
- Kickin Hat 126bpm – 328kB
- Satsuma 125bpm – 331kB
- Trashing Loop 125bpm – 331kB

(Soundisc Series) Sabroso
- Afrosalsa 120bpm – 689kB
- Doischord 100bpm – 414kB
- Giration 130bpm – 318kB

Stray Cat 80bpm   –   1.0MB
Very Shaky 120bpm   –   345kB

(Soundisc Series) Skinny Puppy
  60's Space 141bpm   –   587kB
  Hum Bass 150bpm   –   276kB
  Plonk Riff 150bpm   –   551kB
  Pretty 141bpm   –   587kB
  Really Wasted 150bpm   –   551kB

(Soundisc Series) Smoke
  Dum Dub LP 90bpm   –   459kB
  Hard Ride LP 80bpm   –   259kB
  Howlin Wolf 75bpm   –   551kB
  Rock n Dole 97bpm   –   853kB
  Safety LP 86bpm   –   481kB

(Soundisc Series) Street Level
  Fluffy Bass 98bpm   –   422kB
  Nasty Loop 98bpm   –   422kB
  Scratchy Skip 98bpm   –   422kB
  Uptown Vinyl 98bpm   –   422kB
  Wave Scratch 98bpm   –   422kB

(Soundisc Series) Tremor
  Eightball Riff 165bpm   –   501kB
  Fat Bottom 165bpm   –   501kB
  Flange Shuffle LP 170bpm   –   487kB
  Foot In Mouth   –   324kB
  Metallic BK 165bpm   –   251kB

Backbeat UK would like to thank Zero-G for their assistance and generosity in supplying this disc of high-quality samples to accompany the book.

Important note: *All of the audio samples included on CD2 remain the intellectual property of Zero-G Ltd. They are provided for demo purposes only and as such are restricted to personal use and non-profit. However, purchasing the source product (the product which a particular demo sample is taken from) enables the purchaser to use all samples from that product in their commercially-released music. ©2003 Zero-G Limited. Zero-G® is a registered trademark of Zero-G Limited.*

about the book's author

Coming from a musical family, Daniel Duffell fell in love with Moog synthesisers at the age of 12, before deciding to specialise in recording and music production, serving an introductory apprenticeship at 16 with ex-Motorhead mix engineer Neil Mac.

He then moved to Brighton, where he was to stay for 15 years, working as a venue technician – mostly at the legendary early home of UK dance music, the Zap Club – and as a recording engineer in various studios.

He embraced sampling and sequencing technology at an early stage, and bought his first sampler in 1987 – it was a Casio FZ-10 (rack version of the FZ-1) and cost "a lot". He has since produced a diverse and unlikely collection of commercial (and not so commercial) music encompassing everything from the dance floor to lounge-core to film and performance soundtracks.

Daniel's career as a writer began in 1991 when he took over the role of technology editor at *DJ Magazine*, where he stayed for eight years. He was the launch editor for *DJ Mag*'s UK offshoot *DJeQ* in 1998, before moving to IPC Media, performing technical review duties for *Muzik*, *Melody Maker* and the *NME*.

Dan now writes for *Future Music*, but spends most of his time consulting and writing for various manufacturers of music performance technology.

author's acknowledgements

I would like to thank my lovely wife Amanda for putting up with how much of our lives this book has consumed. Thanks to the publishers for the opportunity to write it, and Paul Quinn for his expert editing. My appreciation goes out to all of the many manufacturers who have helped, not just in the preparation of this book, but over my years of journalism. And I'd especially like to thank the legions of amazing musicians in the world, without whom this book would not exist.

"In the future, records will be made from records." – John Cage (1956)

INDEX